Managing Business C[...] For Dummies®

D0791446

Managing Resistance

Resistance to change has numerous causes. When people resist, ask yourself the following questions about your employees:

- Are they overloaded and stressed out?
- Do they understand why the change is needed?
- Is there a history of flavor-of-the-month changes that have failed?
- Do they believe you are really committed to the change?
- Do they know how the change affects their individual day-to-day jobs?
- Is their self-worth being damaged?
- Do they know they will be recognized and rewarded for making the change?
- Do they believe the change will work?

Managing Your Stress

Recognize when you are becoming stressed — then do something about it.

- Look for those things you can change and accept those things you cannot change.
- Look for something positive in what's happening.
- Stop for one minute and focus on taking deep, slow breaths.
- Take a walk or go exercise.
- Look at the issue from a different viewpoint.
- Recognize that nothing lasts forever.

Keep the Information Flowing

Continual input from people keeps you from being blindsided. Tips for increasing quality and quantity of input include

- Reward the messengers — don't shoot them.
- Get out of the office and informally talk with your people to find out what's working and what's not.
- Hold small group discussions to provide face-to-face opportunities.
- Establish an e-mail suggestion box — and respond to their suggestions and questions.
- Use the questionnaires in this book.
- Let your people do the talking.
- Recognize that you do not have all the answers or know all the problems.
- Concentrate totally on the person talking rather than planning your response.
- Don't interrupt — it's impolite and indicates you are not really interested in their thoughts.
- Use body language to show that you are interested — don't check your e-mail while they are talking.
- Ask your question and then patiently wait for their answer — and stay silent until they respond.

For Dummies: Bestselling Book Series for Beginners

Managing Business Change For Dummies®

Cheat Sheet

Explaining Your Change

Your goal is to maximize understanding and buy-in and minimize resistance to the change. The content of your explanation should include

- What's the change
- What's going right — help keep a balanced perspective and protect people's self-worth
- What is not working and where are the dangers
- What are the benefits of the change and the consequences of not changing
- Where do we want to go — and what's it like when we get there
- What difficulties might we encounter
- What's the implementation plan

Avoiding the Manager Traps

Change can fail when managers forget that they are human, just like their employees. This creates a set of traps unique to the manager:

- Failing to recognize your own resistance — employees see you not changing as you have ask them to change
- Being impatient — setting unrealistic timeframes and implementation requirements
- Building castles in the sky — setting unrealistic positive expectations of the future
- Being misled by employees that everything is fine — because messengers get shot
- Getting surprised by resistance — out of touch with employee issues and therefore unprepared for opposition

Hungry Minds™

For Dummies: Bestselling Book Series for Beginners

Praise for Managing Business Change For Dummies

"A refreshing guide to understanding and managing change in business and in our personal lives. The straightforward advice on addressing resistance to change should be particularly helpful to organizations facing major changes."

— William V. Hickey, President and
Chief Executive Officer, Sealed Air Corporation

"Managing Business Change For Dummies is packed with sound, practical guidance on how to understand, lead, and manage change. It cuts to the essence of change management and offers plenty of on-point lessons for today's manager. Beth and Craig share their insights and guideposts to managing change in a no-nonsense, clear, mildly "tongue-in-cheek" style, which is a pleasure to read."

— Beth Wann, Vice President, Human Resources,
Time Warner Cable

"This book's description of the human side of change is right on. I find Beth and Craig's advice very practical and pragmatic. Managers will benefit from their good, common-sense approach."

— John A. Dorman, President, Business Banking Division,
Independence Community Bank

"I found Managing Business Change For Dummies a treat to read. The book provides a condensed course in understanding the behavior and feelings of workers in times of change. Organizational change can be filled with stress for the people who must implement the change; the authors provide you with the tools to gain your team's support and keep your team, as well as yourself, effective and calm. I plan to use the tools for both my personal and business life."

— Evelyn Greenwald, Chief Operating Officer,
Creativity for Kids, a Faber-Castell company

"Managing Business Change For Dummies offers insightful and practical advice for today's leaders. In a world that is undergoing rapid change, Evard and Gipple have captured the essence of fundamental human relationships in the business environment. This book will be an important resource for successful managers."

— Michael R. Fayhee, Managing Partner,
McDermott, Will & Emery

Managing Business Change FOR DUMMIES®

by Beth L. Evard and Craig A. Gipple

Hungry Minds™

HUNGRY MINDS, INC.

Best-Selling Books • Digital Downloads • e-Books • Answer Networks • e-Newsletters • Branded Web Sites • e-Learning

New York, NY ◆ Cleveland, OH ◆ Indianapolis, IN

Managing Business Change For Dummies®

Published by:
Hungry Minds, Inc.
909 Third Avenue
New York, NY 10022
www.hungryminds.com
www.dummies.com

Library of Congress Control Number: 2001089277

ISBN: 0-7645-5332-1

Printed in the United States of America

10 9 8 7 6 5 4 3 2 1

1O/RW/QV/QR/IN

Distributed in the United States by Hungry Minds, Inc.

Distributed by CDG Books Canada Inc. for Canada; by Transworld Publishers Limited in the United Kingdom; by IDG Norge Books for Norway; by IDG Sweden Books for Sweden; by IDG Books Australia Publishing Corporation Pty. Ltd. for Australia and New Zealand; by TransQuest Publishers Pte Ltd. for Singapore, Malaysia, Thailand, Indonesia, and Hong Kong; by Gotop Information Inc. for Taiwan; by ICG Muse, Inc. for Japan; by Intersoft for South Africa; by Eyrolles for France; by International Thomson Publishing for Germany, Austria and Switzerland; by Distribuidora Cuspide for Argentina; by LR International for Brazil; by Galileo Libros for Chile; by Ediciones ZETA S.C.R. Ltda. for Peru; by WS Computer Publishing Corporation, Inc., for the Philippines; by Contemporanea de Ediciones for Venezuela; by Express Computer Distributors for the Caribbean and West Indies; by Micronesia Media Distributor, Inc. for Micronesia; by Chips Computadoras S.A. de C.V. for Mexico; by Editorial Norma de Panama S.A. for Panama; by American Bookshops for Finland.

For general information on Hungry Minds' products and services please contact our Customer Care department; within the U.S. at 800-762-2974, outside the U.S. at 317-572-3993 or fax 317-572-4002.

For sales inquiries and resellers information, including discounts, premium and bulk quantity sales and foreign language translations please contact our Customer Care department at 800-434-3422, fax 317-572-4002 or write to Hungry Minds, Inc., Attn: Customer Care department, 10475 Crosspoint Boulevard, Indianapolis, IN 46256.

For information on licensing foreign or domestic rights, please contact our Sub-Rights Customer Care department at 212-884-5000.

For information on using Hungry Minds' products and services in the classroom or for ordering examination copies, please contact our Educational Sales department at 800-434-2086 or fax 317-572-4005.

Please contact our Public Relations department at 212-884-5163 for press review copies or 212-884-5000 for author interviews and other publicity information or fax 212-884-5400.

For authorization to photocopy items for corporate, personal, or educational use, please contact Copyright Clearance Center, 222 Rosewood Drive, Danvers, MA 01923, or fax 978-750-4470.

Hungry Minds™ is a trademark of Hungry Minds, Inc.

About the Authors

Beth L. Evard: Beth (Farmington, CT) is an organizational psychologist and the founder of Success through People. She began as a teacher of children with learning disabilities, as well as the learning proficient at the University of Arizona and the New York Medical College. Prior to starting her own company, she worked as a consultant with Coopers & Lybrand. Today, she provides consulting expertise on the human side of change management. She assists leaders to create change-adept organizations — where employees manage more effectively the turmoil, conflict, and stress that come with never-ending transformations.

Craig Gipple: Craig (Wayne, NJ) is president of Leadership Solutions, Inc., a consulting firm specializing in change management and quality. As a consultant, he has assisted a wide range of companies in planning and implementing change efforts. Prior to becoming a consultant, Craig worked at AT&T for 34 years, most of them as an executive leading divisions and teams with up to 6,000 employees. As an AT&T officer, Craig led AT&T organizations through major changes such as Bell System Divestiture, reorganizations, downsizing, process management, reengineering, culture changes, and network modernization.

Blending their two very different backgrounds, Craig and Beth give leaders both an insider's executive perspective, and an outsider's organizational development view. Similarly, they integrate the technical approach to managing change with the rarely seen human focus. For additional information, call 1-800-551-4008 or see their Web site at www.leadersolutions.com.

Dedication

To the women and men who dare the unknown of organizational change.

Authors' Acknowledgments

We owe a special intellectual debt to Daryl R. Connor from whose workshops, books, and conversations both of us first learned in a systematic way about the nature and process of change. Today, anyone who thinks or writes about change inevitably stands on Daryl's shoulders.

Our heartfelt thanks to Ed Knappman, our great agent, who not only connected us with Hungry Minds, but also acted as a caring coach, mentor, and advisor throughout this entire experience. We also want to say "thank you much" to Ed's associate, Vicki Harlow, for skillfully pursuing that unique world of permissions. Vicki, we wish you well!

We also deeply appreciate the editorial assistance we received from Dick Worth, who improved our prose immeasurably and helped us traverse our new path as authors. Without Dick's efforts, this would be a far less readable and enjoyable book. We are also grateful to Karen Garoukian Ferraro for her great job as our technical reviewer.

We are especially appreciative of all the folks at Hungry Minds, especially Holly McGuire, senior acquisitions editor, and Kelly Ewing, project editor. Holly and Kelly have provided the guidance and support we needed anytime we needed it. The third person within Hungry Minds who was most critical to this effort is our project coordinator, Regina Snyder, who was a crucial contact during the production process.

Beth wants to thank a few other people. First, she thanks John Sanger and Natalie Goldberg, who showed her how to translate decades of experience into the world of words. From Gil Fronsdale and Jack Kornfield, she learned how to enter the writing "zone," focusing only on each moment as it arises. And finally, a special thank you to her husband, John, who gave up many weekend mornings to listen, provide insight, and cheer her along.

Craig wants to close this by recognizing the people who worked with him during his career at AT&T and during his present career as a consultant. Those are the people that really taught him about change. And finally a special thank you to his wife, Margaret, who has supported him through thick and thin, including the writing of this book.

Publisher's Acknowledgments

We're proud of this book; please send us your comments through our Online Registration Form located at www.dummies.com.

Some of the people who helped bring this book to market include the following:

Acquisitions, Editorial, and Media Development

Project Editor: Kelly Ewing

Senior Acquisitions Editor: Holly McGuire

General Reviewer: Karen Garoukian Ferraro, Principal, KGF Consulting, LLC.

Editorial Manager: Jennifer Ehrlich

Editorial Administrator: Michelle Hacker

Production

Project Coordinator: Regina Snyder

Layout and Graphics: Amy Adrian, Stephanie D. Jumper, Jackie Nicholas, Barry Offringa, Jeremey Unger

Proofreaders: John Greenough, Susan Moritz, Marianne Santy, TECHBOOKS Production Services

Indexer: TECHBOOKS Production Services

General and Administrative

Hungry Minds, Inc.: John Kilcullen, CEO; Bill Barry, President and COO; John Ball, Executive VP, Operations & Administration; John Harris, CFO

Hungry Minds Consumer Reference Group

  Business: Kathleen A. Welton, Vice President and Publisher; Kevin Thornton, Acquisitions Manager

  Cooking/Gardening: Jennifer Feldman, Associate Vice President and Publisher

  Education/Reference: Diane Graves Steele, Vice President and Publisher; Greg Tubach, Publishing Director

  Lifestyles: Kathleen Nebenhaus, Vice President and Publisher; Tracy Boggier, Managing Editor

  Pets: Dominique De Vito, Associate Vice President and Publisher; Tracy Boggier, Managing Editor

  Travel: Michael Spring, Vice President and Publisher; Suzanne Jannetta, Editorial Director; Brice Gosnell, Managing Editor

Hungry Minds Consumer Editorial Services: Kathleen Nebenhaus, Vice President and Publisher; Kristin A. Cocks, Editorial Director; Cindy Kitchel, Editorial Director

Hungry Minds Consumer Production: Debbie Stailey, Production Director

◆

The publisher would like to give special thanks to Patrick J. McGovern, without whom this book would not have been possible.

◆

Contents at a Glance

Cartoons at a Glance

By Rich Tennant

page 325

page 267

page 7

page 219

page 39

page 145

Cartoon Information:
Fax: 978-546-7747
E-Mail: richtennant@the5thwave.com
World Wide Web: www.the5thwave.com

Table of Contents

THE INFORMATION IN THIS REFERENCE IS NOT INTENDED TO SUB-STITUTE FOR EXPERT MEDICAL ADVICE OR TREATMENT; IT IS DESIGNED TO HELP YOU MAKE INFORMED CHOICES. BECAUSE EACH INDIVIDUAL IS UNIQUE, A PHYSICIAN MUST DIAGNOSE CON-DITIONS AND SUPERVISE TREATMENTS FOR EACH INDIVIDUAL HEALTH PROBLEM. IF AN INDIVIDUAL IS UNDER A DOCTOR'S CARE AND RECEIVES ADVICE CONTRARY TO INFORMATION PRO-VIDED IN THIS REFERENCE, THE DOCTOR'S ADVICE SHOULD BE FOLLOWED, AS IT IS BASED ON THE UNIQUE CHARACTERISTICS OF THAT INDIVIDUAL.

Introduction

● ●

*I*f you want your company to successfully implement any change initiative, you need to know what you can do as a manager. Most changes fail because of resistance, and how you react to it can make or break your change effort. This book gives you ideas and ways to not only understand change, but to help deal with the change you're sure to encounter along the way. You also find out how to plan your change, as well as lead your team. Change doesn't happen overnight or on its own — but change failure happens faster than you realize.

In this book, you discover everything you need to know and more about managing change within your organization — and most importantly, the actions you can take as a manager to help ensure a successful 21st century for your organization. As a manager, you can do a lot!

About This Book

If you're walking on this earth in human form, change walks with you. No matter where you go, it follows. You can't lock it away in a maximum-security prison, nor can you outrun it. Change is here to stay. That's why the more you know about change, the better prepared you are to take life's lemons and turn then into soufflés, or meringue pies. The more change tools you skillfully wield, the more deftly you influence others at work and play. Because knowledge is power, the more knowledge you possess about change, the greater your powers for controlling your own life.

So, this book is for you if you:

- ✔ Have survived working in a flavor-of-the-month environment
- ✔ Work in a stress-filled job with little support and recognition
- ✔ Have gotten a new manager, boss, or administrator
- ✔ Have gone through a merger or acquisition
- ✔ Need to persuade others to change, but don't have the power to make them
- ✔ Have just been promoted into a new job and still not sure what you're doing

- ✔ Work for an organization that's experiencing phenomenal growth
- ✔ Are downsizing
- ✔ Are leading a change that requires people to modify their jobs or thinking

Although you can read this book from front to back if you'd like, you can actually use it as a reference book. If you're in the midst of change and are encountering resistance, you may want to check out Part II. If you're getting ready to implement a change, then you need an implementation plan. Enter Part III.

Conventions Used in This Book

We don't use many conventions in this book, but here are a few that you may want to know about:

- ✔ Whenever you see a word in italics, we are defining the term for the first time in the book.
- ✔ We use the words "employees" or "staff" to refer to the individuals you supervise.

Foolish Assumptions

To write this book, we had to make a few assumptions about you, the reader. We assumed that:

- ✔ You're a manager at some type of organization.
- ✔ You're about to experience or are in the midst of implementing some type of change.
- ✔ You realize that what you do as a manager greatly impacts any change initiative.

How This Book Is Organized

This book is made up of six parts, which each consist of several chapters. Each part focuses on a particular issue, and each of the chapters within the part gives you specific information.

Part 1: Who, Me? Change?

This part explains the intricacies of change and is designed to help you make sense of all the change that is occurring in today's world. In Chapter 1, you not only receive a definition of change, but you discover how you feel when change happens to you personally and to your organization. Chapter 2 examines change as a worldwide phenomenon, as well as its effects on the workforce.

Part II: Over Two-Thirds of Changes Fail — Don't Let Resistance Put You in This Statistic

This part takes a deep look at the inevitable challenge of resistance and what you can do to combat it. Chapter 3 talks about the difference between change winners and losers and how they deal with resistance. Chapter 4 talks about the excuses related to change, while Chapter 5 talks about the reasons people will always resist. Chapter 6 gives you tools for ensuring that you have the information needed to deal with resistance, and Chapter 7 talks about the often unidentified problem of manager resistance. Chapter 8 offers skills for reducing resistance, and Chapter 9 helps you assess how your organization is doing when it comes to handling resistance.

Part III: Planning Your Change — From Calamari to Tiramisu

In this part, you find out about the importance of planning your change. Chapter 10 talks about examining your reasons for changing, while Chapter 11 talks about the early steps you should take when you're considering change. Chapters 12 and 13 help you examine your current world, as well as the post-change world you envision. Chapter 14 takes you through the steps of creating an implementation plan, while Chapter 15 helps you figure out the change message you'd like to send to your staff. Lastly, Chapter 16 helps assess how your management is doing in the area of change planning.

Part IV: Leading the Charge

Change can't happen on its own; you need successful and determined leaders to implement it. In this part, you find out how you can be a successful change leader. Chapter 17 talks about the different roles you face as a leader, while

Chapter 18 discusses the importance of change communication. Chapter 19 examines recognizing change successes along the way. Chapter 20 offers an assessment that you can take to find out how you're doing leading the change.

Part V: Taking Care of Yourself — No One Else Will

This part may seem a little off the beaten path, but it's all related. If stress ties you up in knots and makes you vulnerable to the latest virus, then it's impossible for you to be a change winner. In this part, you find out how you can take care of yourself, both mentally and physically. Chapter 21 discusses the importance of mindfulness and positive thinking, while Chapter 22 talks about the many options you have at your fingertips to relieve your physical and mental stress.

Part VI: The Part of Tens

Lastly, we have the infamous ...*For Dummies* Part of Tens. Each chapter in this part gives you — what else? — a list of ten things that can help you manage change successfully. You discover ten things every change winner does, ten barriers to change, and ten characteristics of a successful change implementation plan. If you like lists, then this part is for you.

Icons Used in This Book

If you're observant at all and you've thumbed through this book, you've probably noticed the little icons located in the margins. Each one is designed to tell you something at a glance.

Whenever you see this icon, we give you a shortcut or some advice.

You'll want to remember the text you see next to this little icon. It's important.

This icon warns you when things may not go your way.

This icon highlights human-interest stories from our experience that you may benefit from.

 You don't need to remember the information next to this icon unless you want to. It tells you the nitty-gritty details of a technical point regarding change.

Where to Go from Here

You can use this book in a number of ways. If you like things nice and orderly, grab a seat and start with Chapter 1. If you prefer to use this book as the reference book it's designed to be, either scan the Table of Contents for a topic of interest or look up a particular concern in the Index. Then flip to that page and read away.

Part I
Who, Me?
Change?

The 5th Wave   By Rich Tennant

In this part . . .

No one needs to tell you that life often spins out of control. In this part, you discover what change really is and how-you and others may feel when uncertainty strikes. You also get a look at the changes that are occurring worldwide — and what changes *aren't* occurring.

Chapter 1

Expect the Unexpected

● ●

In This Chapter

▶ Living with change in and around you

▶ Keeping your cool when things get messy

▶ Getting comfortable with impermanence

▶ Defining the key tools for successfully managing change

▶ Taking stock of the changes going on in your life

● ●

> "I'm sorry to say so
> but, sadly, it's true
> that Bang ups
> and Hang-ups
> can happen to you."

Dr. Seuss
Oh, the Places You'll Go!

*N*o matter how hard you try, eventually your shiny, new car always gets a few nicks and scratches on it, or even an ugly dent. Your closet probably has a few favorite pieces of clothing that now fit a smidgen too snugly. Your company may have been bought, and work-life as you knew it radically altered. Or, maybe, someone else snatched away that promotion or that great deal for which you worked so hard. Face it — in this life everybody meets with a few "bang-ups and hang-ups" — changes that disrupt their plans. The question isn't about how to avoid the bumps and bruises that come with change (because you can't), but rather how you respond when things don't go as you expected or when life as you know it gets turned upside down and inside out.

If you've spent your hard-earned money to buy this book, most likely you want to make change work for you rather than against you. You probably want to take the initiative rather than react defensively or wallow in self-defeating victimhood. And if you manage an organization, you undoubtedly want to lead others into action, not struggle against their self-protective reactions — known as *resistance.* You've come to the right place. You're holding a book that gives you tools and techniques for succeeding with change — in both your professional and personal life (though we focus more on your work world).

It was Louis Pasteur, the 19th century French scientist who developed both the process that pasteurizes your milk and the vaccinations that protect you health, who said, "Chance favors only the prepared mind." You might also say that change favors only the prepared mind.

In this chapter, you jump-start the preparation process. First, we dispel the commonly held belief that change is a now-and-then occurrence. Rather, we show you that change infiltrates every aspect of your life, not just the merger you're grappling with or the new cost-cutting efforts underway. Then we address how the tough part of managing change really isn't mastering the technical tactics, but coping with all the messy human hassles — getting employees to do what they don't want to do. Finally, we present some of the skills that help you become a more effective change manager.

Before you jump into the tough realities and frustrations that come with change, stop a moment. Remind yourself that "information is power." And that the more you know about change, the more successfully you manage it. Also, remember that while change is about losses and endings, it's also about gains and new beginnings.

If You're Breathing, Then Expect Change

You can't escape change. No one has yet found a way to hold back the night or live forever in springtime. Babies and puppies grow up. Indifferent mirrors keep reminding you about the relentless march of time and gravity. When you think about it, your tastes in food, clothes, people, music, and entertainment, just to name an obvious few, have also altered over the past ten to 15 years.

What about the not-so-obvious changes? Did you know that your stomach manufactures a new lining every three days to protect itself from the acidity of its digestive juices? That means your stomach produces up to 500,000 new cells every minute. Your skin is also busily working away, replacing itself every four weeks. In fact, physiologists have established that in a little over one year's time, about 98 percent of your body's cells are new. And then you've got your never-at-rest immune system fighting around the clock against invading viruses and bacteria. Basically, you're a walking, talking change machine.

Now think about work. How much of your job has remained exactly the same over the past five years? Bosses change, peers disappear, and your people find greener pastures. Your customers are fickle, and so, too, is the stock market. The constant centralizing-decentralizing gives you a whiplash. You're forever getting hardware and software upgrades or a new e-mail virus. More and more companies turn to mergers, acquisitions, and reorganizations for what ails them. Oh, don't forget, while playing organizational musical chairs, you just might be going to school at nights to keep your skills up to snuff. No wonder nerves get frayed, with stressed-out employees getting sick or letting out repressed rage in the office instead of on the road.

Now think about personal changes outside of work. You can write your own unique list here — you get married, a child is born, a parent dies, your best friend moves away, you get transferred to another city, you move into a new house that's great, your old car goes kaput, and the personal changes just go on and on. It is important to remember that many changes are in fact good. People often benefit from change. The difficulty is not just good or bad changes, but that so much change occurs.

Welcome to the 21st century.

A New Look at Change

So, what is change? It's adjustments, transformations, transitions, and revolutions. It's the never-ending cycle of birth, growth, and death. It can simultaneously bring joy and sorrow, gain and loss, satisfaction and disappointment, or all those experiences mixed together. Sometimes change happens so gradually that you never notice the subtle shifts in your life. At another time, in one moment, your life, as you know it, is altered forever.

While change defies simplistic definitions and easy explanations, scientists know one thing about it for sure — without change, life on this planet ceases to exist.

Modifications are messy

Human beings have a love-hate relationship with change because it gives them mixed results. It's neither all good nor all bad, but contains the seeds of both. The same biological process that quickly heals a nasty cut can allow cancer cells to run amok. A new manager who fixes long-standing problems also changes the way you work. Reorganizing a company may provide efficiency and better customer service, but it also disrupts long-standing support networks and friendships. Even a dream job comes with an occasional nightmare.

Sir Isaac Newton, the 17th-century English scientist and mathematician, discovered the existence of gravity, invented calculus, and built the first reflecting telescope. He also recognized that "for every action, there is an equal and opposite reaction." (Well, actually he described his Third Law of Motion as "To every Action there is always opposed an equal Reaction.") In other words, a move in one direction causes automatically an opposing move in the opposite

Signs that progress has gotten to you

A friend e-mailed us the following list for identifying when you've had too much technology. Tracing the e-mail chain back, we couldn't discover who began the list, but we did learn that people added to it and modified it as it zipped from person to person. Here it is.

1. You just tried to enter your password on the microwave.

2. You have a list of 15 phone numbers to reach your family of four.

3. You call your son's beeper to let him know dinner's ready, and he e-mails you back from his bedroom asking, "What's for dinner?"

4. Your daughter sells Girl Scout cookies on her Web site.

5. You "chat" constantly with a stranger from Auckland, but you haven't spoken to your neighbors in months.

6. You use your cell phone to see whether anyone's home as you pull into the driveway.

7. You spent a fortune on a new computer, and a month later, it's obsolete.

8. You've stopped staying in touch with family members who don't have e-mail addresses.

9. You consider next-day air delivery frustratingly slow.

10. You get most of your jokes through e-mail — including the ones from the person in the office next to you.

11. You install an extra phone line at home so that you can get voice calls, but the kids have taken that one over to "chat" on the Net with their friends.

12. You get up in the morning and "chat" with your friends before you have your first cup of coffee.

13. You wake up at 2 a.m. to go to the bathroom and check your e-mail on your way back to bed.

14. You're reading this.

15. Even worse, you're going to forward it to others.

---

direction, though it's not often evident what that reaction will be. While Newton focused on the physical environment, you can draw similar conclusions of action-reaction to world and work events. The following are five examples in which "positive" movements in one direction set off unexpected consequences.

✔ The collapse of the Soviet Union brought the end of the Cold War and freedom to millions of people. But with that nation's break up, its stockpiled nuclear and biochemical materials went up for sale. Now cash-rich terrorists and unstable countries obtain the latest weapons of mass destruction. Plus, out-of-work Russian scientists, who specialize in atomic and biochemical warfare, have found ready jobs around the world.

✔ More and more people enjoy the freedom they get from telecommuting — no more commuter gridlock or jammed, noisy cubicles. Along with employees' independence, however, has come the breakdown of teamwork, loss of creative collaboration, and reduced political power for the telecommuters. Furthermore, the Occupational Safety and Health Administration (OSHA) issued a five-page report in 1999 telling employers that they have a responsibility for correcting hazards in the home offices. What that entails, nobody's quite sure, but there's bound to be interesting legal developments in the near future.

✔ The Internet was originally seen as throwing open the doors of competition by allowing the young, David-like entrepreneurs equal access to the customers that antiquated, Goliath-like corporations controlled. Instead, 130-plus innovative dot-coms bit the dust in 2000, while established retail giants reaped the electronic benefits. What's happened? Most Internet-only companies lacked the vital corporate infrastructure necessary to keep customers' happy. Plus, when push came to shove, people returned to the names they knew and trusted. (Even Amazon.com, with its 25 million customers, announced in January 2001 the layoff of 15 percent of its workforce.)

✔ Technology has allowed you to communicate faster with coworkers, friends, and family, as well as prepare fancier presentations easier. But that speed and ease comes with a price — the loss of your privacy. Computers, with their long memories, belong to the company, not to you. Now, every one of your presentation drafts, e-mail messages, Web-sites explored, and to-do list can be (and in some organizations are) scrutinized by management. Many a job has been lost because of the "wrong" e-mail message or Web-site visit. (For more examples of reactions to technological advancements, see the sidebar "Signs that progress has gotten to you.")

✔ Casual-dress enthusiasts believe that abandoning the stuffy, rigid corporate uniform increases creativity, breaks down hierarchical barriers, boosts morale, and lets employees feel that they work for a flexible and open organization. Of course, there has been confusion about what *casual dress* actually means. Employees have been known to show up ready for the weight room or an evening over a candlelight dinner. The fact that apparel-makers report sales for the serious "Wall Street" suit-look have been gaining strength at the beginning of the millennium indicates a reversal of this trend. Some employees feel that the casual look disempowers them, reduces their authority, and makes them appear less executive/partner material.

Impermanence is here to stay

When you're surrounded by flashy glass and steel skyscrapers, encased in a new high-tech car, or work for a company that has a great future, it's hard to imagine that impermanence rules. Like the Seven Wonders of the World (see sidebar about those wonders), powerful companies also live on borrowed time. At the end of World War II, Montgomery Ward was No. 27 on Forbes top-100 companies list; today, it's out of business. During the mid-1960s, the Bank of America ingeniously created the first universally accepted "plastic money," or bank card; today, that company's name still exists, but with new owners and its familiar logo discarded. In 1977, Honeywell was listed among the top 100 companies; today (assuming that its purchase by G.E. is approved), it's just a name on your heating controls. For decades, the Big Eight CPA firms ruled the accounting and consulting world; today, they're down to five, and even they have been torn apart with breakups and lawsuits. The list of companies that are no more could go on — and will.

The wonders that were

According to the ancient Greeks and Romans, the world (as they knew it) contained seven extraordinary sights, which writers of that time called "The Seven Wonders of the World." These architectural marvels represented amazing feats of engineering, construction, and artistic skills. Only one is left standing today, and that, too, is eroding away. They are:

✔ **The Great Pyramid.** Of the Seven Wonders, only Khefre's pyramid remains. Built in 2560 BCE, the 481-foot (145.75-meter) tomb was the tallest manmade structure for more than 20 centuries. Through the years, however, it has lost 30 feet (10 meters) off the top and most of its smooth stone casing. Even now, time, pollution, and sand continue eating away at this great structure.

✔ **The Hanging Gardens of Babylonia.** Some historians credit Nebuchadnezzar II with building the mountain-like terraces in about 600 BCE, 31 miles (50 km) south of Baghdad, Iraq. Archeologists excavating his ancient palace have found 82 foot (25 meter) thick walls leading up from the Euphrates River to the palace, which match closely the descriptions documented by Greek writers. No one knows what destroyed those magnificent gardens.

✔ **The Temple of Artemis.** Built around 550 BCE, in the ancient city of Ephesus in Turkey, this temple honored the Greek goddess of the hunt. Its imposing marble structure, more than 300 feet by 150 feet (90 by 45 meters), served as both a market and place of worship. Surrounded by marble steps and 127 60-foot (80 meters) tall columns, the temple drew people from around the Mediterranean. In 356 BCE, arson destroyed the temple. It was rebuilt approximately 200 years later and permanently destroyed by the Goths in 262 CE. Today, only a few columns remain in a swampy area.

✔ **The Temple of Zeus in Olympia.** In honor of their god, Zeus, the ancient Greeks created the Olympic games. And then around 430 BCE, they built his temple. Zeus rested on a 20 foot (6.5 meters) wide and 3 foot (1.0 meter) high base. The god himself was the equivalent of a four-story building, 40 feet (13 meters) high. His robe and sandals were made of gold, while the rest of his body may have been carved out of marble and ivory. But earthquakes, landslides, floods, and fires eventually destroyed this wonder. Now only rubble remains.

✔ **King Mausolos' Tomb.** On the Aegean Sea, in southwestern Turkey, a simple monument housed the dead Persian satrap (governor) of Caria. Completed around 350 BCE, the tomb was only 140 feet (45 meters) high but was decorated with exquisite statues on the outside and with white alabaster walls and gold art work inside. On top of the tomb, rested a 20-foot (6-meter) statue of a chariot pulled by four horses. For 16 centuries, visitors flocked to see the *Mausoleum* (as it began being called) until an earthquake damaged its roof and colonnades. Then in the 15th century, the Knights of St. John of Malta destroyed it to fortify their crusader's castle. Today, nothing remains of this wonder but the name *mausoleum,* which people still use to describe a large building used for burials.

✔ **The Colossus of Rhodes.** The people on the small Mediterranean island of Rhodes built the 110 foot (33 meter) high Colossus in 280 BCE to celebrate freedom from tyranny. It was so large that only a few people could wrap their arms around the statue's thumb. For 56 years, the iron-reinforced bronze statue stood by the harbor (not straddling it as some pictures show) welcoming all to the island, until an earthquake toppled it.

After lying undisturbed for nine centuries, what was left of it was eventually disassembled by conquering Arabs who packed the fragments off to Syria on about (as the legend goes) 900 camels. The Colossus of Rhodes, however, lives on today as the inspiration for sculptor Auguste Bartholdi's Statue of Liberty standing off New York island and his smaller version that graces the Seine in Paris.

✔ **The Lighthouse of Alexandria.** Also known as the Pharos of Alexandria, this 440-foot (130-meter) tower, or the equivalent of a 40-story office building, was constructed on the island of Pharos about 280 BCE. For centuries, it ensured safe entrance into Egypt's Great Harbor. By day, the tower's "mirror" reflected sunlight that could be seen over 35 miles (50 kms) out to sea. At night, an enormous fire guided ships homeward. By the 14th century, three earthquakes left it destroyed, and by the 15th century, the fallen marble and stones had become part of a fort defending Alexandria. But the vanished Pharos of Alexandria left a legacy. The word *lighthouse* in French is *phare,* and in Italian and Spanish it's *faro* — all derived from Pharos.

Managing business change means acknowledging that impermanence is as much a part of your environment as copiers that break down and friends that take new positions. The best job in the world loses its luster, and the worst job doesn't last forever. Quality circles fade, and reengineering efforts fall out of favor. What can you count on staying around forever? Nothing . . . save change itself.

Managers who successfully lead change don't get too shocked or badly thrown off stride when the unexpected happens to them. They may not be able to predict all the twists and turns of fate, but they never forget that life always provides surprises. Therefore, when the unforeseen happens, successful change leaders quickly pick themselves up, figure out how to win with the new cards they have been dealt, and get on with winning.

Change disrupts everyone's life; the only question is for how long. When you don't expect permanence, but instead expect and prepare for continuing change, you waste less precious time ranting and raving about how unfair life is or how all those problems shouldn't be happening to you. Now you can more quickly:

- **Respond with logic.** The faster you pass through the natural stage of righteous-indignation, innocent-victim, or both, the sooner you move into the "what's got to be done" and "how do we do it" stages. With freed-up energy, you focus your rational powers on analyzing the issues, as well as what you can and can't do.

- **Find a solution.** Time waits for no one — including those who feel unfairly treated. The sooner you harness your ingenuity and problem-solving skills, the sooner you create a plan of action, stop negative consequences from piling up, and start obtaining positive results.

- **Feel less out of control.** For some people, the loss of control can be more devastating than the actual change itself. The more rapidly you develop a well-thought-out strategy for approaching a problem, the less overwhelming events appear, and the more in-control you feel.

- **Focus on what you can control.** Face it: Some things are totally out of your control. You can neither change the direction the wind blows nor stop your department's reorganization — so don't toss away valuable time trying. Save your limited energy for those things that you can influence and that give you a return on your "investment."

- **Avoid getting derailed by anger.** Anger eats away at your health and your ability to think rationally. In fact, Chapters 21 and 22 show you many of the nasty things anger does to you. Even if you have valid reasons for feeling enraged, you're only making yourself sick, undermining your problem-solving skills, and slowing down a future success.

- **Reduce employees' resistance.** If you're thrashing around in confusion and frustration, you won't be much help to your employees. They don't expect you to have all the answers (as much as they might wish it), but they do look to you for a clear direction, for a logical strategy, and for a calm, unemotional focus. The quicker you regain control of yourself and the situation, the more confident your employees will feel in your leadership ability and the more willing they will be to follow you.

The Human Face of Change

When A. G. Lafley took over as CEO of Procter & Gamble in June 2000, he realized that the primary job facing him was to restore the morale of his employees. The company had embarked on an enormous reorganization, which looked great on overhead presentations, but overlooked the disruption in the lives of thousands of people. Only time will tell how well he succeeds with the human side of his job.

There aren't any winners

Here's how employees, from parallel departments in two communication giants, describe what was being heralded in public announcements as an exciting merger.

Company X:

- ✔ "Let's get one thing straight. This was an acquisition, not a merger!"
- ✔ "We'll have to do things only their way."
- ✔ "They don't need two of us, and it won't be [people in the other organization] who hit the street."
- ✔ "Their lack of consideration and common courtesy doing their equipment inventory in our [site] was appalling."
- ✔ "Our technical expertise is no longer valued and is being discounted."

Company Y:

- ✔ "If they were really doing so great, we wouldn't have bought them."
- ✔ "Things are going to change, but my job should probably stay much the same."
- ✔ "It appears that we have less work and three times as many people. Some people aren't going to be here next year. And it could be some of us."
- ✔ "We don't know who we are any more. We don't even have a name [for this new department]. We use to be a great organization. Now everything is in disarray, and we don't know who's suppose to do what."
- ✔ "Now we're treated as numbers instead of human beings. Management's no longer committed to people. All they want to do is just get this merger thing over with. They don't care how we're feeling."

Looking at the merger from the side of the "acquired" group, Company X, we see that they were experiencing damaged self-worth, great uncertainty about their future employment, and feelings of failure that come from being "losers." Now, observing the situation from the viewpoint of company Y, we see, on the one hand, that employees have the satisfaction that comes with being "winners." But on the other hand, they also have fears that accompany destroyed support networks, and a management that has stopped caring about employees.

When you upgrade your accounting system, it's the people who make the new process work. When you merge two departments, it's the people who make the new organization work. (The sidebar gives you a glimpse of how tough department mergers can be on employees.) In truth, it's not the company, association, school district, military branch, hospital, or government agency that changes, but the people.

At least two-thirds of TQM (Total Quality Management) and reengineering efforts have failed. Not because they were bad ideas — there's nothing wrong with wanting to improve quality or streamline work. Rather, leaders forgot that changes are made by people — not a measurement system or a new matrix-reporting relationship.

Braving the unknown

Managing change means motivating employees to leap into an unfamiliar future, as well as getting them to trust that you know where you're going and what you're doing. (Not an easy task with a cynical, change-weary workforce.) Maybe in the good old days, when bosses were emperors, you could issue a decree, and your subjects would obey without question. But as Chapter 2 shows you, today's managers have limited authority over the behaviors of employees. Before you expect people to support your new marketing direction or team-compensation plan with enthusiasm and commitment, you should understand what discomforts and dangers you're asking them to face.

Here's a brief sampling of what employees experience when they abandon the familiar.

✔ **Support network gets disrupted.** As people search to feel more connected with others, work is replacing the community, and in some cases the family. In *The Wall Street Journal* article (1/12/2000), Sue Shellenbarger writes that one of the overlooked casualties of organizational change has been friendships — and with them that sense of well-being that comes with belonging to a group. Along with the breakdown of friendships, employees find their political network (that they've worked so hard to create) unraveling. Now, an environment that once felt secure and trustworthy has taken on a threatening edge.

Not only do employees take a hit when friendships are destroyed, but so does a company's financial results. In the same article, Shellenbarger reported a Gallup study of 400 companies. Researchers found that the strength of work friendships was a top predictor of "a highly productive workplace." In fact, those companies where people reported strong friendships also reported high customer satisfaction, productivity, and profits.

✔ **Conflict increases.** Change often makes people feel more vulnerable and less self-confident. As new ways shove aside the familiar, relationships break down and once agreed-upon roles and responsibilities crumble with the most aggressive employees gobbling up the pieces. Now, employees begin worrying about keeping their jobs, finding enough work to look valuable, maintaining their personal status, and protecting their self-worth. In this kind of stress-filled environment, is it any wonder that people begin building empires, undermining colleagues, and seeing peers as enemies? So, don't be surprised when teamwork begins eroding; change and conflict seem to walk hand-in-hand.

✔ **Mistakes occur more frequently.** As employees grapple with new roles and procedures, they face a steep learning curve before everything begins running smoothly again. If you've ever taken up a sport such as golf, tennis, or skiing, you know exactly what we mean. The process of trying, failing, picking yourself up, and trying again is extremely frustrating — especially for people who were masters of another sport or who were successful in their previous work environment. Therefore, when change hits an organization, two things happen to employees: They become more cautious in order to minimize mistakes and avoid looking dumb; they also become more critical about the mistakes that others make as a smokescreen to hide their own blunders.

✓ **Productivity decreases.** There's no way that employees can maintain the same level of efficiency, creativity, and output when they're in the midst of turmoil. A disrupted support network means that you have more difficulty finding answers, locating resources, and obtaining the help you need. If you're trying to avoid mistakes, then you do your work more cautiously and slowly. Unless you've got effective measurement tools in place, however, this loss of productivity sneaks up on you without warning. Things just start slowing down (and bureaucracy increases) as people protect themselves. Gridlock doesn't only happen on the streets of New York City; it also occurs in offices and cubicles around the world.

✓ **Self-worth takes a hit.** Work not only pays the rent or mortgage. For many people, it's also one way that they define who they are; it makes them feel good about themselves. Yes, individuals enjoy the sense of accomplishment that work gives them. But for some employees, their value as a person is also tied to their job title, the size of their compensation package, the amount of recognition they receive for their ideas, the size and location of their office, and the respect others show them. Change has a way of modifying all that by shifting people's authority, reducing their prestige, and undermining their self-confidence. Figure 1-1 shows you some of the changes at work (yes, you can read "work" as a noun or a verb in this sentence) that batter employees' self-worth. If you want to read more about self-worth, Chapter 5 has a major section on that topic.

Protecting with opposition

When people are faced with disintegrating support networks, escalating conflict, mounting mistakes, decreasing productivity, and shrinking self-confidence, resistance becomes a natural and rational response — all the more so if employees witness incomplete planning of the change effort, receive limited communications from above (not quite as high as the heavens), and remember past change failures. Under the circumstances, can you blame them for throwing up their hands, as well as roadblocks?

Resistance catches many managers unaware and unprepared. They believe that the value of and logical necessity for a change instantly legitimizes the effort. And they would be right if humans, like machines, didn't have professional and personal needs. But they do — people are emotional beings with hopes and dreams.

Loss of valuable work	Feeling out of control	Loss of positional power
Loss of visibiltiy	Reduced compensation	No recognition
Feeling unimportant	Not contributing	Loss of meaningful work
Feeling a failure	Humiliated	Kept uniformed
Smaller span of control	Job not satisfying	Not feeling respected
Feeling excluded	Disempowered	Loss of perks

Figure 1-1:
How employees' self-worth gets damaged.

The following example demonstrates how resistance can catch managers by surprise. Like most companies, leaders in a telecommunications giant used promotions and salary increases as their primary reward for outstanding performance. For the majority of departments, this method was an effective way to recognize successful employees. For one department, however, it proved unsatisfactory. The department's technically brilliant individuals excelled in their engineering specialties, but weren't particularly interested in developing their people skills. As one employee said, "I got my masters in physics because I wanted to do technical work. If I wanted to do this soft people stuff, I'd have gotten a liberal arts degree and gone into human resources." As a result, they were often passed over for promotions and significant pay raises.

To remedy this situation, the department created a "technical track." Now engineers could receive financial rewards for superlative performance outside of the traditional "management track." The department assigned a vice president (a highly technically focused individual) to design their tech track. After spending considerable time and personal effort, he produced a technical path with different levels, multiple compensation ranges for each level and criteria for upward mobility.

Rather than enthusiasm, which he expected, many engineers greeted the vice president with rage. Their comments included

- ✔ "They're insulting us. They're telling us that we're not management material. That we can't work with people."

- ✔ "We're second class citizens."

- ✔ "The technical track is the most abominable thing any group could have done to its people. You have deprived us of an opportunity for promotion outside the organization."

- ✔ "Now I can't hire internal employees [people from other departments] because no one wants to get pigeonholed."

- ✔ "I used to be a second-level manager. . . . Now I'm designated a first level by Human Resources."

- ✔ "This is a bureaucratic nightmare!"

Management quickly labeled the engineers' resistance to the tech track as whining, disloyal, and unprofessional. They failed to look below the surface to see the emotional core of betrayal, pain, and humiliation. The engineers naturally interpreted their assignment to the tech track as tantamount to being stigmatized forever with the labels of "poor people skills" and "poor management material." Individuals, no matter how technically focused, also pride themselves on working well with others — regardless of what the facts show. Without intending to, the tech track labeled employees as "managerially disabled," similar to the educational system of the 1950s that labeled some educationally diverse students as mentally disabled.

By focusing only on surface concerns, the leaders of the engineering department overlooked the real causes of resistance in their employees. They missed the deeper, stronger emotional issues. Five years later, bitterness and distrust remained.

What could the leaders have done differently to avoid damaging employee morale? Rather than focusing solely on the technical design of their program, they could have given technical and human issues equal billing. They could have conducted employee focus groups (see Chapter 6) to better understand peoples' feelings about being assigned to a "technical track." As a result of the focus groups, the original design probably wouldn't have been altered significantly, but leaders would have definitely communicated and marketed their tech track differently.

No matter how great you think your revised appraisal process is or how cost efficient your new shared distribution center makes you, bang-ups and hang-ups happen — and somebody's work world still gets upended. Therefore, successfully managing a change initiative depends upon how well you prepare for and respond to resistance. When you ask people to accept a new way of working, thinking or interacting with each other, you're asking them to modify what has made them successful for years or even decades.

To help you become a change winner, we include six chapters in this book just on resistance.

The Role of a Leader — at Every Level

If you can't stop the tide from rising or employees from resisting, then what can you do? A lot.

First, you can begin by "making peace" with reality, as one vice president in a Fortune 100 company did. After acknowledging how resistance to his change efforts was inevitable, he told us: "At first it was distressing to realize how high the hill was that I had to climb. But then, just recognizing that reality meant that I was halfway up [to the top]." Later he added, "As much as I might want to, I can't make all my changes at once, so just accepting that also puts me ahead of the game. The more I know about what to expect, the more successful I can be."

Accepting a reality doesn't mean you lay down passively letting life roll over you. It does mean, however, that you wisely choose your battles and shrewdly allocate your mental, emotional, and physical resources.

Second, you can focus on strengthening your change-management tools @m particularly the ones in the following list.

- **Becoming comfortable with ambiguity.** When you embark on a change effort, there's always some uncertainty, risks, and loss of control involved. No one has a crystal ball that lets him or her see into the future. You're taking a leap of faith into the unknown — trusting, that regardless of what happens, you'll find the right answers and have the ability to fix problems. As the French novelist and Nobel Laureate André Gidé put it: "One does not discover new lands without consenting to lose sight of the shore for a very long time." Even change winners dislike ambiguity, but they've learned how to work successfully without the "shore" in sight.

- **Practicing persistence.** Intellectually, most managers would agree that change doesn't happen overnight, but in their heart of hearts, many wish that it would. Because managers already have stress-filled and complicated lives, they'd like, just once, for things to run smoothly. And sometimes change efforts do, but more often than not, potholes and roadblocks are the norm. Therefore, change winners are those individuals who determinably stay the course even when everyone else around them wants to give up and look for greener pastures elsewhere. Those who persevere make it across the finish line.

- **Seeing "reality" through your employees' eyes.** If you could "beam-up" changes like Star Trek movies beamed up people, then you'd get along fine on your own. But, alas, you can't go it alone. It's employees who turn your vision into reality by abandoning the familiar and hurling themselves into the unknown. That means you need to understand what motivates the people that your success depends upon, as well as what problems they keep bouncing into — in other words, seeing the change through their eyes. Sitting at your desk, you experience a very different world than the one your people observe from their desks. When it comes to implementing organizational change, nobody's "reality" alone can describe all the issues or provide all the answers. That's why change winners seek to understand the world of their employees which is the only way to get a realistic picture of what's succeeding and what isn't. (For more information about what causes people's views of life to differ, Chapters 3 and 4 are great places to turn.)

✔ **Reducing stress level.** When you're under great stress, seemingly minor irritants escalate into major crises. You begin responding to situations with less logic and see fewer options open to you. Stress in one area of your life doesn't stay put; rather it wreaks havoc in all aspects of your mental, emotional, and physical being. Therefore, change winners make sure that they have multiple avenues for decreasing stress in both them- selves and their employees. If you'd like a sanity check about all the stress that's flooding you at this moment, look at the following sidebar. (And if, you'd like ways to reduce all that stress, turn to Chapters 21 and 22.)

We'd like to add one more tool that you'll need for successfully managing orga- nizational change with a minimum amount of struggle and trouble. That's lead- ing by example — or the shadow of your leadership. How you act — how you personally live the same changes that you ask of your employees — counts big time. In other words, only when your walk and talk match will people take the change-journey with you.

How's your stress level?

In 1967, Drs. Thomas H. Holmes and Richard H. Rahe at the University of Washington Medical School created a scale to help you analyze the amount of stressful events occurring in your life. Since their "Social Readjustment Rating Scale" was published in the *Journal of Psychosomatic Research,* (Volume 11, 1967), similar scales have popped-up in stress reduction workshops, on office bulletin boards and now at Internet sites. In fact, you may have already seen one or two of them.

Holmes and Rahe designed their scale and sta- tistically developed the numerical values after interviewing 394 people ranging in age from 30 to over 60. Their research led to the following conclusions: Different life events cause differ- ent intensity levels of stress; stress is cumula- tive; and change — whether positive or negative — caused stress in people's lives. In addition, Holmes and Rahe found that the more changes people were going through in their lives, the greater their stress levels, and the more susceptible they became to illness.

The following chart is the original "Social Readjustment Rating Scale" created by Holmes and Rahe in 1967 with a few minor adaptations to bring it up-to-date. (Those statements with a "*" were modified.)

(continued)

(continued)

Go through the list and check those changes that have occurred during the past 12 months. Each of the life-events listed has a score representing the magnitude of impact that a particular change will have in your life. Total your scores. *Any total score over 150 indicates that you have enough stress in your life to increase your susceptibility to illness.*

However, you may have many other personal events in your life, such as children in day care, long commute times, aging parents, a sick child, or a child doing poorly in school. All of these additional life events add to your stress level.

The complexity, pressures, and pace of the work place have increased dramatically over the past three decades. If you have to juggle changes at work such as reorganizations, acquisitions, process teams, or a new manager, they will add to the stress that you're dealing with in your personal life.

Therefore, to give you a more accurate picture of your personal stress levels we've included six additional lines for you to list your own particular home and work-related changes. Assign each a value (make a best guess by comparing with the original list) and add them to your total score from the original scale to see if you score over the 150 level. The greater your cumulative score is over 150, the more stress is eating away at your health.

Rank	Life Event	Mean Value
1	Death of spouse	100
2	Divorce	73
3	Marital separation	65
4	Jail term	63
5	Death of close family member	63
6	Personal injury or illness	53
7	Marriage	50
8	Fired at work	47
9	Marital reconciliation	45
10	Retirement	45
11	Changes in health of family member	44
12	Pregnancy	40
13	Sex difficulties	39
14	Gain of new family member	39
15	Business readjustment	39
16	Change in financial state	38
17	Death of close friend	37
18	Change to different line of work	36
19	Change in number of arguments with spouse	35
20	Mortgage more than twice your annual income*	31
21	Foreclosure of mortgage or loan	30
22	Change in responsibilities at work	29
23	Son or daughter leaving home	29
24	Trouble with in-laws	29
25	Outstanding personal achievement	28
26	Spouse begins or stops work*	26
27	Begin or end school	26
28	Change in living conditions	25
29	Revision of personal habits	24

30	Trouble with boss	23
31	Change in work hours or conditions	20
32	Change in residence	20
33	Change in schools	20
34	Change in recreation	19
35	Change in church activities	19
36	Change in social activities	18
37	Excessive or multiple credit card debts.*	17
38	Change in sleeping habits	16
39	Change in the number of family get-togethers	15

40	Change in eating habits	15
41	Vacation	13
42	Christmas	12
43	Minor violations of the law	11
	TOTAL	
Add-1		
Add-2		
Add-3		
Add-4		
Add-5		
Add-6		
	CUMULATIVE TOTAL	

Chapter 2

What Is Changing?

"I wish I could stop the world and get off."

Vice president,
Fortune 100 company

Sometimes it feels like everything around is shifting and sliding — spinning out of control. And at times it is. But the velocity of life's variability wasn't always so dramatic. If you had lived in a Western-world country at the beginning of the 19th century, your life would have been pretty similar to the lives of your parents, your grandparents, or even your great-grandparents. The horse and the sailing ship would still have been the major forms of transportation; long-distance communication still depended on letters and postal service; and manufactured items were produced by individuals working in their own homes.

A century later, all these things were radically altered. The railroad, the steamship, and then the automobile had transformed transportation; a revolution in communication had brought the telegraph followed by the telephone; and mass production revolutionized industry. During the 20th century, the rate of change took on a frantic pace as one technological innovation followed another — the airplane led to space travel, computers produced the Internet, robotic manufacturing gave way to virtual corporations. Indeed, today, change itself seems like the only constant.

Forests have been ravaged to provide books describing all the changes that have occurred, are occurring, and will occur. Thanks to Alvin Toffler, people now know that they hurtle through life in "future shock." Therefore, within this chapter, we focus on only the most recent changes that will likely impact your work world. This is a book to help you manage organizational changes. (If you're looking to manage your wine cellar, never fear; ...*For Dummies* has some of the best books on that topic, too.)

If you are not familiar with Mr. Toffler's work, you would enjoy reading his book, *Future Shock,* initially published in 1971. He predicted the rapidly increasing rate of change we are now experiencing and, most importantly, described what happens when people can no longer cope with the changes. He has since written two related books entitled *Third Wave* and *Powershift.*

The Changing World

One of the indelible images from the last quarter of the 20th century was the collapse of the Berlin Wall, followed by the fall of the Communist governments in Eastern Europe. These events resulted in part from the impact of communication's technology. Television images beamed via satellite showed the people of Eastern Europe all the consumer items available in the West — but not on their shelves. On the Internet, people from both sides of the Iron Curtain communicated about the freedoms available under democratic government. And Communist dictators were powerless to stop the flow of information that eventually led to their overthrow. The world had become smaller.

Increasing globalization

Today, humans live in one gigantic global village. With instantaneous communications, a new idea developed in Vietnam can now be flashed to scientists in Berlin and Oshkosh, Wisconsin, who can then add their own input, via the Internet.

As boundaries collapsed in cyberspace, national borders also began to fall. Mergers occurred between giant corporations from different continents. Daimler Benz devoured Chrysler; Vivendi, a French company, swallowed the Canadian liquor giant Seagram. Hearing multiple languages spoken during business meetings is becoming common place. Managers, who only needed one language, now struggle with speaking and understanding multiple "foreign" languages.

You find the development of a global market reverberating in every nation of the globe. Countries with protected markets have opened them up to free trade (some more than others). This global marketing explosion has led to the collapse of some businesses, while others have grown. Some nations have also begun feeling threatened by the mass invasion of foreign goods — and the culture that comes with them. The golden arches of McDonalds have become easy targets for people fighting to protect their culturally unique, noncommercialized way of life.

While the world market has led to the availability of more and varied consumer goods at lower prices, workers have also paid the price. In the process, many employees have been displaced and their lives unalterably changed, as they were forced to look for new jobs and even move to different parts of the planet.

To remain competitive, American companies have kept wage increases small; indeed, some workers have seen their salaries decline, when adjusted for inflation. Long time American industries have been moved off shore to take advantage of lower wages and cheaper raw materials. Jobs have been lost and workers forced to retrain themselves so that they could move into new positions available in high-tech industries.

Some workers have made the transition, but unfortunately, others got left behind in dead-end jobs. In the developing Asian countries, the demand for low cost goods has fueled their economies by way of escalating the number and increasing the size of sweatshops. As thousands of young people flee the countryside, the urban jungles offer jobs at extremely low wages and extraordinarily long hours — jobs that quickly get filled.

Territorial boundaries continue dissolving with the evolution of television's "reality" and millionaire game shows. Over the past nine years, MTV's *Real World* has kept the world captivated. Then in autumn, 1999, the television series in the Netherlands called *Big Brother* hooked millions of Dutch people. Nine strangers lived together for 100 days in a house with 24 cameras and 59 microphones broadcasting over television and the Internet. The media depicted everything, from the most mundane to the most intimate details of peoples' lives. The show's 24-hour Internet feed had millions of visitors from around the world — even those who couldn't understand the Dutch language. Now *Big Brother* has migrated to Germany, Spain, and America (though *Survivors* did beat *Big Brother* to the U.S. market).

Not to be outdone, *Who Wants To Be A Millionaire* began in Britain, but has successfully migrated to more than 20 different countries. Obviously, when it comes to sharing certain entertainment experiences, cultural walls no longer exist.

Intensifying diversity

Opening borders has meant that more and more people are moving freely from one nation to another, adding to the rich diversity of each country. Food, clothes, holidays, and music from different cultures have all enlivened and enriched lives. In California, for example, "minority" populations, including African-Americans, Asian, and Hispanics, outnumbered whites before the year 2000, giving that state's residents an abundance of cultural delights. Moving into the 21st century, women and people of color are expected to comprise the majority of workers in America's organizations, adding a wealth of creativity never experienced in the monolithic "Father knows best" world.

But diversity has come with a price — the increase of fear, discrimination, and aggression. Skinheads and paramilitary groups target ethnically, religiously, and racially different individuals. As once homogeneous European countries become racially and culturally diverse, they struggle with prejudice, clashing cultures, and conflicting ways of life (problems that were once thought the sole providence of the United States). Pressures abound on the political leaders of industrial nations to "protect" the majority from the growing minority. All these problems and pressures have led to tighter limits on immigration and work permits. Now some governments and some citizens reinforce an "us" versus "them" mentality, rather than encouraging "It's a small, small world" vision of unity.

Collapsing institutions

In the past, individuals looked to "stable" institutions for security — the government, the church, the family, and the company. But now, these institutions struggle with their own change and instability.

Using the United States as an example (because trends that begin in that country often end up in other parts of the world), many people have lost faith in their once dependable institutions. If participation in presidential elections is any indication, now less than 50 percent of eligible voters go to the polls, showing that the government is not a major player in their lives. Americans used to look to their houses of worship for a community and set of values to guide their lives. But, increasingly, individuals seem to be losing faith in established religion and looking inward to find their own spiritual path.

Nowhere has the breakdown of an institution been more apparent than in the family. Today, almost 50 percent of marriages end in divorce. The percentage of traditional two-parent families has greatly declined, while the numbers of single-parent families have increased. Past generations saw the family as a necessary part of their lives; however, many of today's young people are postponing marriage or choosing cohabitation rather than married life.

The breakdown of institutions has left human beings on their own, feeling that they can only depend on themselves and committed only to looking after themselves. This strong emphasis on individualism has brought enormous changes to the workplace.

The Changing Organization and Its Workforce

Perhaps you grew up in a family where one or both parents worked for a single organization until retirement. Lifetime employment was the reward for company loyalty and hard work. No longer! Under the impact of global competition during the last quarter of the 20th century, many organizations began downsizing and turning to temporary, no-need-to-pay-benefits employees.

Growing number of free agents

According to one survey, only about one-quarter of American workers strongly agree that their company feels a sense of loyalty toward them. Among workers themselves, less than half feel any loyalty toward their managers or their organizations. Instead of putting their "faith" in organizations, workers realize that they can only rely on themselves.

Many people now regard their status as being similar to free agents in major league baseball. These players feel little or no loyalty to a particular team. Their primary interest is to negotiate the best salaries possible for themselves. As a result, they may move from team to team constantly looking for a better deal. (And the teams feel little or no loyalty to their players — always on the lookout for new talent.)

Many American workers have begun following the same path. Approximately 45 percent of all workers between the ages of 18 to 25 have been at their current jobs for less than two years. Indeed, the director of human resources at a high-tech company told the authors that if he receives a resume from someone who has been at the same organization for more than five years, he assumes that the employee is neither successful nor ambitious.

To make themselves more "saleable," employees turn to traditional marketing techniques — brand marketing. They're creating the brand "me." Now, enhancing resumes means people create personal Web pages to showcase themselves, their accomplishments, and their sterling references. Similarly, people try to acquire as many skills as possible on every job to make themselves more marketable. Several employees interviewed at a large manufacturing company said they had decided to work there because of the organization's excellent continuous education programs.

Eroding powers of the boss

The decline in corporate loyalty has been paralleled by another development: distrust of authority. This skepticism begins early in the lives of many young people. It's not unusual to find third-graders questioning what teachers say or correcting them in front of the class. Indeed, veteran teachers acknowledge that a major change in schools has been a decline in the respect for authority.

People carry this skepticism into the workplace. No longer do employees assume that the "boss" is automatically right because he or she has a special title. Neither do titles protect managers from public scrutiny. On the front page of "Marketplace," *The Wall Street Journal*'s section B, you can read about the latest trends in your work world. Columnists, often quoting frustrated and angry employees, graphically describe the dumb things that bosses do. At the end of the articles, the writer requests that readers e-mail their comments — ensuring that fresh examples keep flowing. Using the Internet, people now have the ability to trade information about their working conditions and share dirty linen with the rest of the world — and even compete to see who has the worst boss.

Even CEOs are no longer sacred. More and more of the top executive from major corporations get ousted or leave under fire. Along with poor financial showing, these bright, talented people stumbled in many critical areas, not just financial. When these CEOs did trip, they couldn't ask for help from others (it's that stopping the car and asking directions thing), didn't listen to employees, and wouldn't be guided by their board of directors. They also found it difficult to quickly and openly admit problems so that investors didn't get surprised.

The corner suite no longer provides the safe bunker that it once did. To protect themselves, a small, but growing number of CEOs actively solicit formal feedback. Using specially designed questionnaires, these executives get honest "coaching" from other high-level managers and the board. Not a pleasant experience for them to go through, but the alternative is worse.

Differing needs of different generations

As different employee generations — with their diverse needs, values, and lifestyles — converge upon organizations, the impact has forced businesses to change how they relate to employees. One of the most noticeable changes occurred in the way employees dressed for work. From the power blue suit and white shirt or blouse, organizations shifted to allowing dress-down Fridays, and some even moved to a five-day-a-week relaxed dress code.

The Boss from You-Know-Where stories

"Tell Us Your Horror Story! . . . Horns, tails, and no apparent brain cells. Does this describe the person you call boss?" So opened a Netscape contest Web page in conjunction with AOL. From October 6 through November 3, 2000, individuals described, with 50 words or less, their worst boss. Each of the four weeks, four semifinalists were selected by Netscape program managers. Judges used the following criteria: 50 percent for humor and 50 percent for writing style. Each semifinalist won a Netscape t-shirt. At the end of the contest, the grand winner — the one best describing the worst boss — received CDs and DVDs from CDNOW.

Hired hands

The movie industry offers a great example of what the future holds for organizations. No longer do studio's "own" the people who make the movie. Rather, film producers must gather together a team of independent professionals to create a movie — searching for who's available. This team includes a crew of camera operators, lighting people, makeup artists, costume designers, and sound personnel. After they've completed the movie, these freelancers disperse and go onto the next job. Like these ad hoc film crews, those who work as programmers, project managers, HR experts, and user requirement specialists also move from job to job — staying only as long as the projects last.

A major difference between the baby boom generation, now entering their 50s, and their children is that the latter are less corporately driven. These children of the Baby Boomers, who number about 80 million, have watched their parents get laid off due to downsizing, mergers, and acquisitions. While their parents had remained loyal to their organizations, those in the following generation aren't planning to make the same mistake. As a result, many of them find freelance employment far preferable to working for any tradition-bound corporation — forcing companies to rethink their relationship with employees.

Technology is another area of generational differences. Growing up with computer games, the younger generations enter the workforce with a natural affinity for information technology — it's a way of life for them — and an ability to rapidly keep up with advances and new applications. Not so with the older generations. Many baby boom (and older) employees struggle to keep their technical job skills current. They're concerned (rightly so) about becoming obsolete — and this fear hits their self-worth. Ironically, embarrassment and fear of failure often causes them to put off learning the new technology that they need for staying relevant.

Next you've got the personal/family needs of different generations competing for attention and organizational resources. Young, unmarried individuals have one set of requirements; couples starting a family or with small children have different needs; parents with older and college age children have a third set; employees taking care of aging parents require different organizational support; and finally, individuals gearing up for retirement look for something completely different. And within each of these multiple stages of human existence, organizations must still cope with situations unique to each individual employee. And people wonder why companies have become overwhelmed by the multidirectional tug-of-war between generations.

Struggling to keep good workers happy

In many industries, top talent remains in short supply, and fierce competition exists for independent-minded free agents. When you lose a good employee and are lucky enough to fill the position with the same quality person, you should plan on at least four to six months of lost productivity while you get the new employee up to speed. That includes learning the job, fitting in with the culture, understanding how to get things done within the "system," developing a peer network, and figuring out the politics.

So, what should managers do who want to retain a well-trained, highly competent work force? To retain some employees, it means providing opportunities for personal growth and new job experiences. But many other people want more.

More time! With not enough hours in a day to get everything done, you and your family begin to suffer. Time has become a precious commodity. A young engineer at an aerospace company confessed that she envied her husband. Working long hours on her job, she couldn't spend time with her children — time that's lost forever. But her husband, a teacher, had the flexibility to share time with their children. Eventually, she'll quit unless her company finds ways to help accommodate her time needs — and that usually means flexible work hours.

Some other ways that business gives a helping-hand to harried employees include laundry service on the company's site, banking in the cafeteria, car washing next door, and personal time-off — little things that help life run a little smoother. In some high-tech companies, employees get a concierge service that includes running errands, doing grocery shopping, making meals, and picking up the kids.

Still other businesses help the overwhelmed employee by offering flexible vacation time and/or back-up support so that people feel freer to take their vacations. For employees drowning in meetings, a few companies offer monthly or even weekly "No meeting" days. With meetings consuming over 60 percent of many employees' workweek, people treasure those catch-up days.

It's always smart to retain good employees. The degree that you need fancy perks to keep people from jumping ship depends, in part, upon the labor market — how hard it is to fill vacant positions. Even as we write this book, a softening economy and mounting layoffs are shifting the labor market — from a very tight market to one of surplus workers scrambling for jobs. It'll be interesting to see how many of the nontraditional business perks survive the latest economic shift. (That relentless march of change never seems to take a breather, does it?)

When you ask the HR specialists who conduct exit interviews the reasons that people leave, you'll get an earful. What you'll hear is that people usually don't leave because of money but because of other issues. One of the biggest reasons for leaving is employees' relationship with their manager. (Not too surprising, is it?) People don't ask for much in return for hanging around and doing their jobs well. They'd like to be treated with respect, have their talent and hard work appreciated, feel listened to, and not have to fight for their dignity. But when you've got "The boss from hell" contests, obviously many managers haven't yet realized that their actions affect turnover. Perhaps free-lancers have discovered the best way to cope with this unpleasant situation: If you aren't somebody's "loyal" employee, then you don't have to put-up with lousy managers.

Evolving virtual corporations

Allowing employees to work from home provides one way to give them a little flexibility. For decades, salespeople have worked out of their homes. It's cheaper for organizations, which don't have to rent office space, and it gives the salespeople more flexible work schedules.

Because a larger number of employees already have computers at home and access to the Internet, telecommuting, at least for a few days of the week, is a viable alternative for people in many types of jobs. It also allows for stressed-out employees to spend a day *teleworking* in their pajamas, worried parents to stay home nursing a sick child, or concerned individuals to visit and comfort ill parents.

Some organizations have begun relying more heavily on *virtual teams* to accomplish projects. These teams may be organized from different offices in different parts of the world and never meet physically in the same location. Once they've completed the project, employees disperse to other assignments. This means that the old command and control management style no longer works — managers must develop a new way of supervising and supporting people and projects. Specifically, they must now help geographically and culturally dispersed individuals build communication and trust without any face-to-face contact.

With Internet technology, old management structures and functional silos crumble. Departments in different cities, or even different countries, no longer have excuses for not talking with each other. Customers can demand and get faster service from sales support, engineers, or billing departments. Suppliers can fix problems and deliver products or services more rapidly. Virtually overnight, the virtual corporation has reduced borders within and between organizations.

The Things That Aren't Changing

Sometimes it may seem that nothing is staying the same — with employees' basic values and goals constantly shifting. Yet, even free agents working in virtual offices still need some of the things that "old-time" employees stuffed in cubicles desired, including:

- ✔ **The need for recognition.** Contrary to popular opinion, people want more from life than monitoring the value of their stock options. And recognition means more than banking larger checks. People want to hear simple words like "thank you" and "great job." They want to know that their hard work — even when telecommuting in their pajamas — is appreciated. Regardless of what generation a person comes from, most human beings still want to feel valued.

- ✔ **The need for respect.** Employees want to know that they and their work are respected. Yes, recognition is a piece of that, but it goes beyond it. Respect means being treated with consideration, told why a project has been taken away, and not being kept cooling your heels for a meeting that should have begun an hour ago. It's also means being shown common courtesies, not being humiliated (in public or private), and having ideas heard and considered. Managers who respect their employees make sure that the communication channels remain wide open.

- ✔ **The need for trust.** Simply put, people want to know that their manager, coworkers, and employees have confidence in them to do the job right. Without trust, individuals spend their work life with others looking over their shoulders, second-guessing them, and refusing to accept their new ideas. When trust exists, people feel like equal partners in the decision making process, empowered to carry out new ideas, eager to meet customers' needs, and confident to lead their team. Big bosses aren't the only people who need to be trusted.

- ✔ **The need to feel productive.** Work remains central to the lives of most adults. Many people define themselves (some more than others) by what they do and how they do it. Therefore, these individuals want to feel productive in their chosen fields. Recent studies have shown that more and more older Americans are continuing to work at full time jobs long after the conventional age of retirement. They enjoy the feeling of accomplishments that come with work, and in turn, their skills and experience provide a valuable resource to organizations.

- ✔ **The need to grow.** There's a saying, "The only difference between a rut and a grave is the depth." You don't have to be a three-year-old child to get a thrill from learning something new — 100-year-old adults still do. Learning new things keeps people vibrant and energized. And that's how employees want to feel when they come to work in the morning — if not, they should look for new jobs.

Making Sense of All This

One of the differences between the people considered "wise" and those just "ordinary" isn't their brilliance, but their awareness. The wise see what's on the distant horizon that most others miss. They rarely get startled by those events that leave "ordinary" people surprised or stunned. The wise keep their eyes and ears open to the subtlest shifts in sights and sounds. They know that every event or pattern had an insignificant start long before it blossomed in the light of day.

Successfully managing organizational change requires the same type of wisdom. It also means that you constantly recognize the realities of the evolving 21st century organization and the attitudes of the employees who work there. Some of these realities and attitudes are in full bloom; others are just taking hold. For the time being, the people you manage:

- ✔ Want respect for cultural and individual diversity.

- ✔ Feel little or no loyalty to you or your organization.

- ✔ Don't feel the need for lifetime employment.

- ✔ No longer respect titles or people in authority.

- ✔ Want flexible work schedules that allow for more individuality.

- ✔ Are focused on quality of life and family, not staying on the job around the clock.

- ✔ Want the same things out of work that you do — recognition, respect, trust, productivity, and personal growth.

Successful change managers have discovered how to work in this brave, new world.

Part II
Over Two-Thirds of Changes Fail — Don't Let Resistance Put You in This Statistic

The 5th Wave   By Rich Tennant

"I assume everyone on your team is on board with the proposed changes to the office layout."

In this part . . .

Some changes succeed; most change initiatives don't. One of the major reasons is the challenge of resistance. Identifying and dealing with resistance can help make or break your change efforts. In this part, you discover how you can successfully deal with the resistance challenge.

Chapter 3

Resistance: Looking at Losers and Winners

> *"Our process team finally met. Each of us walked into this room totally sure that we knew what our customer complaint process was. Do you believe we couldn't agree on the third step in that process — the one that comes after we pick up the phone and the customer dumps on us? Here we are, 11 of us sitting in the same room day after day, and we couldn't agree on what the third step in our process was. No wonder different departments don't get along with each other. We all walk around here lost in our own little worlds."*

Customer Service Representative
Private company

No one needs to tell you that we live in a world filled with rich variety. You just have to look around, and you'll see the diversity in the kinds of food people eat, the clothes they wear, and the hair color they were given or selected. Each person puts his or her personal stamp on life. They make statements telling others who they are and what's important to them. Yet, you also see trends, with individuals loosely clustering into similar groupings, such as rock fans versus classical music aficionados, free agents versus nine-to-five commuters, or marketing department versus engineering labs. One other such grouping is that of change winners versus change losers. In this chapter, you discover what separates the change winners from the change losers and how you can join the winner's team (if you aren't already there).

Getting That Competitive Edge

Whether it's e-commerce or extreme sports, someone always crashes, while someone else struts around waving his or her trophy. Whether it's having the bigger house or the bigger office, one person sits riddled with jealousy, while another reigns smug and arrogant. So it goes with leading organizational change — some managers bomb, and others get featured in glossy business magazines. Is it luck, or karma, or the stars they were born under? Maybe it's all of the above or none of them.

What we know is that while brain power and advance degrees help, they aren't the answer. We've seen the "best of the best" bite the dust trying to implement reengineering. Similarly, age, gender, or number of frequent flyer miles doesn't seem to separate losers and winners. What does? We shudder to tell you — but here it goes: It's knowing how to motivate human beings. Yup, all that mushy people stuff that they don't teach in college, and even if they did, most students probably wouldn't have paid good money to listen to that gobble-gook.

The simple fact is that implementing change is getting people to do what you want them to do — and that's also what they usually don't want to do. So along with hammering out budgets, designing software, creating marketing strategy, negotiating with suppliers, and manufacturing widgets, you've also got to understand the minds and (and dare we say?) hearts of the people who work for you — or how else will you know what motivates and demotivates them? How else will you get them to willingly follow you — because the "organizational man" who blindly obeys has gone the way of sliderules.

But you're in luck. We're not suggesting that you rush out to hold lunchtime sensitivity circles or drum beating sessions in the desert. (Of course, you can if you want to.) We do suggest, however, that you look critically at what causes losers to bomb and winners to succeed. For, in truth, the people stuff isn't really the "soft" side of managing — it's extremely tough and demanding.

Okay, you say, I'm willing to give winners a try, but what can I possibly discover from losers? Paul Krugman, a professor of economics, can answer that question. He wrote in *New York Times Magazine* (July 26, 1998), "Many people have said that America's worship of success hurts our souls, because we care only about getting ahead. I have no expertise in such matters. But I am sure that our unwillingness to hear about anything but success makes us especially vulnerable to the failure we fear."

And he's right. We love hearing about successes. But what we sometimes forget is that triumph doesn't spring fully grown. It's painstakingly cultivated. Winners got that way because they learned from their own mistakes, and luckily, learned from the mistakes of others — thereby dramatically reducing the mistakes they would have actually made. To help you step into the change-winner's circle, the rest of this chapter focuses on the four areas that differentiate losers from winners.

Difference 1: Recognizing That You Don't Have the Market on Reality

Have you ever driven down the street and seen a house freshly painted the most awful color, say a proudly putrid purple? You know, those people did have a choice of colors — no one forced them to choose purple. Or how about that multicolored, multitextured tie that your office partner so proudly sports when he dresses up for clients? Face it: People definitely do see the world through different eyes.

And as South Africa's former President Nelson Mandela so painfully describes, even his prison guards on harshly desolate Robben Island couldn't agree.

> *"One of the things that we discovered is that men are not the same, even when dealing with a community that has a tradition of insensitivity toward human rights. Because the moment we arrived at Robben Island, a debate started amongst Afrikaner warders, some saying, 'Let's treat these people harshly so that they respect white supremacy, others saying, their side in history will ultimately win, we must treat them in such a way that when they win, it should not be a government of retribution.' Even in a country known for it's absolute and singular vision of white superiority, diverse frames-of-reference still flourished."*

Patti Waldmeir
In Anatomy of a Miracle

How did everyone get to be so different?

Human beings have their own unique *models,* or personal frames-of-reference about how their worlds operate. These models keep most people from becoming overwhelmed by the millions of data bits bombarding everyone each second.

Danish science writer Tor Norretranders explained in his book, *The User Illusion: Cutting Consciousness Down to Size,* how people ignore most of the data bits assailing them. Instead, *filters* or psychological screens, allow in only a miniscule fraction of what is actually out in the big wide world. Then from this tiny amount of data people create a blurry, incomplete, and inaccurate picture of what they now call "reality." While models protect you from drowning in information, they also stop all those valuable ideas and experiences from making it through your protective filters.

In his book *Future Edge,* Joel Barker uses the Swiss watchmaking industry as a real-life example of how your models can lead you into danger. For centuries, the Swiss led the world in watchmaking. Then in the mid-1960s, scientists at the industry's research institute developed the electronic quartz movement.

With the benefit of 20/20 hindsight, this breakthrough could have guaranteed continued Swiss dominance far into the future. But it was not to be. In 1967, the Swiss watch manufacturers rejected the invention. As Barker puts it: "After all, it didn't have a mainspring, it didn't need bearings, it required almost no gears . . . it couldn't possibly be the watch of the future." Confident that their researchers had come up with nothing more than a clever gimmick, the manufacturers raised no objections when the inventors proposed showcasing the newfangled device at that year's World Watch Congress. There, as Barker reported, Japanese executives from "Seiko took one look and the rest is history." Between 1967 and 1980, Switzerland's share of the worldwide watch market dropped from 65 percent to 10 percent, and 50,000 out of 62,000 workers in the Swiss watch industry had lost their jobs.

How do your filters work?

Your models of the world evolve from three interacting and overlapping filters. Only the *biological filters,* such as sight, existed with you when you were born. The other two filters, *cultural* and *individual,* evolve over time. However, even your biological filters don't remain constant throughout your lifetime. As the aging baby boomers know so well, at 50-years-old, they don't have the same visual sharpness or clarity that they once did at age 15.

Figure 3-1 graphically shows you how our three filters create a world of people who often live in their own worlds.

Biological filters

External data must first pass through your senses or your *biological filters.* These filters include the five basic ones of hearing, sight, smell, taste, and touch. But you also have object weight, body position, and balance. And some psychologists would add intuition.

You continually lose a great deal of information because of how your senses are designed. Even with "perfect vision and hearing," you're limited to seeing only what's between 38 to 680 mili microns in our light spectrum and hearing only sound waves that fall between 20 to 20,000 Hz. The rest of the world is locked out to you. How different the same world seems for the snake that uses infrared light or the bee that sees with ultra-violet light, or your dog who howls with pain when sirens scream by.

Take the desk in your office that appears stationary. It's not really stationary. It's spinning around at approximately 17.29 miles per minute or 1,037.60 miles per hour as the earth rotates on its axis. It's also hurtling at 1,110 miles per minute or 66,600 miles per hour through space in the earth's orbit around the sun. Out in space, using one of the military's super-duper powerful telescopes, we can watch our zipping-through-space desk. But back on earth, our less than accurate senses tell us that we and that desk are not moving.

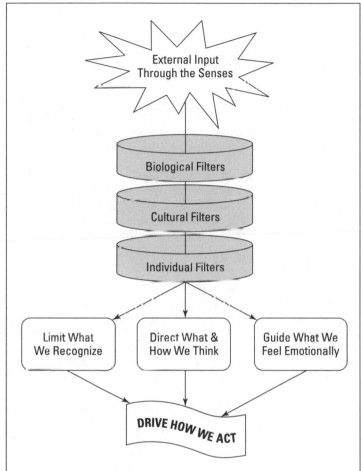

Figure 3-1:
Three filters that cause people to live in their own worlds.

For most people, however, our biological filters allow similar data to get through. Therefore, what creates the real differences among personal models are the next two filters: cultural and individual.

Cultural filters

Cultural filters are the socially transmitted behaviors, beliefs, patterns, and language of the country where you were raised. In one country, wrapping paper taken off of the gift is wadded up and thrown away, while in another country such action would offend the giver. In one culture, diners consume raw sea urchins as a delicacy, and in another, people turn their noses up in disgust.

Your cultural filters:

> ✔ Screen out further opportunities for experiencing the world
>
> ✔ Significantly narrow how you interact with and interpret the world you do get to experience

Within a country, regional or economic subcultures act as additional filters. Growing up in Meridian, Mississippi, is very different than being raised in New York City or Washington, Iowa, or Santa Barbara, California. Sometimes they can almost feel like different countries.

Next we have our family's ethnic backgrounds. Greek, Native American, Brazilian, Ukrainian, African-American, Irish, Moroccan, Chilean, Kenyan, Persian, Norwegian, Jamaican, Tibetan, Mexican, Filipino, or ancestors off the Mayflower — they give different flavors to people's lives and add cultural filters to their models.

Individual filters

Your *individual filters* evolve from your unique, personal experiences. This third filter begins in childhood. Were you the first, middle, or last-born? Did you live with both parents, or one, or multiple sets? Did you grow up in a "Leave It To Beaver" home or have to cope with alcoholism, drug addiction, or mental illness? Were you a parent's favorite, or did you not seem to fit in at all? Did you show interest in sports, opera, or computers? Were you healthy, or did you have physical, learning, or emotional difficulties?

Childhood remains so idiosyncratic that children growing up in the same family often describe totally different experiences — and do grow up to be totally different people. David Kaczynski, for example, worked as a social worker with runaway children, while his older brother Ted, known as the Unabomber, was convicted in 1998 of wounding or killing 26 people with 16 package bombs.

How do change losers and winners see the world?

When you watch how change losers and winners manage, you notice two very distinctly different operating styles. On the one hand, change losers don't respect diverse thinking. For them, all roads lead to their personal opinions. On the other hand, winners respect diverse thinking. For them, other's viewpoints are just as valid as their own.

Change losers see only one way — theirs:

✔ They believe that only their view of every situation is correct. Losers dismiss other frames-of-reference as irrelevant or wrong.

✔ Losers can't take diverse ideas from the four corners of the organization and integrate them into meaningful and creative solutions.

✔ Sadly, losers' models keep them forever blind to the human wealth that glitters in their organization.

Change winners see multiple ways:

✔ They believe that their way of thinking or doing is only one of many — and not always the best.

✔ They take diverse ideas from all across the organization and integrate them into meaningful and creative solutions.

✔ Winners have a model that helps them see the wealth that fills their organization.

Can you win at change without this one?

You can't join the winner's circle without respecting and working well with different types of people, different ideas, and different models of the world.

Recognizing differences is the foundation of everything that winners do. Managers only succeed because they acknowledge and accept their own very human limitations and then skillfully tap into the diverse creativity found in their organizations. For some of you, that's standard operating procedure.

But we still see managers, at all levels, fighting to keep their way as the right way, the only way. To them, we say it one more time, "You can't win if you think you've got the market on right answers. You've got to value the answers of others if you expect to win at managing change."

Difference 11: Planning Before You Leap

Without a good plan guiding your journey, all you do is swim around in circles, getting discouraged, exhausted, and eventually watching your change effort drown. Plus, if you're not sure where you're headed, you certainly won't get your employees jumping in after you. There's nothing earth shattering about this meat-and-potatoes concept — every Business 101 class teaches the need for careful planning. But you'd be surprised how many managers believe that developing a well-designed implementation plan is a waste of their time. In fact, some people hate developing implementation plans more than they do creating meeting agendas and to-do lists.

Get a plan for winning

If you're interested, Chapters 11 through 15, 18, and 19 give you detailed information for creating your own change implementation plan. That's right — six whole chapters devoted just to planning. It's that important for managing successful change efforts.

All we're giving you right now is a brief introduction to your plan. Here are the most basic items that you should include in your implementation plan:

- ✔ Description of what your organization looks like today and what you want it to be like after your change (Chapters 12 and 13).

- ✔ A communications plan for telling people about the change, as well as keeping them up-to-date as your change effort evolves (Chapters 15 and 18).

- ✔ A recognition plan for how you will celebrate successes and reward those employees that support you and your change initiative (Chapter 14 and 19).

- ✔ Guidelines for defining processes, roles, and responsibilities so that you reduce a lot of the conflict and power struggles that are so deadly (Chapter 14).

- ✔ Measurements for identifying accountability and tracking success (Chapter 14).

Understand how change losers and winners plan differently

There's no question, a good change implementation plan takes an extraordinary amount of time, money, and effort. It can also be tedious and laborious. Only winners who truly understand the power of a solid plan willingly put themselves through this initial first step — and then actually use their plan.

On the one hand, change losers find planning a hassle — so they do it poorly or not at all. These managers see themselves as "big picture" people who don't want to get bogged down in detail. They're much too busy doing their "real" work, so they delegate the planning process to others. Whoever develops the plan owns it and feels ownership. So, when the change leaders delegate, they appear as if they are abdicating their ownership and ultimate commitment to what's in the plan.

Change losers who create their own plan, be they line management or staff, do it behind closed doors. Isolating themselves from the people who understand the realities of everyday work life, they can't make its content relevant to employees' needs.

When losers plan, they focus on the mechanical aspects of getting the "job" done and forget about the impact on human beings who have to do it.

On the other hand, change winners find planning a hassle — but they do it anyway. These managers know that without a well-constructed plan, they aren't going to get anywhere — fast or slowly. If it's their change initiative, then winners make sure that it's also their plan. They participate in its creation. They get employee input from around the organization — no job is too inconsequential if it's going to be affected by the change. When determining what to include, change winners focus on not only technical issues, but also employees' concerns and ways for reducing people's resistance.

In addition, every action item has a person responsible for it and is measurable. Winners know that what you measure is what you get.

Because winners see their plans as a "living" documents, they keep them updated and relevant.

Difference III: Making Managing Change a Part of Your "Real" Work

Oh, those wonderful, crazy, lazy days when you could do what you were hired to do. You know, file the returns, respond to passenger complaints, take care of patients, or schmooze with big donors. But now managers also have to get their people to enjoy working in interdepartmental process teams or worry about employee development. What's a tired, overworked, underappreciated, and poorly paid manager to do? Some just tell their people to go do it and then blithely get on with their "real" work. Others consciously lead the charge by rolling up their sleeves — making the same sacrifices and facing the same work disruptions that they ask of their people.

Managing change is part of a manager's job

Simply put, what you get rewarded for is usually what you continue doing. Because most people get promoted for their on-the-job technical performance, that's what they continue emphasizing as they move up the management hierarchy. (And it's usually also those same technical skills that they're good at and enjoy.) Unfortunately, during the scramble up the management ladder, it's often the people side of the business that gets short thrift. Yet, when it comes to successfully managing change, it's the human side of the business that becomes a major part of your responsibilities. This means helping people:

- ✔ Understand the reasons for the change.
- ✔ Accept the need for the change.
- ✔ Implement the change into their day-to-day work.

Of the many people skills you need to accomplish the preceding three tasks, a critical one is actually role modeling the changes in your own work — walking the talk. You know from your own experience, if you don't see your boss doing the same thing that he or she asks of you, you'll think twice about changing the way you work. In Chapter 7, you get a lot of in-depth information about how winners successfully lead the charge.

Looking at the difference between change losers and winners

It all comes down to understanding what motivates people. Change losers either don't understand or underestimate the motivating power of walking the talk. Change winners actually balance their emphasis on day-to-day technical work and personally implementing change in their own jobs.

On the one hand, change losers continue business as usual. These managers see change as an extracurricular activity that doesn't really impact their "real" work. Other people need to change, but certainly not them.

Change losers think that their managing-change job is done when they announce the change, get employees trained, and put up a few posters. Losers forget that they, too, must disrupt their own carefully protected work lives to get the change implemented successfully.

For some change losers, the title of manager means getting a job done, not wasting time pampering employees — to do something they're being paid to do. Therefore, consciously and actively role modeling the change as a way of motivating people never occurs to losers.

On the other hand, change winners make the change effort a part of their daily management responsibilities. They understand that even the smallest change requires that they, as managers, had better start integrating it into their jobs if they expect to motivate employees to also make the change.

Winners know that employees keep them under a microscope. Therefore, every meeting, either planned or spontaneous, becomes an opportunity to discuss and champion the new direction. Similarly, winners painfully carve out of their densely packed calendar time for listening to tales of woe and stories of success. They constantly look for opportunities to show their commitment.

Being honest with themselves, these managers admit that they really hate all the disorder that comes with changing, but they also know that it's the price they must personally pay if they're going to ask others to follow them into the great beyond. For them, being a manager means people-motivational skills, as well as having a technical expertise.

Difference IV: Calling a Truce with Resistance

This section is the shortest in this chapter because the next five chapters give you everything you've ever wanted to know about resistance but didn't know you were suppose to ask. In this overview, we only say that resistance is like the Lone Ranger — initially, you think it's your enemy, but it's really your friend (except there's unfortunately no silver bullets).

Resistance takes a bum rap

Even the toughest, most self-assured managers throw up their hands in dismay when faced with resistance. Yes, it's frustrating, time consuming, and frequently incomprehensible, but rarely is it 100 percent worthless. Actually, employees' resistance provides you with one of the most valuable tools for successfully implementing your changes. Like anything else, you just have to understand it.

Resistance makes the difference

We shock most managers when we tell them that resistance is really an ally they should cultivate, not an enemy they need to destroy. For some reason, losers never break out of the traditionally negative thinking about resistance. But winners manage to escape the conventional negative stereotype.

Change losers struggle forever against resistance. They remain locked into the six myths of resistance:

- **Myth 1:** Thinking that resistance is avoidable
- **Myth 2:** Believing that good leaders eliminate resistance
- **Myth 3:** Judging resistance as bad

> ✔ **Myth 4:** Thinking people only resist those changes they don't want
>
> ✔ **Myth 5:** Considering people who resist disloyal
>
> ✔ **Myth 6:** Believing that resistance has no value

You can get an in-depth look at these myths in Chapter 4.

Fighting against resistance, losers leave wounded messengers, who try to warn them of problems, bleeding on the floor, and littering the officescape. As self-protection, employees take their opposition underground. When that happens, managers have lost control of their change, remain vulnerable to sabotage, and never know when or where subversion will strike.

Change winners harness the power of resistance. These managers escape from the six myths of resistance. They know that the opposition has something valuable to tell them. Sometimes, they may not personally like what they hear, but they put the success of their change initiatives ahead of protecting their egos.

While winners never grow fond of resistance, they work extraordinarily hard to keep it up front and visible. The last thing they want is to "wake up" one day to an organization of dissension and deception.

Making Yourself a Winner

Winners put success ahead of their own personal needs. They may desire the pleasant feelings that come with such small indulgences as shooting messengers or not attending training courses that everyone else must, but they don't give-in to those urges. Self-indulgence is a luxury they can't afford. The price tag for success is nothing less than self-control — first being able to manage oneself. Winners do what loser won't.

Chapter 4

Don't Shoot! Resisters Aren't Your Enemies

In This Chapter

▶ Understanding the six myths of resistance

▶ Analyzing the eight most common excuses for resisting

▶ Turning excuses into solutions

Michael Hammer says, "two thirds of the reengineering efforts he has seen have crashed in flames, shot down by people's reluctance to go along and by management's — especially top management's own ineptitude and fear."

Fortune
April 17, 1995

Resistance from family, friends, coworkers, or employees usually annoys people and can actually fill them with rage. Managers often consider the individual who defies them as illogical, stubborn, disloyal, perverse, and belligerent and sometimes, even a bad person. However, when that same manager opposes another, it's because he or she is rational, clever, and is in the right. You'd better face it: There's nothing logical about the big "R."

It's hard enough forcing three-year-olds to eat their peas, but even more difficult (if that's possible) forcing adults to do what they don't want to do — such as reengineer their jobs out of existence when they need to pay the rent. You can send children to bed without dessert, but how do you force the people in your organization to be good team players who follow the leader? You can't. So what can you do?

Knowing Your Options with Resistance

As it applies to people, *resistance* is a mental, emotional, or physical opposition to changing their world as they know it. In itself, resistance is neither good nor bad — or maybe it's really both, and people simply choose on which to focus. Resistance, like the body's immune system, is a double-edged sword. For example, people may be thrilled when their immune system defends them against the stomach flu that's gripping their colleagues. But when the same defense system turns against them or a loved one in an autoimmune disease, such as lupus or rheumatoid arthritis, they may feel angry and betrayed.

Your job managing an organization is tough enough without also dealing with resistance at the same time you're trying to implement a change. But life doesn't give you a choice in this arena. When you ask people to change, resistance naturally comes along for the ride. When you're faced with rebellious employees, you have four options:

- **You can bury your head in the sand, hoping that resistance magically disappears and harmony miraculously replaces it.** Unfortunately, resistance doesn't vanish; instead, it's your change effort that evaporates.

- **You can attack rebellion with a sledgehammer, hoping to crush it into oblivion and then get on with business as usual.** But if you bludgeon resistance, talented and creative people stampede to the nearest exit; those that do stay go underground becoming bitter, and even subversive.

- **You can use the carrot-and-stick approach, hoping that one or the other will eventually break the logjam and get employees cooperating.** In this method, you're trying to co-opt resistance, but in the long term, resistance proves more resilient.

- **You can turn resistance into a tool that works for you instead of against you.** With this last option, you must make friends with resistance (well, not best friends, but at least a coexistence). Resistance doesn't magically disappear, but it does become less destructive and for some managers, even an asset.

What no one can do is avoid resistance. It's like the ocean's tides, a natural part of our existence. You can no more stop people from protecting their self-interest or self-worth than you can stop the sea from rising and falling. The rest of this chapter shows you how to turn the ever-present resistance from an enemy into an ally.

Avoiding the Six Myths of Resistance

In the same *Fortune* article that introduced this chapter, Michael Hammer, the father of reengineering, saw resistance as "natural and inevitable." He also considered it "the most perplexing, annoying, distressing and confusing part of reengineering."

If we consider resistance as "natural," then why does it still annoy us? What causes experienced and successful professionals to throw up their hands in frustration when confronted with resistance? What makes them turn their back on a gold mine of information? And if information is power, what makes them abdicate such an immense amount of power?

They're hamstrung by the following six myths.

Myth 1: Resistance is avoidable

People tenaciously cling to this myth, ever hoping that some day they will give an order and people will follow. They hang on to it for four reasons:

- ✔ They want to believe that there are still some things in life that they can control — simple things like getting others to accept our brilliant ideas, follow our farsighted direction, or agree with our creative solutions. If we're managers, resistance signals that we can't "control" our employees, and therefore we're bad managers.

- ✔ They need to know that all their careful planning results in a successful change. There's nothing more discouraging than working hard and doing all the right things, only to see resistance undermine everything. Why should managers put out all that effort when it won't ever be enough — when some employees will just never buy-in?

- ✔ They want that new time reporting system, that revised appraisal form, or that merger to be straightforward. And it would be if managers could only focus on the technical parts of their change effort and ignore the human beings who make it all happen. Assuming that resistance is avoidable gives people the okay to avoid the messier, frustrating, and complex people demands and direct their efforts to the easier and less complicated technical issues.

- ✔ They view change efforts as an extra to our "real work." If we can pretend that resistance is optional, then we can spend less time fiddling with the change and more time doing what we enjoy — the work "we're paid to do."

When managers kid themselves that changes occur resistance-free, they set themselves up for failure. Change winners expect and plan for resistance.

Myth 2: Good managers eliminate resistance

Sorry, but good managers can only significantly reduce resistance; they can never eliminate it. Unless you have clones exclusively working for you, you've got people who disagree with your wisdom — and some who even fiercely reject it.

This myth puts managers in a no-win situation.

- ✔ Most organizations equate good leadership skills with control, and resistance with loss of control. If you work in that kind of culture, you're seen as a weak manager. When you admit that you have resistance you're also admitting to yourself and others that you can't control your employees — that you're a "bad" leader.

- ✔ The best approach to managing resistance is providing an environment that encourages questions and challenges management's ideas. At the same time that managers encourage overt resistance, others label them as weak and ineffective.

- ✔ Some time in the distant past, we developed the absurd idea that leaders were supposed to be omniscient — all-knowing. That's an easy delusion to maintain when the accepted management style was "dictator,"but it's deadly today when you're trying to revise a benefit package or introduce a new science curriculum. You'll fail without the honest pushback from the employees who know the job or the customers who are on the receiving end of your new program.

Contrary to prevailing beliefs, leaders who successfully manage change, don't eliminate resistance — they encourage it, minimize it, and learn from it.

Myth 3: Resistance is bad

It's annoying to think that 95 percent (or maybe it's 91.7362 percent) of the time, resistance isn't 100 percent bad. Yes, we had the Luddites in England who erroneously believed they could protect their jobs by destroying the new machines of the Industrial Revolution. But then we've also had the Ukrainian people who successfully rebelled against the old USSR in order to govern their own country.

In organizations, we've seen individuals who have opposed a technical track or a mommy track, professors that wanted to teach rather than only publish, and medical interns who fought to reduce 48-hour hospital shifts. These people had valid reasons for their resistance.

Rebellious employees may also have legitimate reasons for not immediately signing up for a new way of doing business. From their point of view within the organization, they see and experience things that remain hidden to you, their manager. If you knee-jerk and shoot messengers as the enemy, then you'll be left operating from a data vacuum and vulnerable to surprise attacks from hidden problems. If you keep an open mind, however, you become richer for the valuable information that resisters pass on to you. True, occasionally their message may be about your own leadership imperfections, but then sometimes (as much as it's tough to admit) people are not always perfect.

While resistance can be destructive, the ultimate destruction comes from managers' unwillingness or inability to listen and respond to the message.

Myth 4: People only resist those changes they don't want

People also end up resisting those changes that they initially wanted.

You've probably heard the saying, "Be careful what you wish for; you just might get it." We have a friend who ecstatically plunked down money on the house of his almost-dreams — it needed a lot of fixing up. Five frustrating years and a $100,000 later, he has almost brought it up to his standards. While he's still glad he bought the house, the honeymoon was short-lived, and discouragement quickly set in. Sometimes people are like our friend, going after things that look good, but turn out so radically different once they get into it.

In his book *Managing at the Speed of Change,* Daryl Conner explained why people often end up resisting the very changes that they once worked so hard to get. When embarking on a new journey, we do so with "uninformed optimism." We naturally focus on all the great and wonderful things that will happen. Think about starting a new job, taking your marriage vows, having those 1.5 children, or getting that promotion — didn't you mostly imagine the opportunities, excitement, advantages, and possibilities of your new adventure? Many of those expectations may have come to pass. But so, too, did a lot of unexpected and unpleasant experiences. Even if you had tried to predict and prepare for all the things that might have gone wrong, there's no way you, or anyone else, could have done it. People just aren't as creative or crafty as life seems to be.

Here people are celebrating their new-and-improved circumstances, when Murphy's law crashes the party, ants invade the picnics, and their parades get rained on. All it takes is a good dose of reality to knock people into Dr. Conner's next phrase, "informed pessimism." The stronger the uninformed optimism, then the greater the informed pessimism will be — and the more disillusioned, bitter or angry people become. And then voilà, they're now resisting the very thing they worked so hard to get.

So, you needn't wonder any more why people who once supported your wonderful recommendations turn on them, and maybe even turn on you. In the words of the late 16th century, English theologian, Richard Hooker, "Change is not made without inconvenience, even [when going] from worse to better."

Larry got what he wanted, but it wasn't what he expected

The following was originally reported by the Associated Press and subsequently recounted in *The Darwin Awards: Evolution in Action* (2000) by Wendy Northcutt.

Larry Walters, a 33-year-old truck driver, had a lifelong dream of becoming an Air Force pilot, but poor eyesight kept him grounded in his North Hollywood, California, home. Every weekend, he would loll around in his backyard lawn chair longingly watching as jets from Los Angeles International Airport (LAX) flew above him.

One day, Larry realized life was too short to let it go by "grounded." Off he went to his local Army/Navy surplus store to purchase 45 weather balloons and several tanks of helium. He would build his own flying machine, thank you.

In the backyard of a friend's house in San Pedro, he attached all 45 weather balloons to his well-secured Sears aluminum lawn chair. Once they were inflated, each balloon measured six feet across. On the morning of July 2, 1982, Larry loaded himself up with a six-pack of Miller Lite, some sandwiches, and a pellet gun. His goal was to gently float 30 or 40 feet in the air to enjoy a vista across sprawling Los Angeles. When he was ready to come back to earth, he expected to pop a few balloons with his pellet gun and just as gently land.

With great anticipation, Larry climbed into his "cockpit." His cheering friends cut the ropes anchoring his "plane," and Larry began his first solo flight. Instead of peacefully gliding into the smog-filled LA sky, Larry's lawn chair blasted off like a rocket ship. It didn't stop at 40 feet, 400 feet, or even 4,000 feet. In fact, it wasn't until he reached an altitude of 16,000 feet that the thinning air checked the lift of the balloons, leveling him off.

Horrified that he might unbalance himself if he popped a balloon, Larry drifted for nearly an hour contemplating his options and feeding his courage with beer and sandwiches. Eventually, Larry found himself floating into the primary approach corridor for jets landing at LAX. Delta and TWA pilots, who were the first to spot Larry, radioed the tower that they were passing a guy in a flying lawn chair.

Cold and increasingly desperate, Larry finally found the courage to pop a few balloons. His descent went smoothly until he landed on a power line, briefly blacking out a major area of Long Beach. Climbing out of his lawn chair, Larry was led away in handcuffs by waiting police officers.

Yes, Larry got what he wanted, but it definitely wasn't what he expected.

Myth 5: People who resist are disloyal and bad

Every now and then, you'll find a rotten apple in the bag, but not too often. So, too, resistance may occasionally come from disloyal employees. But just like most of the apples you buy, the majority of individuals who oppose your "great leap forward" are good.

They're just human beings struggling to protect themselves and their families. When they undermine your change efforts, employees do so for five very legitimate reasons. Resistance occurs because people:

- ✔ Feel a loss of control and want to keep what little control they may have left.

- ✔ Are experiencing too much change in their lives and can't cope with more.

- ✔ Honestly believe that the change effort is wrong for them or the company.

- ✔ Have seen previous change initiatives crash in flames or die a lingering death — so they don't want to invest in something that'll also fail.

- ✔ Want to avoid damage to their self-worth by a change that reduces their power, makes them appear useless, or makes them feel inadequate.

In Chapter 5, we discuss these five reasons in-depth, including how to minimize their impact on your employees.

Myth 6: Resistance has no value

Just as resistance isn't 100 percent bad, it also isn't 100 percent without value. In fact, behind all your employees' "whining," "bellyaching," and "ungratefulness" lie hidden the answers that'll make you and your change effort a success. But first, you've got to control your frustration and resentment at the people who throw up roadblocks to your change. Then you've got to rummage through employees' excuses to discover both what's about to blow up and how to fix it before it derails you and your change effort.

Figure 4-1 shows how you can travel from the myths of resistance to reality.

Long live the opposition

"The opposition is indispensable. A good [leader], like any other sensible human being, always learns more from his opponents than from his fervent supporters. For his supporters will push him to disaster unless his opponents show him where the dangers are. So if he is wise he will often pray to be delivered from his friends, because they will ruin him. But though it hurts, he ought also to pray never to be left without opponents; for they keep him on the path of reason and good sense."

Walter Lippmann

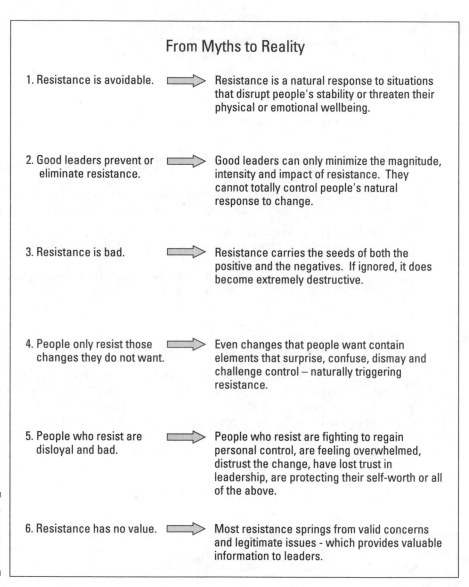

From Myths to Reality

1. Resistance is avoidable. ⟹ Resistance is a natural response to situations that disrupt people's stability or threaten their physical or emotional wellbeing.

2. Good leaders prevent or eliminate resistance. ⟹ Good leaders can only minimize the magnitude, intensity and impact of resistance. They cannot totally control people's natural response to change.

3. Resistance is bad. ⟹ Resistance carries the seeds of both the positive and the negatives. If ignored, it does become extremely destructive.

4. People only resist those changes they do not want. ⟹ Even changes that people want contain elements that surprise, confuse, dismay and challenge control – naturally triggering resistance.

5. People who resist are disloyal and bad. ⟹ People who resist are fighting to regain personal control, are feeling overwhelmed, distrust the change, have lost trust in leadership, are protecting their self-worth or all of the above.

6. Resistance has no value. ⟹ Most resistance springs from valid concerns and legitimate issues - which provides valuable information to leaders.

Figure 4-1:
Breaking away from myths.

Unlocking the Power of Resistance — Listen to Excuses

Although you may intellectually see some value to resistance, what about some hard, real-life examples of how resistance can actually help you? The following eight most common excuses are your keys to benefiting from employees' resistance. When people refuse to march to your drum beat, examine their excuses rather than hitting them over the head with the drum. You can discover a surprising amount of riches.

The protective power of excuses

Few people are dumb enough to tell their boss to go pound sand, or that the joker sitting in the next cube isn't their "internal" customer — "and no way am I going to treat him like a customer." Nor will employees tell the powers-that-be how overwhelmed they feel having to deal with one more crazy new thing. And certainly no one would admit how demoralized they feel seeing the special project that they've worked on for seven months handed over to someone else — especially someone who they intensely dislike.

Along with the need for showing political correctness and saving face, people also want to wake up in the morning believing that they're good human beings — not lazy, disloyal troublemakers. So, employees need credible explanations to justify, to themselves and others, their lack of cooperation — their legitimate reasons for not being "good" employees.

Don't overlook the riches in your own backyard

In the mid-1800s, a farmer decided that he was not making enough money. Writing to his cousin in Canada, who was working in the recently developed coal-oil business, he asked for work. His cousin responded that he couldn't hire the farmer because he lacked knowledge of the oil business. The farmer studied everything there was to know about oil until he knew what it looked like, how it was made, and how to refine it. He was hired.

According to county records, the farmer then sold his farm for $833 and moved to Canada. As the new owner was herding his cattle to the brook, he found that the farmer had put a plank edgewise across it to skim a dreadful-looking black scum off the water.

And so in 1859, was launched America's first oil discovery — the multimillion-dollar oil fields of Titusville, Pennsylvania.

Russell Conwell
Founder of Temple University

That's where excuses come in. They give individuals reasonable, rational, and recognizable explanations for resisting. But just as importantly, they also provide managers with the opportunity to hear employee issues, fix present problems, and avoid future disasters.

Even though every change initiative has its own list of excuses, we have found a core of eight excuse categories that pop-up the most frequently. Unless you have a huge change effort underway, you won't be faced with all eight excuses. Now, here they are to help you locate the riches in your own organization.

Excuse 1: Change isn't consistent with present culture

> *"The big push now is for team work. But the only people who get the big rewards are the heroes who single-handedly save projects. We're still creating a company of lone-rangers, not team players. Why should I risk my bonus to help some one else get theirs?"*
>
> Supervisor of Fortune 200

The underlying problem in the preceding quotation is that management underestimated the power of its existing culture. Briefly, *culture* is the underlying values and beliefs shared by a group of people to support a common purpose and shape acceptable behavior. Like a big octopus, its tentacles reach out to all parts of your organization. Whether it's teamwork or quality, nothing succeeds unless your organization's underlying values and outward behaviors continuously reinforce that new direction. In fact, culture ruthlessly undermines anything that doesn't fit in with the status quo. Just as our body rejects transplanted organs such as liver, kidney, and heart — organs desperately needed to sustain life — so, too, does an organization's culture reject changes needed for its survival.

In the introductory quotation, the Fortune 200 company that wanted teamwork unfortunately had underlying values and behaviors that were reinforcing individual performance. In fact, they had a culture that actually worked against teamwork. By keeping the old culture in place, leaders loudly communicated that they were not serious about teamwork. If managers had listened to the excuses for not supporting the new direction, they would have quickly learned that their change was headed for failure — unless they created a teamwork-friendly culture.

Hearing Excuse 1 means that you better make your organization's culture compatible with the change or the change will be destroyed. Please think about the following three red flags before proceeding.

1. Look for the places where the change and the existing culture clash. Any place you find a conflict between your change and the organization's culture, the culture always, always wins.

2. Make sure that you really do need that change before mucking around with your organization's culture. Changing a culture is very complex and exceedingly difficult process. It actually becomes a huge, separate change effort in itself.

3. If you do decide to modify your organization's culture, every morning take your patience pills along with your vitamins. Changing a culture is a long, drawn-out, and frustrating process. Just look at GE — it's taken Jack Welch over 15 years to change GE from a traditional, sleepy manufacturing company to the powerhouse that it is today.

Excuse 2: Employees don't understand why they need to change

> *"Don't tell me to change how I've worked these past 17 years unless you can also tell me why it's all of a sudden wrong. I haven't heard my customers complaining."*

Manager, government agency

In the preceding quotation, management forgot to sell the change. All too often, managers think that great ideas should sell themselves. But they don't. Just because you think that decentralization or reengineering would make your organization more customer responsive doesn't mean that your employees share your views. In the new business age, where managers are no longer kings and employees subjects, good ideas need champions.

Excuse 2 signaled that these government-agency employees received incomplete communication about the change. People neither understood how very unhappy their customers (taxpayers) were nor how the proposed change would help employees do their jobs better. Management lacked an employee "sales package" that specifically spelled out the current difficulties and benefits of the change, as well as how to help people see the significant disadvantages if they didn't change.

Further more, employees felt demoralized — that all those years of hard work were wrong. You won't buy something that makes you feel bad about yourself — nor will your people. The managers in this government agency forgot to preserve employees' self-worth. All people heard was how bad everything was, which translated into what a bad job everyone was doing.

You have to start selling your change so that employees understand the reason to "buy." Here are some ideas for convincing your employees to make the purchase.

1. See your employees as customers — make sure that you understand their needs and expectations. This concept can be a radical one for some managers, but you have to decide how important getting employee buy-in is for you.

2. Sell. Sell. Sell. And if at first you don't succeed, then sell, sell, sell some more. Advertising experts tell us that a successful sale requires people to hear a message at least three times. Similarly, public speaking gurus chant the mantra, "Tell them what you're going to tell them, tell them, and tell them what you told them." Managers must also have the same focus and consistency when selling to employees.

3. Include in your advertising campaign, not only what's going wrong and why everyone needs to change, but also what employees have been doing right. And they have to be doing a lot right, or you wouldn't still be in business.

Excuse 3: This change is poorly planned

"We're all running around like chickens with our heads cut off. Management doesn't know what they're doing or what they should be doing. It's one crisis after another and I'm beginning to feel like some paramedic."

Supervisor, software company

In the preceding quotation, it looks like nobody's in control. There's nothing more damaging to your credibility than to have your change running out of control — unexpected problems, missed delivery dates, power struggles, and confusion over who does what. In other words, management doesn't know what they're doing, so why should anyone risk following them?

With the small software company talked about in the quotation, employees' frustration loudly told management that they lacked a credible implementation plan. In fact, leadership not only created an incomplete plan, but also never shared what they did have with employees. This meant that people faced a change not knowing where they were headed. Nobody knew who was supposed to be doing what, when, how, and where. Not trusting that management knows what they were doing, employees felt discouraged, angry, and resentful.

The military historian S.L.A. Marshall wrote in his book, *Men Against Fire*, " . . . faith in the rightness of a cause cannot sustain the fighting will of troops unless they believe that the larger military undertaking will succeed." Well-developed change implementation plans give employees the feeling that you will succeed. And without those plans, you'll be lucky to get even a few brave souls following.

A winning plan

In 1944–1945, one of the most complex military undertakings in history occurred — D-Day and the battle for northwestern Europe. Military leaders coordinated land, sea, and air invasions against the brutal forces of nature and the entrenched Nazi army. They succeeded — not only because of the soldiers' courage and tenacity, but also because of extraordinary pre-invasion planning.

An implementation plan that covers all critical steps and issues demonstrates that you know what you are doing. Let your employees help you.

1. Use your employees to help you decide what's lacking or what needs greater focus in your implementation plan. One way you can do this is with the employee focus groups that we describe in Chapter 6.

2. Go back and update your plan based upon your people's input. Yes, it takes a lot of time and effort, but you'll now be able to show your employees that you know what you're doing and where you're all headed.

3. Make sure that you always share that implementation plan with the people who are being affected by your change. It's not just a three-ring binder for you. That plan also signals to your employees that you know where you're going and what you're doing.

Excuse 4: There is no communication

"I feel like the proverbial mushroom — you know, kept in the dark, fed a lot of stuff, and waiting to be canned. All we get are memos and newsletters telling us what we've already heard from the rumor mill. Nobody's talking to us."

Employee, manufacturing company

In the preceding quotation, management did not understand the needs of its employees. Like a lot of organizations, managers in the preceding manufacturing company focused solely on the messages that they thought were important and then used the easiest way to present those messages — written. They forgot to check to see what issues were also critical to employees. And they didn't realize that people get the most information from face-to-face communication.

Whenever you communicate with someone, your success depends upon presenting information that is meaningful to your listener. You might say that your listener becomes your customer. Whether it's an international marketing meeting or a small accounts payable department, your listeners have specific issues and questions that they need you to answer in order to walk away feeling satisfied and informed.

Furthermore, the most effective way to communicate with people is actually talking with them. Of course, that takes a lot more time and effort than sending memos or zipping off e-mails. And when it comes to talking about a new direction, you'll also most likely have to deal with an auditorium packed with or a room full of frustrated people. But when done well, you'll find that the greatest payoffs, to you and employees, come from taking that risk and personally talking with them.

If you're interested in more information about how to communicate your change efforts, check out Chapter 18.

You need to customize your communications to meet the listener's requirements. Each group you speak with will have similar but different requirements.

- ✔ Use multiple ways for communicating with your employees, but make face-to-face discussion your primary method.

- ✔ Apply the customer-supplier model to when you communicate with employees. Ask yourself: What are my employees' (customers') communication requirements? How well am I meeting those requirements? How can I do a better job?

Excuse 5: People don't know what the change means to them personally

"I'm willing, but my manager hasn't told me yet what she wants me to do differently. I'm waiting to hear it from her."

Accountant, bank

In the preceding quotation, the bank had just announced a new customer care program. The presentations to employees were at an impersonal, corporate level. Management did not show people how this change related to their personal day-to-day work.

Remember that old saying, "You can lead a horse to water, but you can't make it drink?" The same thing goes with your change initiative. You've got to convince employees to "buy" into it — force just doesn't work. And that means putting on your marketing hat. Just as individuals purchase a product or accept an idea based on how good it makes them feel or how it can personally help them, so too with managing change. Just because you think something is great, doesn't mean that your people will feel the same way.

Make it face-to-face

Numerous studies have found that people get more information from face-to-face communications than written because approximately:

- Seven percent of information comes from the words.

- Fifty-five percent comes from facial expressions and body language.

- Thirty-eight percent comes from vocal intonation and inflection.

Therefore, you've got to create the conditions and provide enough information so that employees convince themselves to "buy" your latest-and-greatest idea. It is hard to even "accept" a change unless you understand what it means to you.

If you look at successful marketing you see that specific customers groups get targeted — age, economic levels, cultural backgrounds, past buying practices. Similarly, selling to internal customers requires that you target specific departments or functional groups. Different employee groups will

- Have different reasons for needing the change
- Use it differently
- Gain different benefits
- Struggle with different problems

You need to help employees relate the change to their own specific workplace and needs. Unfortunately, this means that the same cookie-cutter speech won't quite do the job. You want the same message, but with different related examples. This also means that you need to know a bit about the work of the group in front of you.

1. Package your change effort to both the general organization, as well as to specific job groups. This way, employees will see how the new direction fits into the their organization and relates to their personal jobs.

2. Go to other companies and benchmark both their success and, yes, even failures. Make sure that you look at not only at how the change succeeds in the entire company, but also what it looks like in individual departments.

3. Talk to your employees using lots of user-specific examples from your benchmarking. Show how the same change succeeds in organizations and departments *similar* to their own and explain what problems they might encounter on their change journey.

A peek in the personnel manual

Here's a quick guide into what makes up your organization's policies and procedures.

Policies are written rules or guidelines that tell employees what's acceptable. Examples include

- ✔ Having employee raises and bonuses based upon their annual appraisals.

- ✔ Requiring a vice president's approval for overtime.

- ✔ Forbidding any type of discrimination and harassment.

Procedures are the "how to" steps for implementing the policies. Examples include

- ✔ What does the appraisal form look like, who fills it out, how is it reviewed with the employee, what input does the employee get, who signs it, and who determines compensation based on the job evaluation.

- ✔ When you can request overtime, the form used to make your request, who you give it to, and who approves it.

- ✔ How employees report discrimination or harassment and the actual step the organization takes to respond and follow up.

Excuse 6: Policies and procedures don't support the change

"Nobody's ever appraised me on 'delighting the customer.' I get paid for doing my own job. People who get paid for keeping customers happy can worry about that."

First-level manager, telecommunications company

The comments of the first-level manager in the preceding quotation occurred as a result of the leaders not ensuring that policies and procedures were consistent and aligned with their "delighting the customer" program. Sure enough, the appraisal form made no mention of the customer, which only reinforced employees' old behaviors and habits. Whether it's appraisals or overtime policies, day-to-day practices that don't reinforce the new effort only undermine it. Because managers left a disconnect between their change initiative and their procedures, employees had a built-in logical reason to say, "No! You're not serious about the change."

People constantly scan for cracks and crevices of inconsistency. One of the first places they look is the "written laws" that govern how employees and the organization work together. Keeping the old policies and procedures only reinforce the old behaviors. If you want to change behavior, change the ties that bind. If you want to make a culture change, define the new culture you want and then be sure to compare it with the personnel manual and other pertinent practices.

You need to modify your policies and procedures to fit your change effort. Excuses can wreck your change, so eliminate the grounds for the excuses.

1. Go through your policies and procedures with a fine-tooth comb to indentify inconsistencies with the new way of thinking and acting. Particularly, you should review how you evaluate and reward people — those are two biggies. What you measure and what you reward is what you get.

2. Rewrite policies and procedures that conflict with your new direction so that they now support your change. Each change has it own set of issues. The following are modifications made by the telecommunications company that introduced this excuse:

   • Developing a new set of operational goals related to customer satisfaction.

   • Creating a new set of performance measurements based on customer satisfaction. That might also mean requiring managers to actually talk to customers before writing-up employees' appraisals.

   • Adding a section to the appraisal form that focuses on customer satisfaction.

   • Adding new training courses for "delighting" the customer.

Excuse 7: Nobody knows who's supposed to do what

"This whole decentralization's a disaster. When I ask for help I'm told, 'Well I don't really do that anymore — only when the sky's blue on the fourth day of the sixth month.' And then that same person had the audacity to call and tell me that I'm doing his job!"

Marketing supervisor, software development company

Many changes create different work processes and require employees to take on different roles and responsibilities. The need for redefinition or at least clarification of processes, roles, and responsibilities is often overlooked. Plain and simple, without a common understanding about how the new work gets done — it doesn't. As with the preceding software company, people waste precious time trying to figure out who does what, when, and where, as well as rush to protect their jobs. Work stops, customers suffer, and the reorganization grinds to a halt.

When processes start breaking down, so, too, does accountability — who is responsible for getting what job done. You start finding important work falling through cracks. Too late you realize that no one is there to catch the work as customers also start disappearing. And you don't have anyone to fill in the cracks before even more work gets lost.

All work is part of a process

When things get jammed up, the experts say, "It's the process that's broken, not the people." They're right. You don't work in isolation. You need things from others to get your job done, and you give your work to others so that they can accomplish their jobs. Thus, when a process breaks down, so, too does your productivity.

Briefly, a *process* is a set of interrelated activities that follow a defined flow. Every process starts with some input, usually a customer's (internal or external) request, then moves sequentially through a number of specific work tasks and ends with an output. Only after you

document a process can you then assign clear responsibility for each task to an individual or work group. You avoid lots of headaches if everyone associated with a specific process understands and buys into the workflow and who-does-what responsibilities.

The combination of defining a process, role, and responsibility clarifies "how we do work around here" and "who does what around here." This helps people to feel good about their job, produce quality work, increase productivity, and keep happy customers. You can't beat that!

Additionally, in times of change, employees naturally look after themselves. To be blunt about it, protecting one's job always comes first. But power struggles over who-does-what is more than just fighting for personal power. It's:

- Justifying one's job — read paycheck
- Protecting one's self-worth
- Maintaining a smidgen of control in a world out of control
- Protecting one's standard of living

And you can be sure, wherever power struggles occurred before the change — they become World War III as people's control disintegrates during the change.

 You've got to make sure that each of your people know what their job is and how all the jobs work together. Not knowing "who's supposed to do what" is a reasonable excuse for holding back and not trying too hard to make the change work. It's a great excuse for resisting.

1. Document all work processes affected by your change. This documentation may mean getting the cooperation of other managers in other departments. That's because start-to-finish work rarely gets accomplished in only one isolated work group or department.

2. Once you know how a process works, then help employees clarify their roles and responsibilities in that particular process. Just as important as getting the mechanical requirements of your change effort in place is making sure that all people understand how their work fits into the greater whole.

3. Now, share your documented process and redefined roles and responsibilities between different departments and individuals so that everyone knows how jobs all fit together.

Excuse 8: Management's not serious about the change

"We're pushing to become a paperless company, but my boss only uses his computer for e-mail and stock quotes. So, why should I change the way I'm working?"

Graphics designer, advertising

The "leader not serious" excuse provides ample reason for employees not supporting the change — they believe it will go away anyway. There are many ways for the employees to conclude that their manager is not really serious about the announced change. It is particularly easy to reach that conclusion if the manager's actions do not match the words.

Whoever came up with the saying, "Don't do as I do, but do as I say," didn't know anything about managing change. In reality, it should go, "We don't do as you say, we do as you do." That's because, at the first sign of inconsistency, employees dismiss a manager's words and focus on the behavior.

Nothing kills a change effort faster than having employees hear their managers say one thing, but do another. Blind obedience is dead. Now, employees demand that leaders earn trust and loyalty. If you have any inconsistency between your words and actions, it:

- ✓ Signals dishonesty to employees
- ✓ Breeds mistrust of your leadership
- ✓ Ferments anger toward you
- ✓ Results in resistance to the change

Rightly or wrongly, managers unwilling to make the same changes they demand of everyone else loudly communicate that they're not honest and trustworthy — traits people consider the most important in a leader.

Employees aren't mind readers. (Thank heaven!) It doesn't matter how strongly you think you support a change, only that employees clearly see your commitment — over and over and over again.

Your credibility is oh-so-fragile

In a study sponsored by the American Management Association, nearly 15,000 managers nationwide were asked, "What values (personal traits or characteristics) do you look for and admire in your superiors? Analysis identified 15 categories. The most frequently mentioned were

✔ Integrity (is truthful, is trustworthy, has character, has conviction)

✔ Competence (is capable, is productive, is efficient)

✔ Leadership (is inspiring, is decisive, and provides direction)

You need to critically analyze your own behavior to see how well you role model the change. Some leaders even ask others to monitor and coach them on the role-modeling task. Forget about having the luxury of keeping any of your old, comfortable habits during times of change (even if it's only one or two of them). You must always (and we do mean always) live the new behaviors day-in-and-day-out to maintain your integrity in the eyes of your employees. Once you've lost your credibility, you've lost your ability to lead others.

We know that this recommendation sounds harsh and rigid. But, we have learned that role modeling is one of the most important and powerful tools you have for success and that the lack of role modeling is your fastest way to failure. You can find more information about role modeling in Chapter 17.

Words of Wisdom

We can all take a lesson from Hamlet's comment to Rosencrantz and Guildenstern: " . . . there is nothing either good or bad, but thinking makes it so." When faced with resistance, how we think about it determines whether it balloons into a monster that devours our change effort or evolves into an ally that ensures success. The choice is yours.

Chapter 5

Why People Will Always Resist

"After 30 years of treating patients, I can honestly tell you that I understand how the human mind works, less now than I did when I got out of medical school. I'm constantly amazed by how smart people become prisoners to their emotions. And you and I aren't any different. We're all trapped by our emotions."

Psychiatrist

*O*h, why can't people be like computers? When computers talk back, you can hit a different key. When they freeze, you can turn them off. But human beings are completely different. People have no keys to hit, and no switches to turn off when they're uncooperative. In fact, psychiatrics and world-renowned experts in neurobiology still have a universe to discover about how individuals' "minds" and emotions actually work, let alone, how to reprogram them.

Face it, for all the brainpower that people run around with, they're also creatures of deep, difficult-to-understand emotions. Often people try to delude themselves into believing that they always act logically. But what about road rage, fear of flying, and love at first sight — nothing very logical about these responses. If you're on this planet in human form, you operate using both orderly intellect and messy emotions — and, at times, emotions rule with a far firmer hand than anyone cares to admit.

Therefore, if you want to reorganize your accounting department into process teams, get the principal's buy-in for your new athletic program, or convince a customer to accept a different delivery schedule, you need to become ambidextrous. That is, you must understand both their thoughts and feelings. You must understand what causes them to accept or reject change.

Your vast educational system has prepared you (well, most everyone) to succeed in the world of technology and logical thinking. But, unless you've spent years in psychology classes, and devoured self-help books you usually get blindsided by resistance. And even then, even after you've mastered all this "soft" human stuff, you can still get baffled and bewildered by resistance. (That's because the "soft" stuff is really the harder stuff to deal with.)

This chapter helps you become more ambidextrous in managing resistance. First, you must understand the five reasons that cause people to resist your brilliant ideas. Those five reasons are

- ✔ Feeling out of control
- ✔ Drowning in change
- ✔ It's a terrible idea
- ✔ Too many past failures
- ✔ Protecting self-worth

After you grasp the reasons, you're ready to move into the tools that reduce resistance. As you read this chapter, please keep in mind that:

- ✔ No matter how pigheaded, disloyal and crazy people's resistance appears — it's usually rooted somewhere in realistic concerns.
- ✔ Understanding those concerns is the first step to gaining people's support.

Reason 1: Feeling Out of Control

Life is often like trying to sit down on a chair that some one has pulled out from under you. You expected solid support, but instead got shocked with a painful free-fall. People expect life, like chairs, to remain predictable and dependable. And, in a strange way, it is. Life's predictably unpredictable and dependably undependable. You can never know when a drunk driver will crash into a school bus, when a breast cancer gene kicks in, or when a plane will crash. . . .

Hey, wait a minute, you say — *For Dummies* books are supposed to be fun, lighthearted reading. Not this heavy stuff of planes falling out of skies. And you're right. They usually are. But as hard as we tried, we couldn't find a jovial way to treat one of the most important subjects in people's lives — their quest to live free from fear, their quest to minimize life's pains and maximize its pleasures. And that's what control is all about — to make your lives and the lives of your loved ones safe from harm.

Please keep a balanced perspective. Remember, you're managing resistance to make your change successful. Then remind yourself that there will be a time to celebrate and feel good about a job well done.

What we can count on

Even though you can't stop tornadoes, prevent Alzheimer's disease, or fix world hunger, you can at least control some things in your lives. How about preventing the printer from never jamming, your boss from stealing your ideas, and U.S. car companies from becoming foreign owned? No? Well what about counting on customer loyalty and supplier dependability, or never going through another reorganization? Not these either? With very little that people can control, it's not surprising — when they do have something that seems reliable — that they don't want some one mucking with it. Take that tried-and-true manufacturing process that's always worked pretty well, thank you — someone's going to fight to keep it from changing. Or when you've shined like a star and received large bonuses, you're not likely to welcome the uncertainty of team compensation. Everyone knows that Sally, Tom, and Morris are just mediocre performers and will destroy your rating.

Where does this leave you? With one thing that you can count on — people will wage war to keep control. So when resistance pummels you, the first question to ask is: Do people feel out of control? Is your simple change in HR benefits or your new better-than-ever way for moving inventory demolishing people's sense of control?

What it feels like when we lose control

Think back about a change you've gone through that stripped away your sense of security. You probably experienced one or more of the following feelings:

- Fear
- Denial
- Vulnerability
- Confusion
- Helplessness
- Defensiveness
- Bitterness
- Depression
- Anxiety
- Anger

HUMAN INTEREST

What people say when they feel out of control

Listen to the people who resist the latest and greatest changes in their organization. Beneath their words, you will hear the struggle to keep what little control they have from slipping away. They say things like:

☛ "Nobody's telling us anything. Just call us the middle-manager mushrooms."

☛ "Will doing this role and responsibility stuff change my job?"

☛ "Reengineering will only break something that's not broken."

☛ "I should head a team to oversee this [employee] taskforce. They may not see all the important issues that I do."

☛ "It's all moving too fast for me to know what to expect any more."

☛ "What's going to happen to me?"

Your tool: Communicate more and better

Communication? That's nothing new. Everyone knows that communication's important. Yes, they do, but many leaders (at all levels) still don't do it. Communicating well takes soooooo much time, and the communicators frequently find themselves in vulnerable positions. (Who likes standing in front of a room full of angry people?) Our experience has shown us that people implementing change efforts are usually so focused on getting the technical steps right that they forget about talking to the people. Furthermore, these more-comfortable-with-technical-issues managers usually shy away from the messier emotional sides of leadership, never becoming ambidextrous.

Good communication gives people greater direct and indirect control over their lives. The best way of understanding these two types of control is to think about driving a car. When you have direct control, you make the car turn, change lanes, and stop. As much as you might wish, you can't drive any of the other cars around you.

Avoiding the other car is where indirect control comes in. As a defensive driver, you watch other cars and their drivers. Say that you're zooming down the highway at 70 mph to make a meeting. You sense that the car on your right, without a flashing turn signal, is going to cut in front of you. You have two choices: Speed up and keep that car out or slow down and let it in. But you can't actually take over the steering wheel of that other car. With indirect control, you get enough information to make informed decisions — even if you can't be in the driver's seat of that other car.

Helping people achieve direct control: They feel that their concerns are heard and acted on

As you read the following recommendations, you may find yourself thinking how basic they are — how every good manager should already be doing them. But reality is much different. Using the following upward communication's tools takes a lot of time, patience, skill, and hard work.

- ✔ Giving employees a structured and anonymous (safe) way to communicate with management, such as annual upward-feedback surveys. But that's not enough. You must also respond quickly to the feedback by summarizing people's concerns and then either fixing the problems or telling them what you can't do and why. If you don't take this step, then don't ask for feedback. You'll only reinforce people's fear that you don't care about what they think. Feedback without your response is one of those cases where doing nothing is better than doing it badly.

- ✔ Making employees feel safe in meetings so that they can ask tough questions and tell you what's really worrying them. And remember, the instant you lose your cool with one person, you've lost everybody's trust.

- ✔ Giving people multiple ways of letting you know, in real-time, what's happening in their organization. Chapter 6 gives you specific tools for doing this information gathering. But, again you must act on that feedback or explain why you can't.

- ✔ Creating employee teams to fix problems. Individuals who live with the problems are often the best ones to fix them.

- ✔ Showing that you are truly listening to people by:

  - • Looking at them when they're talking and using other body language that shows you're interested. Appearing interested is a difficult skill to fake for more than a second or two.

  - • Summarizing important points. Summarizing shows that you're listening and lets you check your own interpretation of what people are saying.

  - • Respecting their opinions, even if they differ from yours. Most of us intellectually agree with this concept, but have difficulty putting it into practice. See Chapters 3 and 8 for help.

  - • Listening patiently and not interrupting even when people are irritating. This ability to restrain yourself depends upon your emotional intelligence — which we discuss in Chapter 8.

Helping people experience indirect control: They feel that you keep them informed

Most managers do a good job talking with their people about the "job." But when it comes to managing change, communications seems to get clogged in the bureaucratic pipeline. During times of turmoil and uncertainty, people need to hear from you, even if it's only for you to tell them that you don't know anything. In other words, even when you're emotionally talked out, you've got to keep talking.

Here are some of the things you can do to help your people feel indirect control:

- ✔ Keeping them ahead of, or at least even with, the rumor mill by providing timely and accurate information. You can keep them informed with informal walking around, quick staff meetings, videos, electronic alerts, and newsletters.

- ✔ Telling them not only how good the change is, but what's bad and ugly. By explaining the downsides, you're not only protecting people from being blindsided, but also showing them that you're on top of things.

- ✔ Sharing status reports and other change-tracking data. Even if you're behind schedule, share this with them. This way, people know what's happening, that you know what's happening, and that you're still in control.

- ✔ Inform the people affected by a decision as soon as you've made it. If they don't hear the facts from you, they'll grab on to the latest rumors. Besides, that's just treating people with basic respect and common courtesy — the same way you'd like to be treated.

And now you know why many managers do only a fair to less-than middling job of communicating. It's hard work, demands well developed people skills, requires that you place your employees' needs before your own, and eats up a lot of precious time. But it's energy and time well spent, because good communication is one of your most powerful tools for reducing resistance. And reducing resistance will ultimately save you time in the long run.

Reason 11: Drowning in Change

Remember the dark age of computers — about eight years ago? While working on your now-antiquated desktop, you might have had a screen saver in the background, a proposal in word-processing for a perspective client, a customer database, and Solitaire (that was the time before Free Cell) — and your boat-anchor of a computer slowly chugged along. Everything stopped when you tried opening the slides for your intercompany-pricing presentation. You had exceeded the computer's RAM (Random-Access-Memory). Up popped the message telling you that you had insufficient resources and had better shut down a program or two.

Well, your employees are still like that old computer. They only have so much RAM or emotional energy to operate all the programs running in their lives. And more powerful models are not expected in the near or distant future. So, here's this brave individual attending law school at night, teaching

TIP

What people say when they're sinking

Resistance is their self-protective mechanism when employees feel overwhelmed and have nothing left to give. And then they still have to go home to face a difficult roommate or take care of a sick child, or maybe even both. When people are swallowed by waves of change efforts you hear comments like these:

- ✔ "I can't take it any more. How many times do we have to redesign our purchasing program? Enough's enough."

- ✔ "Stop the world! I want to get off!"

- ✔ "I'd rather quit and then look for another job than go through another acquisition. I can't take it any more."

- ✔ "I hate waking up in the morning. I don't have the energy to get dressed, let alone come in here."

- ✔ "All we do is fight over the little stuff, and our real problems never get solved. You should see the backstabbing that goes on in this division. People are so stressed out, and we're taking it out on each other."

junior-high math during the day, trying to understand the state's new math curriculum, planning a wedding, adjusting to the school's new principal, spending time with the family because Dad's been diagnosed with prostate cancer, and now the school board wants to implement some quality program. No wonder people shut down.

Resistance is a lifeboat

As members of the human species, people don't have separate energy sources for home demands and work demands. They both drain the same power reserve. Unfortunately, many managers assume, in their mad rush to stay abreast of the competition, that people continuously produce unlimited energy. Piling on the changes at work, they forget about the maelstrom of change at the home front. First it was decentralization, then TQM, a culture change to treat employees nicer, followed by a new appraisal process, major cost cutting efforts, then reengineering, downsizing, upgrading the e-mail, a push for a paperless environment, process teams, and then back to centralization. Instead of a workforce enthusiastically lining up for another tour of duty, organizations get people who pile into the resistance-life boats because they can't cope with any more change. They feel

- ✔ Stressed out
- ✔ Angry
- ✔ Physically, mentally, and emotionally exhausted
- ✔ Sick more frequently

↳ Reluctant to take risks

↳ Combative

↳ Less mentally flexible

↳ Edgy

↳ Less tolerant of ambiguity

↳ Impatient

↳ Less forgiving of mistakes

Your tool: Limit changes while increasing support to people

Again, none of these recommendations are rocket science. They're just good basic management principles and tools. But in the push for increasing market share and profits, managers sometimes lose sight of the human face that goes with the revolving names on organization charts.

Re-evaluating all the changes you've got going and those on your wish-list

The action items associated with this recommendation are directed toward leaders who make the decisions. For managers without the authority to control the changes foisted on their organizations, you can use the items listed under the next recommendation.

You can help your employees stay afloat by:

↳ Prioritizing all your current and hoped for changes. Then only do those that your organization's very survival depends upon or that offer a-once-in-a-lifetime extraordinary opportunity.

↳ Evaluating critically those changes that you keep to see what, if anything, is going wrong or causing trouble — then fix it. If you're unsure of what's not working right, your people will be glad to tell you — they've probably been trying to for a long time.

↳ Telling employees how you're prioritizing your various change efforts and what criteria you're using. It'll pleasantly surprise and re-energize those people who expect to see change initiatives eternally bobbing about like unwanted trash.

↳ Taking those few change efforts that you're keeping and integrating them into a single plan. Unless tightly interwoven, they're bound to unravel and jerk people in multiple, competing directions, all over again. You can find more information about creating your implementation plan in Chapter 14.

Helping people cope with stress

This section is for you managers who don't have control over what changes your organization latches onto or eliminates. Even while you may feel like you're drowning, you've still got a responsibility to help your people survive — because without them no work gets done, and no change gets implemented. (Chapters 21and 22 will give you personal tools for taking care of yourself so that you can successfully cope with all the changes pounding you.)

If you want to successfully implement these next action items, you must intellectually and emotionally believe that employees are more than worker bees sent from above to make you look smart and competent. However, even if you don't believe this, do these action items anyway. In this case, something is always better than nothing. And people who aren't fighting for survival do a better job meeting the needs of their patients/customers/clients, and, of course, bosses.

You can reduce employees' resistance by:

- ✔ Monitoring their stress level so that you know when to provide extra support:

    - • Walk around and informally talk with people. For example, you may find out about a moving expense report bogged down in Human Resources (HR), and a call from you may put a check in your employee's hand — thereby reducing some stress.

    - • Keep an eye on increasing absenteeism and illnesses. You can't prevent people from getting sick, but you need to know when stress is eating away at employees' health.

- ✔ Knowing what your organization's in-house employee assistance program has to offer and the process for using it. If your organization doesn't have such a program, then ask HR what community resources they recommend. If you work for a very small company that doesn't have a formal HR department, then use your network, friends, neighbors, and the yellow pages as a resource. However you do it, give your employees some type of support system when things get tough.

- ✔ Sending your people to resiliency training and stress reduction courses. See what HR (again, if you have one) offers, talk to peers in other departments or friends in other companies. But if you're going to send people to courses, make sure that you go first or go with them. You can bet that your own stress contributes to theirs.

- ✔ Finding multiple ways to compensate people for working long hours. While many organizations have overtime policies, they often frown upon excessive use (or even any use) of them. Therefore, come up with creative ways to accommodate flexible work times, telecommuting, and time off. Having a little flexibility in one's life is a great antidote to stress — and a lot better than over-the-counter or prescription drugs.

> ✔ Helping increase your employees' feelings of control by implementing the recommendations in Reason I (the preceding section). The more sense of control people have, the more physical, mental, and emotional energy they have to deal with nonstop changes.

Reason III: It's a Terrible Idea

Sometimes even great ideas turn out bad. It's a rare leader that intentionally sabotages his or her own organization. In most instances, changes backfire because leadership had insufficient information about the change and its impact on the organization.

A great idea + a great company = a great failure

In 1992, the venerable jean maker, Levi Strauss & Co., radically changed its manufacturing process. The company needed to reduce the soaring number of repetitive stress injuries due to piecework, as well as lower costs, increase productivity, and keep their U.S. plants running. They stopped paying workers for independently performing repetitive tasks, such as only sewing seams or attaching waistbands. Instead, teams of 35 people manufactured the whole product and received team-compensation based on the number of items they finished. Even the unions thought this change an improvement for the workers.

Six years later, Levi was forced to admit that it had made a terrible mistake as *The Wall Street Journal* reported on May 20, 1998. While the company had achieved some successes, there were many more failures. The quantity of garments produced per hour plummeted. Overhead and labor costs, as measured per pair of pants, skyrocketed. A company known for its high employee morale and quality of work life now had hostile workers verbally abusing each other — even making death threats. And 11 U.S. plants closed with 6,395 employees, or a third of the workforce, laid off.

What went wrong? Team work, the darling of management gurus, failed. Leadership discovered that:

> ✔ Skilled and faster workers lost money because of slower, less skilled ones.
>
> ✔ Production broke down as garments piled up in front of slower workers.
>
> ✔ All team members lost bonuses because of one worker's mistakes.
>
> ✔ Injured workers got harassed because they couldn't keep up.
>
> ✔ People spied on each other to make sure that no one stayed in the bathroom too long.

> ✔ Supervisors, lacking skills for resolving conflicts, left workers struggling alone with their bitter quarrels.

After Levi's problems came to light, experts, with hindsight, had a field day dissecting them. Could this disaster have been avoided? Probably, if Levi had intimately and actively involved plant workers in the up-front planning. But some consequences, no one could have foreseen — until hands-on experience brought them to life. No manager, at any level, has a crystal ball.

Ignorance isn't always bliss

Sometimes ignorance feels like bliss. It doesn't keep people awake until 2 in the morning or jolt them out of sound sleep at 4 a.m. Those individuals don't sweat the small stuff, because they don't even know what it is. But there's no place for ignorance when you're leading an organization into the 21st century. Not when people's jobs, mortgages, and the college tuition for their kids depend upon your decisions. Keeping your head buried in the sand may make you feel good in the short term, but it has ruined many a career and destroyed many a company.

For those people who expect to effortlessly implement organizational change, it's time to clear the sand out of your eyes. Every change comes prepackaged with its own set of potential dangers. If you don't hit landmines, then at least some major potholes surprise you. It's usually not the change initiative itself that's the problem. It's how it interacts with the organization's culture and people, as well as how it's actually being implemented. Success in one company doesn't guarantee success in another.

Personally, you can only anticipate some of the future dangers — not all of them. Therefore, you shouldn't rely solely on your own experience and intuition. The best way to anticipate problems is to see the change through the eyes of the people in your organization. The knowledge of your people can help you avoid smacking into unexpected obstacles and minimize the natural resistance that accompanies unpleasant surprises.

When disloyalty becomes loyalty

It's amazing how a different perspective often changes what we see. Take the square in Figure 5-1. Looking at it from another position it becomes a diamond.

The physical characteristics of the shape never changed. What did change was the angle from which we viewed it. We just rotated it 45 degrees, changing our vantage point. We can do the same thing with employee's resistance. From one vantage point, we hear "whining," "laziness," and "disloyalty." From another angle, we hear warnings of danger, calls for help, and concern about the organization. The choice of what we hear is ours.

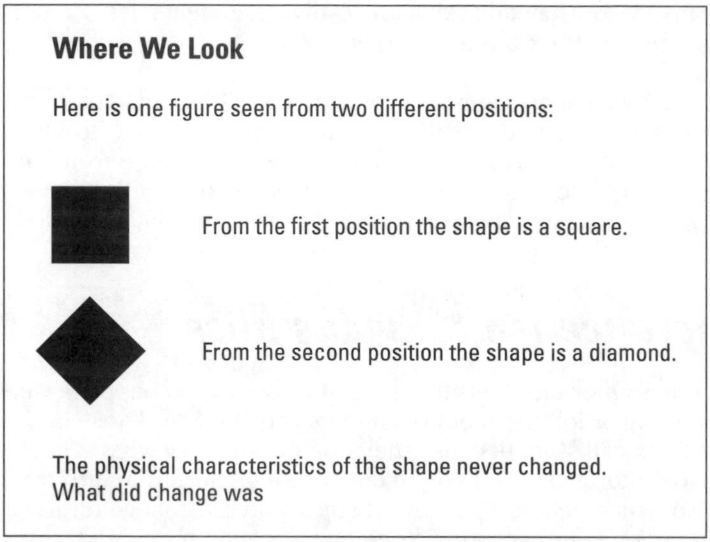

Where We Look

Here is one figure seen from two different positions:

From the first position the shape is a square.

From the second position the shape is a diamond.

The physical characteristics of the shape never changed.
What did change was

Figure 5-1:
It all
depends
on your
perspective.

Your tool: Protect the change, not your ego

Most people don't like making mistakes. Depending on the "size" of that mistake, they feel dumb, humiliated, angry, or worthless. And when they do "screw up," they would like to keep it private — not advertise it in front of 10,000 people or even one. Unfortunately, looking smarter sometimes means appearing dumber — allowing your employees to be your eyes and ears because you can't be everywhere and know everything.

Choose knowledge over ignorance

As part of your formal planning process for implementing change, ask people in different organizational areas and levels where they think the landmines are. Be prepared and willing to make modifications based on their feedback. Although you make modifications, it's still your change effort, but you want to do it right. Chapter 6 offers you ways to collect all this information.

✔ Any time you hit employee resistance, ask yourself:

- Where is the fire in all this smoke?

- How well am I listening to what people are telling me?

- Could I just possibly have made a mistake? (Tough being human, isn't it?)

- What can I do differently? (Don't worry about what "could have been;" stay focused on the "now.")

- How can I become less defensive in the face of their resistance? (Everybody gets defensive — nobody likes facing another's resistance.)

✔ If you don't hit resistance, quickly look around to see what's forcing it underground. You might think of resistance as similar to earthquakes. You want all those little tremors that naturally release the pressure build-up so that the "big" one never materializes. So, work hard to bring resistance to the surface. If you don't find it soon, you're in for a nasty shock.

✔ The employee feedback process you (hopefully) created provides valuable information. Constantly scan it to see if people keep resurfacing old issues and warning you about new ones. The earlier the warning, the less well rooted the problems and the easier for you to fix it. In other words, smaller potholes get repaired faster and cheaper than bigger ones.

✔ On March 8, 1987, the London newspaper *The Observer* recorded President Ronald Reagan as saying: "You know, by the time you reach my age, you've made plenty of mistakes if you've lived your life properly."

Test the waters

No matter how desperately you need that change initiative, try to start small and move slowly. With a pilot test, you can modify, change direction, or call a halt before you cause too much damage to customers, employees, or your organization. If your organization's survival depends upon your change, it also depends upon you doing it right.

✔ If your change effort affects a large number of people, then create a pilot with a small group. You may be able to do a pilot during the planning stage and use the feedback to guide your plan. If only a small organization is affected, then phase in the change — fine-tuning and digesting each segment before moving on.

✔ Make sure that you have the support of your direct reports' before you introduce your change effort to the next level. Nothing kills a great idea faster than managers who don't enthusiastically believe in it. Even if they did try to sell it to their employees — nobody would buy it.

Reason IV: Too Many Past Failures

Whether it's on a battlefield or in a boardroom, people want leaders who succeed. In exchange for following them, individuals ask that leaders know where they're taking everyone and how to get them there. And when leaders don't, you stop following.

HUMAN INTEREST

A self-fulfilling prophecy

You can listen in on a focus group of first line supervisors in a telecommunications company. They are discussing not only their latest change, TQM, but also the effects of past changes.

Person A: "They're upset that we're not all jumping on the quality bandwagon? I'll tell you why. It's not going anywhere."

Person B: "I've worked with this company for 14 years, and nothing that we've started has stuck around."

Person A: "We've seen it all: quality circles, QWL [Quality of Work Life], MBO [Managing By Objectives]. We even had the Managing for Excellence Library that had a whole list of things we were supposed to be doing as managers."

Person C: "I still use that. There's some great things in there. Whenever I have an issue with one of my people or it's time for appraisals, I go there to get my ideas."

Person B: "You're probably the only one in the company using it."

Person D: "I've also got sitting on my shelf a box for some professional development, or another, that I've never taken the wrapping off. I don't even know what's in the books."

Person C: "Is that the reddish-brown box?"

Person D: "Yea."

Person C: "Don't waste your time on it. It's their first semi-attempt at doing quality without knowing what they're doing."

Person E: "If you haven't figured it out already, we weren't born yesterday. We know to wait, and eventually they'll all go away."

Change efforts quietly fade away or end in public failure when leaders have either selected the wrong direction, or chosen the right one but didn't know how to achieve success. Either way, they haven't proven themselves trustworthy.

Resistance as messenger

Successful change managers understand that credibility and trust are rare and precious gifts. They know that a title alone can't guarantee that employees will believe in and follow them. Rather, they must earn these gifts — over and over again.

TIP

So, when change winners run into resistance, they listen, act quickly to understand the messages, locate potential dangers, and fix the problems. These managers remain acutely aware that they have a narrow window before failure takes hold and employees stop believing in them. The last thing successful change managers want is to create a "program-of-the-month" culture that causes people to ignore new ideas or efforts. Once employees see a revolving door of changes, your ability to lead quickly disintegrates.

Your tool: Keep earning employees trust

You need to let history be your guide. What's your organization's track record when it comes to changes? In the past five to eight years, how many changes initiatives have you had (big and small)? What percentage are still successful? What percentage have faded or failed? If some of your change efforts have fallen short of expectations then employees may question whether to follow you on future journeys. To reinforce your people's trust in you as a change-manager, you *must* succeed with your next change efforts. You can start to rebuild trust by:

 ✔ Analyzing exactly what went wrong with past changes so that you don't make the same mistakes again, and again, and again. The best tool for getting this information is employee focus groups (which you can read about in Chapter 6).

 ✔ Explaining honestly to employees what went wrong with past changes and how you plan to do thing differently. But remember, when you tell them how you're doing things differently, they won't believe you until they actually see you in action.

Even if you have a 100 percent change success rate, you don't have the luxury to rest on your laurels. With each new effort, employees put you and your change under the microscope — which means that your hard-won credibility always remains vulnerable. People keep searching for signs of failure. Here are ways to show them your commitment and reinforce their trust in your change-management skills.

 ✔ Talking about the change often enough that you hear yourself in your dreams, and employees hear you in theirs, too.

 ✔ Going to every training course (related to the change) that you ask employees to attend.

 ✔ Starting all your staff meetings with change updates.

 ✔ Making every change yourself that you ask others to make. (Role modeling is so important, you can read more about it in Chapter 17.)

 ✔ Celebrating publicly both small and large successes. (For more information about recognition, take a look at Chapter 19.)

 ✔ Holding the people reporting to you accountable for success in their organizations. What people get measured on and paid for drives where they put their energy.

Reason V: Protecting Self-Worth

One of the ways that many human beings define themselves is by what they do. Whether it's raising children, manufacturing elevators, creating Web sites, styling hair, healing patients, policing streets, flying airplanes, repairing vacuums, negotiating contracts, typing letters, auditing financials, or teaching students, part of a person's identity and self-worth comes from his or her "profession." Yes, work pays the bills, but it also tells the world who people are, and helps them feel good about facing the day.

Whatever the job, it's important that individuals feel respected, feel that their work is appreciated. Whatever threatens that job threatens their self-worth — their value as a human being. Therefore, managers should take care when they (knowingly or unknowingly) stomp on their employees' self-worth — because people can turn into righteous warriors.

Oh, how tender self-worth is

What endangers self-worth? The list could fill a book. So, we'll just focus on a few heavy hitters in the workplace that push most everyone's buttons. These are

- Being treated with disrespect
- Losing power
- Feeling ignored
- Losing influence
- Being kept uninformed
- Feeling humiliated
- Lacking recognition
- Losing control

These self-worth missiles come at people all the time — in meetings, around "water coolers," during presentations, through e-mails, with notes, at appraisals, and in voice-mails. Employees are forever picking themselves up, patching their damaged defenses, and charging back into the fray. Just to make sure that they don't miss anything, people keep their insult-sensors revved up and super-sensitive, always programmed for nonstop scanning. These missiles affect everyone because even the toughest, gruffest, and roughest people still have their self-worth soft-spots. Those soft spots are their vulnerable areas, which, when jabbed, leave them devastated and feeling worthless.

Into this daily fray comes organizational change — where jobs get changed, control taken away, responsibilities reduced, and information withheld. Often, the way changes get implemented cause people to feel, as expressed by one manager, "like chopped liver." Is it any wonder that, when the latest-and-greatest change is announced, people create firewalls to protect themselves from further attacks?

Change my computer's software, but leave my "humanware" alone

You have two general areas in which you and your employees face personal change. These are

- Technical areas such as mechanical, electronic, industrial, chemical, nuclear, and medical
- Human areas such as leadership style, change management skills, teamwork, relationship building, conflict management, and political skills

And as you would expect, the changes in the technical areas are much easier to swallow than those in the human arena. Individuals' self-worth usually takes less of a direct hit when they must upgrade their e-mail system than when they must improve their communication styles with employees. Or when they've got to learn a computer assisted design program as compared to figuring out how to get their work done while working with others on a process team. This greater impact from the human changes happens for three reasons.

- **Continuous improvement:** Because of all the rapid scientific developments, managers expect to continuously improve their technical skill — and would probably feel inadequate if they weren't up to date. They aren't conditioned to think the same way about their people skills. Working with others is a part of employees' self-concept, not external to them. Therefore, changing people skills means, to many individuals, a fundamental change in who they are as individuals. One leader told us, "I'm a good person, and if I have to keep improving the way I lead, then there must be something wrong with me."

- **Measurability:** Technical systems, by their very nature, lend themselves to measurement. Not so with human behaviors. How do you measure your conflict-management skills, and against what standards? You can't measure these types of skills, and there aren't any standards. So most employees don't think there's any reason to go through all the frustration and pain of changing the way they handle conflict (or other people skills) when there's no empirical evidence telling them that they're doing it the wrong way.

✔ **Accountability:** Individuals don't feel personally accountable for not being a whiz with the latest electronic bells and whistles. Figuring out their new handheld computer isn't the stuff that heroes are made of. But when they're told that their team-building skills aren't first-rate, they then feel personally accountable for this "flaw." Up pops their defensive shields.

What's interesting in all this is that becoming a change winner is really less about improving technological skills than it is about improving how you actually work with people. So, for managers, leading change more effectively means tinkering with or even making major adjustments to their people skills — who they are as human beings. Yet, every organization has managers who willing put their self-worth at risk to ensure that their change succeeds. You can read more about these change winners in Chapter 3.

Your tool: Protect others' self-worth as fiercely as you protect your own

Yes, you've just read a cousin of the golden rule in this business book. (Now, pick yourself up off the floor.) You can add this one to all the others that have come to us over the past three millenniums. Table 5-1 shows you how this basic value has remained consistent across 3,000 years, among different parts of the world and diverse cultures.

Put very simply, employees are human beings, like you, who want to be treated with dignity and respect. You can demand productivity, quality, and all that other good stuff, but these things only happen with willing people who feel good about themselves. Just as your self-worth determines what changes you accept or reject, so too, does it affect what others choose.

✔ When discussing the need for making a change, balance your presentation with what's also going well and what people are doing right. Every first-level management course teaches the need to maintain a balanced perspective, but you'd be surprised how rarely it's used. (Or maybe you wouldn't be.)

✔ When discussing problems, stay specific. In other words, keep away from all-encompassing statements and solutions. Rarely does life give us people or situations that are all good or bad. For example:

• Use "sometimes" and "lately" in place of "always"

• Use "occasionally" instead of "never"

• Zero in on specific problems rather than generalizing to the entire organization/change effort/team

• Search for processes that need fixing, not people to condemn

✔ Make sure that your words and actions accurately represent your intentions. People can only judge you by what you actually say and do, even though you judge yourself by your intentions. Many a person's self-worth has been demolished by the "best intentions."

✔ Make a list of the ways that you want to be treated. Put it by your office phone and read it in the morning. Then at the end of the day, before rushing out, quickly review how well you applied your list to others. Okay, we're being idealistic, hoping that some of you will give this list a try. But you never know — and besides, wouldn't you like to work with people who did?

✔ Every time managers cause injury to another's self-worth, even unintentionally, they damage their relationship with that person. If we do it too often and with too many people, we find ourselves isolated — or even the focus of sabotage. However, the reverse also holds true. When you treat others with consideration, you create an invaluable support system that you can turn to in times of need.

This concept of treating others as you want to be treated is not new. In fact, it goes back at least 3,000 years (see Table 5-1).

Table 5-1	3,000 Years of Wisdom
Religion/ Philosopher	*Versions of the Golden Rule*
Hindu	This is the sum of duty; do naught unto others which if done to thee would cause thee pain. (1000 BCE)
Zoroastrian	That nature alone is good, which refrains from doing unto another whatsoever is not good for itself. (600 BCE)
Jain	In happiness and suffering, in joy and grief, we should regard all creatures as we regard our own self. (600 BCE)
Taoist	Regard your neighbour's gain as your own gain, and your neighbour's loss as your own loss. (500 BCE)
Confucian	Do not unto others what you would not have them do unto you. (500 BCE)
Buddhist	Hurt not others in ways that you yourself would find hurtful. (500 BCE)
Aristotle	We should conduct ourselves toward others as we would have them act toward us. (300 BCE)
Jewish	Do not do to others what you would not like others to do to you. (50 BCE)
Christian	Do unto others as you would have them do unto you. (30 CE)

(continued)

Table 5-1 *(continued)*

Religion/ Philosopher	Versions of the Golden Rule
Islamic	No one of you is a believer until he desires for his brother that which he desires for himself. (600 CE)
Sikh	As thou deemest thyself, so deem others. (1500 CE)
Kant	Act only in accord with a principle that you would at the same time will to be an universal law. (1700 CE)
Bahái	Ascribe not to any soul that which thou wouldst not have ascribed to thee, and say not that which thou doest not. This is my command unto thee, do thou observe it. (1800 CE)

Chapter 6

If Knowledge Is Power, How Do I Get More Of It?

- -

In This Chapter

▶ Protecting yourself from being blindsided by resistance

▶ Acquiring tools for collecting vital information

▶ Using the information you gather

- -

"If they want to know why reengineering isn't working, they just have to ask. We'll tell them. And that's what they're afraid of. We'll tell them more than they'll want to hear."

> Middle manager
> Fortune 100 company

*W*hoever came up with the idea that "what you don't know won't hurt you" probably didn't live to a ripe old age and definitely didn't make a lot of money. He or she most likely ignored signs that said, "BRIDGE WASHED-OUT" or "DANGER — NO SWIMMING." That person probably thought he or she knew what was best for customers instead of listening to the customers themselves.

The great economist and writer John Kenneth Galbraith understood the power of knowing when we don't know.

"One of the greatest pieces of economic wisdom is to know what you do not know."

> John Kenneth Galbraith, economist.
> *Time* Magazine (1961)

Your very survival, both personal and professional, depends upon getting the right information at the right time. What you don't know leaves you vulnerable to physical injuries, fiercely competitive rivals, greedy peers, and unhappy employees. (We won't even get into all those untidy "personal" issues such as your love life.) There's a catch, however. Valuable information becomes worthless unless we use it.

In this chapter, you find multiple ways of gathering lots of valuable data that will help you to avoid both small and large disasters and manage resistance more effectively. The rest of this book helps you successfully use all the great stuff that you've so carefully unearthed.

The Inside Scoop from Friends and Favorites

Everyone needs a good internal network for obtaining real-time information about what people are saying when standing around a jammed copier or at the local coffee bar. But you shouldn't solely depend on it. The picture you get from your internal sources usually provides incomplete and, at times, distorted pictures. That's because:

- ✔ They filter the data through their own personal biases, axes to grind, and self-interests. Their goal isn't to give you incomplete or inadequate information; it's just their three filters naturally at work (see Chapter 3).

- ✔ They are unable to appear everywhere at all times, work in every position, and understand the needs of all your people or organizations.

- ✔ They may get labeled as your "spies" and therefore be seen as untrustworthy. Employees willingly share their true feelings only with people they trust.

- ✔ They hear only what's politically correct. What they won't hear is all the politically incorrect stuff that you need to avoid future pain and grief. However, even if they did get politically damaging news, they'd probably clean it up before repeating it because they wouldn't want to damage their relationship with you by making you angry.

So, if you really do want to know what's going on in your organization, what's fueling resistance, and how to make sure that you and your change effort succeeds, don't rely solely on your friends.

The Power of Employee Focus Groups

Originally, focus groups were the darling of marketing departments. But then human resource professionals, consultants, and presidential advisors discovered the powerful synergy generated when eight to ten people get to talking.

Focus groups for physicians

Survival for one major metropolitan medical center meant recruiting a large number of experienced family-practice doctors to their medical staff. The medical center turned to focus groups. Three focus groups, each with ten local-area physicians, were held. The doctors sat around a table for two hours bluntly sharing what they liked and didn't like with their respective medical affiliations and what they required to join another hospital. The information from these three focus groups gave the hospital administrators exactly what they needed to attract and retain a staff of loyal doctors.

Focus groups are carefully planned and structured group interviews that encourage participants to talk with each other, not the interviewer. The energy generated by these discussions produces an amazing outpouring of honest feelings, hidden attitudes, and buried beliefs. Individual interviews simple can't provide the insight or depth of information that focus groups do.

If you want to understand employees' deep thoughts and feelings about a specific topic, you can't do better than these facilitated small-group discussions. And if you've got food in the room, watch out — two hours later, you'll have trouble getting people to stop talking (as we did with the doctor focus groups). It's almost as if individuals have ventured out of their protective caves and discovered that, in fact, they're not alone in an impersonal and infuriating world. Here's a room full of people, just like themselves, struggling with similar problems.

With focus groups, you can

- Gain greater understanding of existing issues and their solutions.
- Travel into the future to explore what could be and ought to be.
- Gain data to market your change effort to specific employee groups.
- Create customized employee questionnaires that address concerns relevant to people.

Knowing when to do focus groups

Like all the tools in your mechanical and management toolbox, nothing works for you in all situations. So, too, with focus groups. The best time to use them is when:

- ✔ You want to identify specific problems that are causing resistance or potential problems that could trigger resistance.

- ✔ You want solutions for those problems and ways to prevent future problems from occurring.

- ✔ You want to understand what people are actually feeling and take the pulse of employee morale.

- ✔ You want to know what issues you should focus on in planning your change initiative.

- ✔ You want to test the viability of a new effort before you spend the time or money going in the wrong direction and ending up with egg all over your face.

- ✔ You want a follow-up on your employee survey to clarify particular trends that don't quite make sense or what you can do to stop a downward spiral. (See the section "Here a Survey, There a Survey, Everywhere a Survey" later in this chapter for more on employee surveys.)

Getting the most out of your focus groups

No matter how good a tool is (mechanical or management), its true value comes from knowing how to use it. While focus groups appear straightforward and simple, they're just the opposite. In truth, they demand intensive preplanning, highly skilled interviewing skills , and strong knowledge of group dynamics. To help you get started, here are some of basics for forming focus groups.

- ✔ **Keep the number of people from eight to ten within each focus group.** With fewer than eight, you start losing the synergy between people, and it becomes more like individual interviews. With more than ten, you get people who can hide and valuable information gets lost.

- ✔ **Don't mix levels of management.** Every person should be at the same level. As soon as you put a higher level person in the room, the dynamics change and employees clam up.

- ✔ **If you know that two departments are at war, keep them apart.** You want participants to focus on the problems, not use your session as a battleground.

- ✔ **For organizations of greater than 100 people, three focus groups provide the most reliable information.** If you use just one group, it's to gain a high-level overview, never for in-depth understanding. We have found that the first group usually provides breadth of data, while the second group gives more depth. The third group then fills in most of the missing pieces, hones in on the biggest issues, and refines your recommendations.

Marketing professionals and campaign managers rely heavily on focus groups because they provide great insight into the wants, needs, and feelings of a large group of people (such as sports car buyers, cookie eaters, and soccer moms) without having to interview thousands of people. If you want to know what your organization of 500 people think about the new benefits package, only three focus groups of eight to ten people give you a good picture of their perceptions. True, you won't get person-specific gripes, but you do get the heavy hitters — trends and issues upsetting most of your people. And fixing those issues early on gives you a lot of credibility — even when you can't eliminate individual sore spots.

Of course, if you have an organization of 5,000 or 105,000 employees, you may want to zero in on specific functional groups, such as manufacturing, finance, headquarters staff, sales reps, and marketing, with two or three focus groups per department. Or if you have people spread out all over the globe, do the focus groups by location, which mixes departments. However you choose to group people, just make sure that you decide up front and remain consistent.

✔ **Keep the number of issues you want discussed small — three to five is a good number.** Each issue will have numerous subissues and will naturally branch out into related territory. You need time during the session to clarify, verify, and solidify. You want to keep a set of consistent questions between all focus groups so that you can add apples to apples. But because each group has their own particular personality and set of concerns, you also create group-specific questions real-time.

✔ **Don't create a tight agenda that you must follow rigidly.** In fact, a page with just a few questions and issues works best. You want to trust the process and let it flow wherever it needs to go. Good listening is the greatest stimuli for getting people to talk.

✔ **Make sure that you have the right facilitator.** He or she understands and enjoys people, listens well, and has the analytical skills required for digging through lots of diverse opinions and facts, and then can come up with trends. A good facilitator also establishes trust with strangers easily and quickly and knows how to gently coax people to open up, as well as getting others to talk less. This person isn't afraid of conflict and manages freewheeling discussions without appearing to manage. He or she isn't afraid to give you or even the CEO straightforward feedback from the groups and maintains confidentiality at all costs.

Grab a Chair and Sit Right Down

In the 1980s, the buzzword was "managing by walking around." One corporate officer called it "sitting on desk corners" (that was when desks were built sturdier). Simply, managers were told to get out and talk with employees. This was supposed to help them find out more about what was happening in the "real world" and to help employees feel appreciated.

HUMAN INTEREST

Dropping in on a focus group

Here's an excerpt of first-line managers discussing their TQM program. These telecommunications supervisors talked about a whole range of issues from how their own managers were living quality (not very well) to how the company was doing a better job meeting customer expectation. Of course, our editors wouldn't let us give you a right-from-the-tape-recorder transcript because people rarely talk in complete, grammatically correct sentences — and that's the way books are supposed to be written.

Person A: "As part of recognition this quarter, HR rolled out quality awards. And they gave these awards, not for process teams, or not for getting the job done better. They gave them for going to class."

Person B: "They've geared the prize to the class you go to. The longer the class you went to, the better the prize."

Person A: "What I got going to the three-day one was a little stick-on Q pin. What someone else got for going to a five-day class was a nice duffel bag."

Person C: "There was another prize for someone going to a class where they got the water jug with the plastic straw."

Person A: "They're going to do this on an ongoing basis now every quarter. Now people are saying, 'I really like that sports bag. So I'm gonna go to that class!'"

Person C: "I was one of them. I said, 'OK, how do I get that bag?'"

(Everyone laughs.)

Person B: "They're driving the wrong behavior. Because the incentive is not to do quality, not to go through the process management, but it's just to get the classes under your belt."

Person C: "Hey, don't go ruining this for the rest of us. My husband wants one of those bags, too."

Regardless of what you call it, if done right, informally talking with your employees at their desks, in the mailroom, or on assembly lines is a great way to find out what they're thinking, even if you never get their deepest, darkest secrets.

Admittedly, chatting with employees devours huge amounts of time, which may give short shrift to some of your other responsibilities, like preparing for meetings, reading reports, networking, and responding to phone and e-mails. So, what do you get in return for sacrificing time out of your harried schedule? A lot. You get

✔ Detailed knowledge of what's actually happening in specific jobs as it effects both your change effort and the organization.

✔ An understanding of what's on people's minds (depending on how comfortable they are with you) and where many of the problems are festering.

✔ A sense of how teamwork is working.

✔ The latest rumors and how well your communication is working and what's getting distorted.

✔ A chance to talk with people who don't report directly to you and get a sense of how well the chain of command is working.

✔ The state of morale — just looking at people's body language and hearing the tone of their voice will tell you whether they're overwhelmed and discouraged which nourishes resistance.

✔ Satisfaction (and some managers even get enjoyment) from helping people feel valued by talking to them and listening to what they tell you.

✔ The opportunity to reinforce key messages both personally and through the grapevine.

✔ The opportunity to lead and demonstrate your personal commitment to the change effort.

Sitting down and talking with people sounds easy, and it can be. But don't forget, you control their paychecks. Naturally, employees will feel cautious the first time a big mucky-muck comes strolling over to them for a "casual" chat. But if you do it right, over time, people will begin to trust you and open up. Here are some things to remember on your tour around the organization.

✔ **You're not checking up on people to see whether they're working instead of playing hearts on their computers.** It's designed to make you a smarter manager.

✔ **Except for a few questions, let the employees do all the talking.** Your focus is on them and their needs, not on yourself and your issues.

✔ **Don't be afraid to ask questions:**

　　• How's the job going?

　　• What problems are getting in your way?

　　• How can I help you?

You can also ask other questions about specific issues that you've picked up from previous walk-abouts and focus groups.

✔ **Show *genuine* interest in your employees as people.** Are they new parents? Going back to school? Returning from chemotherapy? Or just coming back from a vacation to Timbuktu? Then spend a moment talking about what's important to them, besides work. If you don't know, just look at the pictures and quotations they keep on their desks or walls for areas of interest.

✔ **Work hard at keeping an open mind.** You probably will hear stuff that you don't like or vehemently disagree with, but remember, they may be seeing a diamond, and you're looking at the square (see Chapter 5).

✔ **If you tell them that you're going to deal with a problem they've raised, then do it and tell them when you've done it.** Also, if at all feasible, do it within 24 hours of your conversation.

✔ **If you're not their immediate boss, make sure that he or she is not present for the conversation.** This talk is between you and the employees. You don't want their manager hovering around, making employees feel intimidated or influencing what you hear.

✔ **Don't take your newfound information and use it to pound on the employee's manager or other people.** If employees see their honesty with you being used to hurt others, they'll stop talking to you.

✔ **Be honest.** If you don't know something, then say so. Bluffing only destroys your credibility.

✔ **Thank people for taking their time to talk with you.** It's not only common courtesy, but it also shows your employees that you value their input.

✔ **Above all, remember that everything you do must stem from a sincere interest in people both as unique individuals and as your employees.** (And if you're really not interested in what your employees think, don't do this. They know it and resent your lack of sincerity.)

Here a Survey, There a Survey, Everywhere a Survey

"Oh, gosh, not another survey. We just had one last year, and nothing's changed." Sound familiar? For both good and bad reasons, organizations have turned to the survey (sometimes to the exclusion of other valuable options) to discover what's on employees' minds. When done correctly, questionnaires provide great information. When done poorly, they're a horrible waste of time and money — and turn people off.

Over the years, employee surveys have gotten a bad rap — and that's because companies have abused and misused them. Some employees see them as trash can material because:

✔ They rarely see the summarized results of their and others' time and honesty.

✔ They've got to answer a load of questions, many of which are redundant. In fact, many surveys try to solve the problems of the United Nations rather than zero in on specific issues appropriate to each organization.

✔ Questions are often not relevant to employees' day-to-day struggles.

✔ Surveys are cold and impersonal leaving people feeling that they've become one more don't fold-or-staple employee.

✔ Managers don't do anything with the input, and if by chance they do, people often don't learn about what's been done.

Keep the baby, throw out the bath water

Don't give up on surveys, just modify what you do with them and how you do it. When used correctly (isn't that the way with most things) questionnaires give you a valuable tool for zeroing in on causes of resistance, understanding trends and tracking progress. You should use surveys if you:

✔ want feedback from a large number of people

✔ want quantitative data

✔ want to compare year-to-year progress

✔ want to make comparisons between departments or organizations

How to get the most for your money

If you think of employee questionnaires in the customer-supplier model, then the people who actually receive and fill-out the survey are the customers. Therefore, you must develop employee-friendly surveys — ones that meet customer requirements, which means, you've got to find out what those requirements are.

More surveys than you can count

You can find hundreds of different canned surveys out there. General and specialized human resource consulting groups offer all manner of questionnaires — on any topic you could possible want.

If you're going to use a survey either from a traditional or e-company, make sure that you first "talk" with the developers to determine whether:

✔ You can customize it.

✔ They will do the analysis and at what price or whether they will give/sell you a data analysis software to use yourself.

✔ They have a database collected from other companies for comparing your results. However, you should realize that any comparative data they have is only for their standard question set and not for you if you're customizing. Or they may be willing to provide comparative data on individual questions that you use unmodified.

First and foremost, make sure that all questions address people's issues and needs. Even if you're using a canned questionnaire from some company or off the Web, run it through two to three focus groups to let them customize it. (See the section on focus groups earlier in this chapter.) You'll find that this extra effort is truly worth your extra time. Depending upon your organization, you'll want to sample different technical functions or departments to make sure that you get diverse perspectives. You'll be amazed at the questions and quality of your final product if you let your "customer" help.

Other things to remember:

- **When you hand out the survey, tell employees the cut-off date for returning the questionnaire, the expected time required to do the analysis, when they will get a high-level summary, and when they can read the actual report.** Make sure that the dates you give them are the ones you can actually meet. Obviously, the length of time required for analysis depends upon the number of people taking the survey, how many questions, whether sections exist for comments, and whether those comments are analyzed and categorized.

- **At the same time that you design the distribution process for the survey, also decide how you'll share results with all employees.** Then do so within one month (less is even better) from the time you get the analysis of the results.

- **Ensure confidentiality.** If you're going to have people respond to an electronic questionnaire, use an outside supplier to collect responses.

- **For tracking purposes, keep most of the questions consistent year after year.** But each time you reuse a questionnaire, pass the questions through at least one focus group to see what's no longer a problem and what new issues have arisen. The little tweaking that occurs won't hurt your year-to-year comparisons.

- **Provide opportunity for comments — either after each question (only if it's a short survey), at the end of each section, or at the end of the questionnaire itself.** But you must give people a chance to individualize their responses. Letting employees personalize the questionnaire acknowledges that their individual issue and concerns are important — and therefore, that they as human beings are also important.

- **Keep it short — not more than 20 questions.** (Okay, okay, you can have 23). The focus groups will help you pinpoint the most important ones so that you don't have to include the bathtub. (See the section earlier in this chapter for more on focus groups.)

- **Make sure that within a month of sharing the results of the survey with people, you have begun fixing the easy problems and shared your on-going efforts with them.** Then tell people what your plans are for tackling the tougher issues.

> ✔ **Check the effectiveness of your survey with focus groups six months after employees received the results.** Ask participants questions such as: Did the survey ask the right questions? Was the analysis accurate? Was the feedback of results timely? Has management responded to the issues identified? Would you take this survey again?

Here are actual examples of employee survey statements that focus groups in different organizations created. Employees responded to each statement with their reactions, ranging from Strongly Agree to Strongly Disagree.

✔ I can readily obtain the resources and information I need to do my job.

✔ All people are treated with respect and dignity.

✔ People want to be on quality teams because these teams improve work processes.

✔ My internal suppliers are working with me to understand and exceed my expectations.

✔ I am asked my opinion about day-to-day work decisions.

✔ All my team members take pride in their work.

✔ My manager helps us integrate the quality process into our day-to-day work.

✔ When I get feedback from my supervisor, it is specific and helpful.

✔ My supervisor is open to discussing viewpoints that are different from his/her beliefs.

✔ We support and reward messengers that deliver unpleasant information.

✔ My manager shows that he/she appreciates my work.

✔ Everyone I work with on interdepartmental teams shares the same goals and priorities.

✔ I believe our leaders support Quality because of the way they talk and act.

✔ Upper management both listens to and acts upon our ideas for improving customer/client satisfaction.

✔ The leaders of this company care about me.

Munching Biscuits with the Boss

Food, food, glorious food! Nothing breaks down barriers better than sharing a little sustenance. It's such a powerful force in lives that manufacturing, selling, and providing food is an international multibillion-dollar industry. Whether you're bringing doughnuts in for a staff meeting or taking your project team out for pizza after work, food provides both nourishment and nurturing.

What happens to your surveys?

After you and your employees take precious time away from a jam-packed day to conscientiously fill out your survey, it often feels like all your efforts just vanish into a cosmic black hole. Some surveys do evaporate into the great beyond, but the majority of them actually go through an indepth analysis and get sent back to management.

Whether your own human resources department or an outside consulting firm conduct the survey, most analysis follows a general process. After you've sent in your questionnaire, data entry people manually enter each answer to every question and comments into a predesigned database. They also enter any identifying data such as department, what vice president's group you're in, or your job level. After all questions from all questionnaires have been entered, then comes the number-crunching. Each question usually has an overall average and range of results computed based on all the people responding to that question. Next each question gets analyzed according to predetermined subcategories, such as the distribution department, first-line supervisors, or nursing staff.

If the questionnaire also has places for your comments, then those are usually just sorted according to the various departments or groups. But here we find a lot more difference between organizations. On the one hand, managers in one company may just get a printed list of comments in the order they were entered. On the other hand, managers in another company get comments categorized by topics with summaries for each category. Because computers aren't yet smart enough to analyze comments, humans do all this work. As you can imagine, it's very mentally and time intensive. The greater the number of employees responding and the greater the number of comments written, then the greater the labor required (and we should add, the more expensive).

Some survey results come with specific recommendations, and others leave the what-to-dos up to each manager. The more tailored the questions are to each company and the more employee comments, then the easier it becomes to create recommendations and specific action plans.

So now the results have come back to your organization. How do you get to see them? That all depends upon how much genuine interest your leaders have in the survey. We know of companies where leaders read the reports and then file them in desk drawers, never to look at them again. Yet we also know of leaders that created special processes for cascading the survey results down the chain of command — until every person either got their own summary copy for their organization or attended a formal presentation. And, of course, most organizations fall somewhere in between these two ends of the continuum. If you want specific detail about how to communicate results of surveys turn to Chapter 18.

Regretfully, between cost-cutting and virtual offices, the opportunity to bond over bagels has become far too rare. Don't let this stop you, though. You'd be amazed at the great information you'll get sharing snacks with employees. So, whether it's breakfast buffets, brown bag lunches, or dans.com chocolates at meetings, you can always find ways to stimulate the palate and, thus, the mind.

HUMAN INTEREST

Food for thoughts

At the time that Craig had an organization of 3,500 people, he also had the luxury of providing breakfast buffets. Needing to spend quality time with employees from all levels, he held two-hour breakfast meetings with 25 to 30 employees every two weeks. At first, people were dubious about having breakfast with their boss's, boss's boss, but eventually they began looking forward to, as they called it, "Grits with Gipple."

One week before each breakfast, Craig's administrative assistant called all district managers (middle managers with anywhere from 40 to 150 people in their organization) asking for names of people to attend. By the next day, she had a filled breakfast list. This way, breakfast always had different organizations and different professional levels represented. Sometimes, a manager would put his or her name on the list.

During the first few breakfasts, Craig spent the initial 45 minutes with people walking on eggshells as they went through a silent buffet line. This was followed by superficial conversations while eating freshly scrambled eggs. At the end of the time set aside for eating, he stood up and shared "what's happening" for about five minutes. He then asked people to tell him what was on their minds. As people brought up topics, he wrote them on a flip chart and discussed them. Slowly, everyone relaxed, allowing politically sensitive conversations to flow. Craig always left the meetings with a long list of to-dos — problems that he needed to fix. And either he or one of his people followed up on all of them — immediately.

An active employee grapevine spread the word about Grits with Gipple. Within three months, even before they lined up for their eggs, people began airing their frustrations. Their openness allowed Craig to address problems before they became burning issues and a rallying point for resistance.

You don't need a huge organization or catered meals to meet informally with employees. We know one manager who held monthly bring-your-own-brown-baggers — his attendance lists filled up months in advance.

Sometimes more can be better

When you've got a lot of employees in your organization, informal chats at each person's desk, while valuable, leave many people feeling out in the cold. Meeting with small groups of 20 or more (but don't go much bigger than 30, or you'll lose that special personal interaction) is a more efficient way to learn what's going on in your organization. For the price of a pita sandwich, pickles, and chips, you get

- ✔ Time to establish a comfortable atmosphere while people are eating.

- ✔ People building on each other's ideas which helps you to see a more complete picture of problems; rather than limiting yourself to individual, and possibly, isolated issues.

✔ An opportunity to discuss a greater number and variety of issues than the one-on-ones. You also don't have to listen to the same problem over and over again as you travel from desk to desk.

✔ The chance for the more timid employees to see that the bolder ones don't get tarred and feathered for speaking their minds; which means that you get more participation as time goes by.

✔ To spend more time with employees than you would with just the 15 minutes or so at each person's desk if all you did was the walking-around data gathering.

Menu for success

Employee meetings, even with lots of food, aren't a slice of pie (or is it a piece of cake?). They take lots of skill on your part. You'll need to:

✔ Get to the room early so that you can greet people, shake hands, and, if you have a humungous organization, ask where they work.

✔ Immediately thank people for taking their time to talk with you.

✔ Tell people up front that you won't disclose who says what unless they agree that it's okay. You should expect them not to believe you at first, but if you maintain confidentiality, trust will build.

✔ Not be the first one through the buffet line. But if it's only cookies on the table, do take the first one to show people that it's okay to chow down. But please, don't take the last cookie.

✔ Record issues on a flip chart, which lets everyone see that their concerns will be addressed.

✔ Keep your responses short. This meeting isn't the time for three-ring-binder answers. People want to know that you've heard what they've said. They also want a brief, meaningful explanation, as well as the assurance that you'll act to deal with their problems.

✔ Remember that you hate being lectured to, and so do they. Here are some tips for not lecturing:

- Talk in the "us" and not "you."

- Tell stories as examples.

- Describe what *you* will do, rather than what *they* should do.

- Poke fun at yourself (and that means making yourself vulnerable).

- Remember that you're there for information gathering.

✔ Keep eye contact with the speakers. Even if they're longwinded, don't let your mind wander. You're under a microscope with people looking for the slightest hint of insincerity.

- Show respect for all people, even the ones that are too angry to show respect for you.

- Ask whether others also have the same problems as the one being discussed. This way, you will get greater depth of information.

- Tell them what you'll do with the issue list. And then do it.

- Close by thanking them for their input.

The Suggestion Box — With or Without Paper

Your success in managing change depends as much upon getting timely and reliable information as it does your experience and talent. Therefore, don't limit yourself to one or two ways of data collecting. You must keep open as many channels as possible. One opportunity for great information is the old-fashion, out-of-fashion suggestion box. After you and your people create a process that works for the team, you'll be surprised and pleased by the volume pouring in.

You can make your suggestion box paper or e-mail, it doesn't matter. What's important is that you have a process for people to pass along concerns real-time. Yes, you'd think that intelligent and mature employees should bounce into your office as problems arise. But they won't and don't (except for your friends and favorites). You need to keep information flowing for the 98 percent of the time that you're not analyzing focus group and survey results, holding lunch meetings, or visiting cubicles.

Keep it simple

Your suggestion box doesn't have to be anything fancy. But whatever you do, make sure that employees in your organization clearly understand that you're looking for and relying on their input.

Here are two basic options for your suggestion box. Of course, you and your employees can, and should, create your own personalized variation.

- **The old-fashion suggestion box** works great with smaller organizations or project teams. If you don't get grossed-out by the tacky look, attach an extra large envelope to the side of your room-divider or next to your office door. Like a newly installed bird feeder, your suggestion "box" will remain lonely for a while. But slowly, one or two hardy souls will stop by. If they find that you pay attention to their suggestions, other employees will join in, too.

✔ **The electronic suggestion box** takes less effort and doesn't look funny. It also gives work-at-home or work-on-the-road people a chance to pass their headaches on to you. What people lose, though, is anonymity in exchange for speed and ease. And initially, many people may stay far away from zipping you suggestions. But over time, seeing how the team benefits and how their coworkers remain safe from reprisals, most people will eventually begin contributing.

Either way you choose, be prepared for a lot of little piddly stuff, petty complaints, or plain off-the wall ramblings. But in all that mass of messages, you'll find a disaster waiting to occur — one that you can prevent. You'll also discover simple ways that you can help people get their work done faster and smarter. And you'll get a window onto what's causing resistance and what you can do to reduce it.

Getting the most out of your suggestion "box"

If you're going to go through all the work creating some form of a suggestion box, you want it to work efficiently and effectively. Here are some suggestions for you. As you read through them, you'll find that everything we list is just good basic management stuff. And for a lot of managers, these things are easier said than done.

✔ Maintaining confidentiality

✔ Thanking people for their input

✔ Keeping an open mind

✔ Responding quickly to problems or telling people why you aren't

✔ Respecting views different from your own

✔ Remembering that, as much as you may wish, you can't be everywhere and don't have all the answers

What to Do with All That Knowledge

Making momentous decisions depends upon having critical information. And once you have it, you need to heed it. Otherwise, your story may end in tragedy (see the sidebar "Use it or lose it").

Use it or lose it

Acquiring knowledge is about more than simply knowing — it's about using what you know. When you choose to ignore a piece of information, you'll have to face the consequences — and, unfortunately, sometimes they're deadly:

✔ On January 28, 1986, the world watched in horror as the Space Shuttle Challenger exploded 72 seconds after lift-off. A hardware failure of a solid rocket booster (SRB) "O" ring caused the disaster that destroyed seven lives. The Thiokol engineers directly responsible for the development of the SRB "O" rings initially recommended not to launch the shuttle until the outside air temperature reached 53 degrees Fahrenheit. Unfortunately, both Thiokol and NASA executives pushed the engineers to withdraw their recommendations — forcing

public relations objectives ahead of safety goals.

✔ On May 4, 2000, the National Park Service authorities began a controlled or "prescribed" burn to clear underbrush at Bandelier National Monument. By ignoring the National Weather Service's warning that conditions were unfavorable for burns with dangerous winds possible, 44,000 acres of New Mexico woodlands went up in flames, 400 homes were incinerated, and several buildings in the Los Alamos Laboratory were destroyed. Just prior to setting the fire, the Weather Service faxed a special forecast to officials warning of increasing winds and the high rating for potential fire hazards.

While managing change projects probably isn't as monumental as deciding to launch a space shuttle, your success as a manager depends upon having accurate information and making right and timely decisions with it. If you don't want your new customer care program derailed or your joint venture sabotaged, you'd better know what's not working, who's disgruntled, and where hidden dangers await you. You'll also need to keep a mind free of I-have-all-the-answers so that you can profit from your information treasure trove.

Chapter 7

Managers Resist Change, Too

• •

• •

"Nobody ever told me that the hardest part of modifying our culture would be getting myself to live the new behaviors."

CEO
Software company

*W*hat makes or breaks your wonderful new customer care program or your latest cost cutting drive comes down to one simple question — are you, as a manager, making the same changes that you're asking of others? You can have the best designed implementation plan, the finest training package, or the most creative recognition program — but all of them come to naught, if employees don't see you and the other managers leading the charge.

While it's now a cliché, "walking the talk" is one of the best vaccines or antidotes you have for resistance. Even other managers say that role modeling is possibly the most important thing they can do to motivate their employees. So, why don't they always walk the change-talk? What makes smart and organizational-savvy people personally abandon the very changes that they, at one time, championed? In this chapter, you see that:

✔ Managers may be powerful, but they're human beings first, subject to the same vulnerabilities that plague everyone else — but only under a much brighter public spotlight.

✔ Managers can easily get caught in five traps that undermine their resolve to support a change, but they do have escape tools.

Managers Are Human, Too

Many employees expect perfection in their managers; they forget they are dealing with people who have human imperfections — just like they do. Beneath a manager's special title, big office, fancy perks, and tough exterior hides a human being with feelings that need protecting — no different than every other human. In fact, managers too have a self-worth that they must safeguard. They also need a certain amount of stability and control in their lives. So, naturally managers reject changes that make them appear inadequate, feel foolish, or disrupt their lives.

What hurts managers' self-worth?

Titles can't protect people from their humanness. Even managers aren't immune to the following "traumas" of life:

- Making mistakes in public
- Appearing ignorant
- Being wrong
- Missing goals and deadlines
- Appearing misinformed
- Being unprepared
- Losing power
- Appearing weak and indecisive

How do managers protect their credibility?

Credibility comes down to being respected for the job you do. If you're a manager, that means inspiring trust in the employees who report to you, the people you work with, and the person you report to. To have credibility as a manager, individuals must appear strong and in control, and they must get things done. Then employees willingly follow them. Managers who don't have credibility look weak and out of control. Nobody follows them.

Managers live with a Catch 22. If they publicly "walk the talk" by using the new software, improving their communication skills, or trying the quality improvement process, they'll look and feel just like everyone else — incompetent as they struggle to learn something new. So "walking the talk" risks a blow to their self-worth, but not "walking the talk" risks losing their credibility. But unlike most employees, managers' success and failures play out on center stage.

Managers take a double-blow to their self-worth. While feeling the personal frustration of learning something new, they must also make their mistakes in public with the whole organization watching and dissecting their performance. Faced with such no-win situations, it's no wonder that many managers find "logical" excuses for resisting the very changes they're asking of everyone else. These excuses include

- ✔ "I don't have time."
- ✔ "I've got fires to put out."
- ✔ "I've said I believe in this. . . . That should be enough."
- ✔ "There's no rush, it's something I can do later."
- ✔ "That's someone else's responsibility."
- ✔ "I made the decision, now they have to implement it."

During times of organizational change, life seems to conspire against managers. Not only must you protect your self-worth from the ravages of public scrutiny, but also you must do so while trying not to get ambushed by the five resistance traps.

Five Resistance Traps to Avoid

As tough as it is for managers to protect their self-worth under intense public scrutiny, it's downright humiliating to get caught in one (or worse, more than one) of the five resistance traps. Now you've got employees watching — second-guessing your actions, criticizing your decisions, and judging your struggles to rescue yourself from a trap.

It doesn't matter if you have 1 person or 10,000 people in your organization, the traps lay in wait for all managers. And we do mean *all*. We've seen some of the brightest and most talented leaders get ambushed. What makes the five traps so treacherous is that they give limited warning before they seize you in their iron jaws. But don't give up. Now that you know they're out there, you can remain vigilant, take precautions, and if caught, extricate yourself. Armed with the information in this chapter, you can show employees that you know how to manage changes — that you deserve their trust.

Trap 1: Failing to recognize your own resistance

Around 300 BC, the Chinese general, Sun Tzu wrote *The Art of War*. In his classic treatise about winning on the battlefield, he counseled military leaders to "Know the enemy and know yourself; in a hundred battles you will never be in peril. When you are ignorant of the enemy but know yourself, your chances of winning or losing are equal. If ignorant of both the enemy and of yourself, you are certain in every battle to be in peril."

The general omitted what would happen if you knew the enemy, but remained ignorant of yourself. Most likely, he considered that an impossibility — believing that knowing the enemy first depended upon knowing ones self; and that lack of self-knowledge did not just bring "peril," but rather defeat.

The general's advice still holds true in the 21st century. Managers who remain "ignorant" of themselves — who don't know when they're hamstrung by their own resistance — leave their changes, organizations, and themselves in peril. And often they lose the battle.

Finding your resistance in different shapes and sizes

Just because something looks good on transparencies doesn't mean that it'll work the same way in the harsh light of day. Just because people see the need for reducing costs, increasing customer loyalty, and improving employee productivity doesn't mean that they like the price they have to pay to get there. And nothing in the titles of "leader" or "manager" exempts any one from sticker shock. (In Chapter 4, you can read more about the why's and how's of people resisting changes they originally wanted.)

How do you know when you're the one who's doing the resisting? You can review the following list. As it relates to a specific change, if you find yourself doing one or more of these things, most likely you're caught in Trap 1.

- ✔ **Canceling meetings and not rescheduling them.** What do you do when you must cancel a meeting that's near-and-dear to you? You reschedule it, of course. But if that same meeting focuses on a topic that you'd rather not deal with, it's far more convenient not to find time for another date. When this happens, you're telling your employees how little you respect the subject of the meeting and your commitment to them.

- ✔ **Avoiding the training that all your employees must take.** Let's be honest, if there's something that you really want to learn, you'll sign yourself up (even if you pay for it yourself). But if it's not a topic high on your interest list, somehow, there's just no time left on your calendar for that class. Or you may have something more important pop up the morning you're suppose to be sitting in the workshop. If you don't go, why should your people?

✔ **Having more important work to do than appearing at change-related meetings.** If the company's holding a meeting about a change in the compensation guidelines, it's a pretty good guess that you would find time in your packed appointment book for it. But if you just can't seem to clear your calendar for the quality kick-off rally or even one of the four employee suggestion program orientations, it's a good bet that your own resistance lurks in a dark corner.

✔ **Not holding your direct reports accountable for supporting the change initiative.** When you believe that something is important, you make sure that the people in your organization also support it. If your company is on a team building push but you see no value in touchie-feelie activities, you won't ensure that your direct reports attend team-building workshops with their people. Neither will you evaluate and compensate them on how well they pull their employees into teams.

✔ **Not following through to see that decisions are implemented on time and correctly.** On pet projects, you probably make sure that everyone is meeting their commitments. Yet, forced to manage a merger of your department with another, you may not be terribly concerned about missed dates and incomplete deliverables. It's natural to turn your back on something that may steal away your power.

We don't want to do process management

The first year that managers in a research and development department began using process teams, their resistance almost brought the effort to a screeching halt. The managers, used to a high degree of independence, resisted the idea of having to work as part of a process team. Here are some of the reasons the managers gave for not forming or half-heartedly forming teams:

✔ "We're too busy; we don't have time to meet." (*Process team never met.*)

✔ "I don't understand what we're suppose to do." (*Process team met once.*)

✔ "Your list of processes is wrong; that's not the way we work around here." (*Process team met once and agreed not to meet again.*)

✔ "Every project's different. We'll have to design a process for each project." (*Process team met once and agreed not to meet again.*)

✔ "This is great for factories, but not for highly technical professionals like us." (*Process team never met.*)

✔ "I have other higher priority work that they pay me to do." (*Managers missed meetings.*)

✔ "You can't measure our processes. We don't produce 100 widgets per hour. We may work six months on a project. How do you measure that?" (*Process team completed first two steps, but stopped meeting when it came to the third step, which was developing measurements.*)

Without the personal involvement and consistent support of their vice president, the managers' process teams would have failed. Slowly, over a three-year period, the majority of managers worked through their own resistance and led process teams that eventually made significant productivity growth and financial improvements for the company.

Sometimes being a manager puts you into a double bind — having to support the party line, but not believing in every part of it. You're not alone. All leaders face that natural dilemma in their careers. What's important is not that you believe in everything that comes down from up high, but that you don't say one thing to your employees and then do the opposite. Inconsistency between your words and actions destroys your credibility, their trust in your ability to lead, and their willingness to follow you in the future.

Escaping Trap 1 — Scrutinize yourself with the same intensity that your people scrutinize you

Successful actors and athletes watch tapes of themselves to analyze their imperfections so that they can improve their performance for the next time. They willingly do what most people shy away from — taking an honest look at themselves in the mirror. You can conduct the same analysis by doing the following:

- **Acknowledge that you're the last person to know when you're resisting.** Therefore, keep the upward feedback channels wide open. (We show you how to do that in Chapters 6 and 18.) If your people feel safe giving you feedback, they'll let you know when your "walk" and "talk" conflict.

- **Look at what your employees are resisting and then examine your own actions.** You'll often see a one-to-one relationship.

- **Do a reality check.** List all the things that you must do differently because of the change and circle the ones you don't like, don't think apply to you, or don't think you need to do — but still expect others to do.

    1. Start with the least offensive items — go do them, in spite of all your logical reasons why you don't need to. By not doing something, you're telling your employees that it's okay for them to also ignore it.

    2. Go through your list systematically implementing the other items. You don't have to do them all at once, but your employees need to see that you are taking action to support the change.

    3. Watch for a "just doesn't apply to me." If you can't find any justification for doing an item, then there's probably no reason for your employees to be doing it, either. Eliminate it.

Trap 2: Being impatient

While you may not yet travel at warp speed, your life still zooms about at a point-click velocity. Whether it's selling your old dirt bike to the highest bidder or just buying chocolates, you'd probably like most things sooner than later. Documents that once crawled by snail-mail now arrive in a matter of seconds by fax or e-mail. With faster computers come the expectations of a faster way of living and of doing business, including implementing organizational changes.

Advertising specialists and political analysts tell us that, unless we're obsessed with a titillating scandal, most people's sound-bite attention span lasts for about three minutes. Anything longer, and they're gone. So is it any wonder that managers wait impatiently for quick results? However, asking people to abandon years of experience, demolish long-term relationships, and willingly face chaos is not the same as surfing cable channels. Transferring your have-it-faster-technology expectations to human beings sets them, your organization, and yourself up for very frustrating times.

Recognizing the "use before this date" syndrome

Newsweek describes the business environment as one "where management plans often have the shelf-life of cottage cheese." One reason that change efforts sour so quickly is that people, conditioned to quick fixes, expect quick changes. And when they don't see the spectacular results in their arbitrarily decided-upon time frames, they become disillusioned and head for the next quick fix — and the next.

TQM (Total Quality Management) is one such example. Unrealistic time-frames contributed to disillusioned leaders and employees, which in turn caused more than two-thirds of the quality efforts to fail. Philip Crosby, in his landmark book *Quality Is Free: The Art of Making Quality Certain,* told readers that it "took five to seven years of unrelenting effort to achieve the [quality] revolution at ITT." He warned people not to "expect too much too soon," never to relax their attention and "stay at it continually." Even with all of his admonishing against unrealistic expectations, Crosby still sees managers who believe that merely announcing quality is the signal for arranging victory dinners.

One vice president told us that he expected to "get quality up and running in six months. I don't care what the other fellows do. I know what I'm going to do." He couldn't do it and decided to try reengineering.

Knowing when impatience has trapped you

If you're human, you're probably impatient to get the job done. You've got a lot on your plate — both personally and professionally — so you don't have time to dilly-dally with indecisiveness. That means you're most likely to

✔ **Set short due dates.** You want to get one job over with so that you can get on with the next dozen. Quick action works for some things, like implementing flextime or adding a mid-year employee review. But all the pushing and pulling in the world won't get a culture change or process teams established in a year or two. What it does do is destroy your physical and mental health and those of your employees.

✓ **Challenge people with "stretch" implementation dates to get them motivated.** Unfortunately, unreasonable goals have the opposite effect. Right or wrong, employees assume that you don't understand "reality" and/or don't know what you're doing. Either way, impossible time frames fuel resistance — big time.

✓ **Think that announcing your new direction means that people are willing and able to dump the old and embrace the new — and that they'll naturally switch into fast forward.** Don't get comfortable. After your great video presentation or intricately designed organizational chart, your work is just beginning. Now, you must start selling your ideas to employees. You have to convince them why they should follow you, and how all of this new stuff isn't just another flavor of the month. You find more information about selling organizational changes in Chapters 15 and 18.

✓ **Figure that once everyone is properly trained, they're ready to go.** Regretfully, book knowledge can't substitute for hands-on, mistake-wiser learning. People need time to understand how classroom theory translates into real actions. In fact, sometimes employees need multiple training sessions to help them make the transition — along with lots of practice in between.

✓ **Get frustrated when you see, at first, only miniscule success, instead of quickly getting the big saving or productivity gains.** It's easy to get caught up in the success of companies featured on business magazine covers and forget that they were at it for 10 years or more. Similarly, when you buy packaged change programs from venders, their primary goal is selling and they may slightly enhance how quickly you get all those great results. Bottom line — hoping for big results early, defeats you and your employees.

✓ **Flood the workplace with directives and memos, but don't take the time to personally discuss with people what's actually happening to them.** Are you telling yourself that "I don't have time to hold employees' hands, I just want them to go do it?" Maybe if this were the "good ol'days" when managers were kings, you'd get away with royal demands. But not so now. Edicts don't get the work done faster but, in fact, create walls of resentment and resistance that actually slow everything down.

Identifying when impatience is necessary

By now, life has probably taught you that many rules often have their exceptions. Here's one of them: You need impatience, and lots of it, when:

✓ Competitors are eating your lunch because you're having trouble getting that new product to market.

✓ Customers' desperately need your latest new product.

✓ Cash flow is sinking to a dangerous level and costs are soaring out of control.

✔ Internal auditors have found significant irregularities.

✔ Market window for your new program is closing and you'll go the way of manual typewriters if you don't move quickly.

✔ Customer complaints have skyrocketed.

But being impatient doesn't mean being closed minded. When people tell you that something can't be done the particular way you want it, they may actually see problems that you're missing. So, remain open to discussing alternative approaches in order to achieve vital successes in the timeframe you need them.

Escaping Trap 2 — Research realistic timeframes

Many managers run into trouble when they plan their change in isolation. There's a world of valuable information out there that can help you determine what's practical and doable within certain timeframes.

1. **If you're planning (or even smack in the middle) of a major change effort, take the time to see what others have done in that area.** *Benchmarking* is using the experience of other organizations to help you set realistic timeframes, goals, and standards, and it's time well spent.

2. **Ask the people most affected by the change what they think are practical deliverable dates.** Some managers think that employees automatically give "false" estimates because "they're basically lazy and will try to get away with murder if you let them." We've found, when given the chance, most employees honestly give you realistic estimates — because most people do have high work standards.

3. **Review with your team, during your status update meetings, all target dates to determine how realistic they are.** Over time, experience has a sneaky way of showing you what's actually feasible.

If you're really courageous, you can also look in the mirror. Based upon your benchmark data and employee input, are your timeframes realistic? And if they aren't, what's actually motivating you? Are you facing imminent destruction from galactic competition? Or do you just want to look good for the higher-ups? Is your organization about to go under? Or does your self-worth occasionally depend upon moving at the speed that breaks the sound barrier? What you might also find is that, at times, your impatience is causing you to look out-of-control rather than like a super manager.

Remember, even when your organization's very survival depends upon speed, it also depends upon getting the change initiative implemented successfully — and you can't do that without a realistic time plan.

Trap 3: Building castles in the sky

What you consider a success or failure often depends upon your expectations. Take skiing, for example. On the one hand, a person terrified of skiing might feel thrilled just staying upright while going down a gentle incline. On the other hand, to a highly experienced skier, success may only mean zooming down the most challenging, gravity-defying slope known as triple black diamonds.

Unfortunately, many new adult skiers venture up on the slopes with expectations of glory, rather than terror and humiliation. They start their lessons fantasizing about soaring down majestic slopes, only to be faced with the reality of the earth sliding out from under them as their skis meet snow for the first time. No wonder ski resorts bemoan flat revenues. Frequently, beginning skiers, with their unrealistic expectations, quickly become disheartened after a lesson or two and never return.

In place of skiing, you can substitute establishing an e-business, reengineering, snowboarding, culture change, process teams, or golf. The activity doesn't matter. When people, including managers, start out with starry-eyed high hopes, the results invariably lead to discouragement and often times to abandonment.

Thinking there's only one side — the positive

Few managers who set forth on an organizational-change adventure concentrate on what can go wrong. They naturally focus on the glorious possibilities. Even when listening to employees of successful companies bluntly discuss the exorbitant prices they had to pay — the frustrations and failures — most eager-to-buy managers concentrate mainly on the awe-inspiring results. But once they start down their own change path, these same gung-ho managers find themselves mired in the disappointment and discouragement of reality. It's not surprising that so many better-than-sliced-bread changes end up in the dustbins of history.

Expectations, in themselves, are neither good nor bad. The problems arise when people build expectations on incomplete information, faulty data, or their own unsubstantiated wishes — then managers leave themselves vulnerable to the shock and disillusionment of reality. Whether it's skiing lessons, marriage, a new job or a new accounting system, the more accurate a picture you have, the less betrayed you feel when you smack into reality, and the more likely you are to hang in there.

Looking through rose-tinted goggles — real-life examples

Just like people, expectations also come in different shapes and sizes. In Trap 2, we discuss an important expectation: wanting things in a hurry. But there's a slew of others that also trip up managers.

High and often unrealistic hopes lead to disillusioned managers — and employees' accusations of a flavor-of-the-month management style. Managers can build unrealistic expectations in the following situations:

- ✔ **Managers, who try to replace months, and even years, of team building work with a one-day or one-week workshop, set themselves and their employees up for a big letdown.** Team building workshops — you know, the kinds where employees swing from trees, share deep personal experiences, or construct designs with toothpicks — all to make everyone a big happy family. While valuable, these experiences only crack open the door to team synergy. The real progress comes from day-after-day hard work — the ways people resolve conflict, earn trust, and treat each other.

- ✔ **Managers, who organize employees into process improvement teams, often reduce head count (because of expected savings) long before they get their new processes in place.** Somehow, "doing process improvement" automatically bestows great cost savings on the organization. Yes, some teams do eventually provide great financial rewards. But that's only after people have struggled over trying to agree on the present work process, designing the new one, and finding ways to eliminate work — sometimes their own. Most often, frustrated managers give up.

- ✔ **Managers can have unrealistic expectations of redesigned appraisal forms.** Employees' appraisals remain a constant source of frustration for leaders who want to improve employee development. With high hopes, leadership expects the new form to improve how managers' provide feedback and coaching. Truthfully, what form managers use and what they record on paper have little effect on their actual style when giving an appraisal. Improvement comes from changing managers' view of the boss-subordinate relationship and the basic way they relate to people. Instead of improved employee development, nothing changes, but management can now think that all is well and move on to bigger and better things.

We could go on for pages with other examples, but a couple of these should be familiar to you.

Escaping Trap 3 — Balance your enthusiasm with objective data

Information is power, so you need to find out not only what has worked for others, but also what hasn't. If you benchmark, keep your focus on the early struggles, not the great, after-many-years benefits. You already know the gains you want, that's why you're spending all that time and money.

Feeling disappointed about your results? Maybe the change isn't the problem — maybe you need to take a hard look at your expectations.

 1. **Honestly answer these questions about your change:**

    - Why am I *really* putting myself and my employees through all this chaos?

- If life were perfect, what wonderful things would I hope to get?

- Based on my benchmarking and employee comments, how realistic are my expectations?

- Given this imperfect world, what (modified) expectations can I live with?

2. **Create a detailed list of all the things that you think are going wrong — including the small irritations.** Now take that list to employees and get their opinions as to why these problems are occurring. You'll find some real problems that you can fix immediately, others that will take longer to remedy. You might also find that some frustrations are to-be-expected natural growing pains, or that people are on a steep learning curve and haven't quite mastered the new skills.

You must keep in mind that creating new expectations doesn't mean lowering your standards. Rather, it means that you rethink and rationally develop realistic ones.

Trap 4: Being misled by employees that everything's fine

Wouldn't it make your job easier (and also your life) if you always got accurate information about what was happening in your organization? No more surprises jumping up to bite you. But, of course, you know that's not how reality operates. Your employees don't always warn you in advance when the project is running behind schedule and over budget. You just motor along thinking that everything is hunky-dory, until an irate customer (either an internal or external one) calls you out of the blue, demanding that you fix everything — now.

It's not that employees want to mislead you; it's just that they don't always get rewarded for bringing bad news — nor do they find it personally rewarding. Basically, there are three reasons why you don't always receive accurate and timely information.

✔ When you control people's mortgages, kids' tuition, stock options, and promotions, they usually try to keep you happy (as long as it's legal). Therefore, if you dislike hearing bad news, you probably won't have to. Your employees will tell you only the good stuff, omitting what makes you disgruntled or displeased. And if there aren't any glad tidings out there, well, people will most likely present a watered down version of the mounting dangers — at times so diluted that you won't realize that the sky's about to fall on you.

✔ Like many other creatures on our planet, human beings are also territorial. While individuals may like to play in other peoples' sandboxes, they usually keep a large "No Trespassing" sign prominently displayed on theirs. And one of the last people anyone wants digging around is the boss. Whether it's a two-person project team or a huge department, employees want to remain in control. Therefore, one of the best ways for people to protect their little (or not so little) corners is to keep their managers feeling safe and satisfied.

✔ People want to feel and appear competent, both to others and themselves. If bringing bad news means that some of it will stick to them, they'll find a way to minimize the negative information they're delivering. The next-to-last thing most employees want is a boss thinking that they're part of the problem rather than part of the solution. And the last thing they want is actually feeling like a part of the problem. (It's that self-worth issue that we talk about in Chapter 5.)

Shooting yourself in the foot

Without realizing it, some managers actually destroy the very information channels that they need for survival. In their desire to look professionally proficient and feel personally proud, they unwittingly set the stage for misinformation. In other words, the fewer problems they have to deal with, then the more competent they appear to the world and themselves. (You're right, it's another self-worth issue.)

In their own words, employees explain reasons for not sending accurate information upward:

✔ "Our manager came in yesterday morning for our monthly staff meeting, and the first thing he did was show us the headlines of how McDonnell Douglas let go all these people. Then he said, 'Aren't you glad you don't work there? Now what problems do you have?' We're no fools. We didn't open our mouths."

✔ "About a week ago, I went to my manager with a problem. She told me, 'I don't want to hear what's not working. Just tell me how you plan to fix it.'"

✔ "We work in a company that rewards heroes, not whistle-blowers."

✔ "At our annual officers meeting, the chairman stood in front of his officer team of a 125 people. After his presentation, he asked for questions. One person asked a question, and the chairman immediately fired back, 'That's the dumbest thing I've ever heard. Anymore questions?' No one said a word."

In a perfect world, employees would put the needs of the organization ahead of their own political gains, financial security, and personal needs. In fact, some do. But for many individuals, experience has taught them that job success comes from pleasing those in power — not antagonizing them.

Success in organizational change comes from receiving accurate and timely information about what's going well and what's not. While we've never met a manager who consciously wanted to be kept ignorant about what was happening in his or her organization, we've met many managers who contentedly operated with limited data. Martin Luther King, Jr., understood how dangerous lack of information was when he wrote "Nothing in the world is more dangerous than sincere ignorance and conscientious stupidity."

Escaping Trap 4 — Create a safe environment for messengers

If you're really honest with yourself, you know that nothing goes absolutely right the first (or even the second and third) time. If you're only hearing the good things about your change effort, start worrying. You'd better get out and look for the bad news or even the glimmer of trouble-to-come. Start asking your people:

- How's it going?
- What problems are we running into?
- How can I help you?

Are you finding yourself getting blindsided? If so, you may want to take a look at how comfortable your employees feel bringing you "bad news" and what you may be doing to shut down the information pipeline. Here are some ways to find out. (But remember, none of these options bring quick results. Creating trust takes work and time.)

- If you work for a company with a large human resources department, they can help you unclog the communications channels. They have professionals skilled in organizational development (OD) who can interview employees and offer ideas for improving upward feedback.

- If you work for a smaller organization, but can still hire outside support, then bring in a specialist to talk with your people and help you design a plan of action for strengthening upward communications.

- If you don't have access to an OD specialist, then implement some of the recommendations in Chapter 6. You'll see results less quickly than if you had professional support, but with consistency and patience, you can build credibility and gain your people's trust.

Count your blessings. Every time you get bad news, tell yourself that it's better than being kept in the dark. Over time, you'll discover it's true.

Above all, reward messengers — and never ever shoot them, even when they may be wrong. When employees see that messengers remain safe, or are even rewarded, people begin believing that they can trust you. And then you'd be amazed at all the great information that starts pouring in.

Trap 5: Getting surprised by resistance

You probably like surprises when they come as prettily wrapped gifts, but most likely not when they come as resistance to your new patient care program or new product launch. Problems that catch you unaware cause others, namely your boss, peers, employees, and customers, to think that you don't know what you're doing, that you've lost control, or both (not a good situation in which to find yourself).

Most successful managers stay ahead of surprises by maintaining a vast, carefully developed working-overtime network. Yet, even armed with their fierce drive to avoid looking incompetent, they often get blindsided in one area — employees' resistance to change. For a variety of reasons, detailed in Chapter 4, managers mistakenly think that they and their changes can remain untouched by resistance. The truth of the matter is, no one (and we do mean no one) who manages organizational change avoids resistance. Try avoiding turbulence in the sky, delays at airports, or ants at a picnic. You can't. And the same goes with avoiding resistance.

Slipping from hope to disillusionment

There's no question that facing a room packed with people who hate your new organizational design is an unpleasant experience. (All right, that's an understatement.) Yet, you'll find one thing more disagreeable — walking in expecting support and being surprised by enraged employees. Now, you're not only facing an angry audience, you're doing so minus a carefully pre-planned strategy. Furthermore, when coming under unexpected assault, it's difficult to blithely produce calming answers, valid arguments, and clarifying antidotes.

Here's how some managers describe what it's like colliding with unanticipated resistance:

- **Angry (with themselves) because they didn't do their homework.** "I should have seen it coming before it hit me smack in the face. It doesn't take a rocket scientist to know that combining two departments will threaten people and scare them about job security. It's my own [darn] fault for not taking the time to get a handle on it all."

- **Angry (at others) for raining on the parade.** "We've got no time for whiners here. If they can't understand what's got to be done and do it, then I don't need them. That should be clear enough for everybody."

- **Discouraged by the amount of work needed to win people over.** "You know, getting this expense-reporting system up and running wasn't as simple as they [venders] told me it would be. They've left and here I am with a company full of angry people filling my mailbox with nasty e-mails and expecting me to fix their problems yesterday. I'm tired."

✔ **Helpless because they don't know what to do next.** "We all put so much effort into developing this new benefits package to help people with kids and aging parents. But now we've got everyone else [mad] because they feel discriminated against. It's a lose-lose situation for us. I just don't see anyway out of this mess."

Regardless of the emotions managers experience when hit with unexpected resistance (yes, even the toughest, meanest manager has emotions), the end results look pretty much the same — feeling betrayed, followed by loss of enthusiasm for the change. Now, employees have the opportunity to chalk-up another failure.

Monitoring resistance like you monitor the weather

Sit in any airport with droning televisions suspended from the ceilings and you'll see people stop what they're doing to watch the weather forecasts. They want to know what's happening in the skies outside and what to expect wherever they arrive. In other words, will they take off and land on time and have a relatively smooth flight?

While meteorologists aren't always accurate, they don't allow you to exist totally in ignorance of the elements. When your plane finally does depart, your pilots fly armed with the latest weather conditions for their entire flight path. (Of course, that doesn't mean you'll soar turbulence-free, but only that you'll miss the worst of the rough air.) Besides the aviation industry, other industries such as shipping, agriculture, river control, and public utilities also receive special weather forecasts to help them prepare for difficult conditions ahead. No, you can't control the weather but you can predict — and thereby at least partially protect yourself and your change effort.

If you understand and expect resistance, you can put in place a resistance monitoring process that helps you during the planning. You also want to monitor the implementation process so that you identify new resistance clouds as they appear.

Missions for prediction

Here are two missions. One for the weather service and the other written by a human resource executive. Both missions focus on preventing damage through prediction and planning, not avoidance or elimination.

Mission of the National Weather Service: "To protect the life and property of our citizens from natural disasters by using warnings and forecasts for hurricanes, tornadoes, floods, winter and summer storms, and all manner of severe or extreme weather."

Mission of a Human Resource Vice President: "To make our [culture] change successful, we prepare for resistance before it strikes. And when it does, we have strategies that reduce, defuse, and use it to strengthen our new direction. . . ."

Like the weather, you can't always predict when and how resistance will strike, but you aren't left vulnerable and powerless. When resistance storm clouds appear (and they always will), you can quickly mobilize your damage-control efforts and implement your resistance-reducing strategies.

Using your common sense, past experience, and knowledge of your organization, you can make a fairly accurate prediction of the probable types of resistance that will be encountered and where it will be encountered. The problem with predictions is that they all have a margin of error. Your challenge is to reduce that margin of error. The secret for error reduction is input from your people during the planning stage, followed by continuing input from your people during the implementation stage.

Escaping Trap 5 — Prepare, and prepare some more, for resistance

When dealing with resistance, others and yours, you can either become a victim or take control. If you want to ignore it's existence, you're just allowing resistance to run riot over your change efforts — which still keeps you in the victim mode.

Probably the most important thing you can do to escape Trap 5 is to accept that employee resistance is inevitable. After you're made that mental and emotional leap (and for some managers it's so huge that they never make it) here are some things you can do to protect your change initiatives:

✔ **Look at the source of resistance during past changes.** While your change efforts may focus on different areas of the business, employee concerns often cross boundaries, just like they cross departments.

✔ **Plan for resistance at the same time that you create the technical components of your implementation plan.** This means that you:

- Get employee input while the idea of changing is just a gleam in your eye. They can tell you where peoples' hot buttons are and also alert you to other problems that may jump up to bite you. One of the best ways for you to collect data is focus groups. You can read about them in Chapter 6.

- Make sure that you schedule small group communication meetings at the very beginning of your great-leap-forward. You want employees to feel comfortable asking questions and you want to provide accurate answers before the rumor mills work overtime. For more about these meetings, Chapters 6 and 18 can assist you.

- Add action items that minimize or remove anticipated excuses for resisting. You don't have to wait until excuses take on a life of their own; early on, you can get hints of why people are not supporting you. Chapter 4 discusses eight of the most common excuses.

✔ **Keep upward communication channels open during the entire implementation phase.** Make sure that you give your employees multiple ways to let you know how things are going, before you get blindsided by unexpected problems and resistance. While you may be receiving warnings all the time, ask yourself: How clearly are employees communicating? And how well are you listening? Again, Chapter 18 gives you information in this area.

✔ **Enhance your communication and interpersonal skills for successfully dealing with frustrated, angry, and fearful employees.** The style you use when responding to emotionally upset people can either reduce or increase their problem (and can actually create new problems). In Chapter 8, you have tools that help you face 1 or 100 unhappy employees.

The Higher You Rise, the Less You're Forgiven

One first-line supervisor told us how he felt about watching his manager quietly avoid implementing quality. "If she doesn't think it's good enough for her, then it isn't for me." Of all the excuses that employees create to reject your new direction, the ones that give them the most legitimacy comes from your own actions. If people don't see you walking the talk then you've given them a perfect excuse to say, "It's not for me, either."

One of the things that makes managing change so difficult is that you don't have much room for mistakes. Any movement away from 101 percent personal commitment, loudly communicates to people that you aren't committed at all. You can't afford losing precious opportunities to role model by getting caught in even one of the five manager-resistance traps. Your own frustrations, disillusionment, and disappointments erode your own ability to lead your employees through organizational change. So, when it comes to resistance, the best place to begin is with yourself.

Chapter 8

Skills for Working with Resistance

"I don't know how she did it, but our director never lost her cool. Here she is facing a room of 60 or so very upset people because the company's moving us in with the marketing group. Now most of us will have to commute an hour or more a day. No moving package, nothing. Just, 'Here's where your desks are now going to be. Show-up in two weeks.' This move wasn't her idea, but she's still the one who had to tell us. At least she listened to us and tried to come up with ideas to help. And given how ugly we were that wasn't an easy task."

Supervisor, finance department
Private company

Dealing with resistance often feels like a Sherman tank rolling over you. If you lose your temper and fight back — becoming sarcastic, issuing dogmatic directives, refusing to listen — then you only end up in the same emotional quagmire as your employees. Instead of helping them deal with a difficult situation, you become part of the problem. But if you keep a grip on your own emotions and remain capable of understanding theirs, then your self-control becomes a tower of strength for them and for you.

The first step for successfully managing resistance — and this giant step is one that some managers have difficulty making — is keeping your own emotions under tight rein. Before you start working on damage control, you have to make sure that you don't cause more damage — add more fuel to an already roaring fire. You've neither the time nor the luxury to indulge your anger. You need to maintain employee trust in order to obtain their cooperation.

The next step is ensuring that your people feel heard — that you understand their concerns and are working to fix their problems. You must show them that part of your commitment to the change is being committed to supporting them.

As you discover in this chapter, all the skills for managing resistance depend upon first managing yourself.

Controlling Your Emotions — Don't Be Pavlov's Dog

If you're a manager reading this book, then you've demonstrated the ability to think clearly and rationally. However, facing complex technical problems, delayed projects, or unhappy customers (even all at the same time) is child's play compared to facing irate employees. But managers have done it and survived — some have even come out looking like heroes. And so can you — by demonstrating a little emotional intelligence (EI). EI may have become one of the management buzzwords of this decade, but don't dismiss it as another academic curiosity. It's real.

Understanding emotional intelligence

EI is your ability to manage your own emotions so that you use them for creative and productive purposes, rather than letting them damage or destroy your efforts. According to Daniel Goleman, the author of *Emotional Intelligence: Why It Can Matter More than IQ,* EI has five characteristics or "domains":

1. *Knowing one's emotions.* Self-awareness — recognizing a feeling *as it happens* — is the keystone of emotional intelligence. . . . [T]he ability to monitor feelings from moment to moment is crucial to psychological insight and self-understanding. An inability to notice our true feelings leaves us at their mercy. People with greater certainty about their feelings are better pilots of their lives, having a surer sense of how they really feel about personal decisions from whom to marry to what job to take.

2. *Managing emotions.* Handling feelings so they are appropriate is an ability that builds on self-awareness. . . . [We must] examine the capacity to soothe oneself, to shake off rampant anxiety, gloom or irritability — and the consequences of failure at this basic emotional skill. People who are poor in this ability are constantly battling feelings of distress, while those who excel in it can bounce back far more quickly from life's setbacks and upsets.

3. ***Motivating oneself.*** . . .[M]arshaling emotions in the service of a goal is essential for paying attention, for self-motivation and mastery, and for creativity. Emotional self-control — delaying gratification and stifling impulsiveness — underlies accomplishment of every sort. And being able to get into the "flow" state enables outstanding performance of all kinds. People who have this skill tend to be more highly productive and effective in whatever they undertake.

4. ***Recognizing emotions in others.*** Empathy, another ability that builds on emotional self-awareness, is the fundamental "people skill." . . . People who are empathic are more attuned to the subtle social signals that indicate what others need or want. This makes them better at callings such as the caring professions, teaching, sales, and management.

5. ***Handling relationships.*** The art of relationships is, in large part, skill in managing emotions in others. . . . These are the abilities that undergird popularity, leadership, and interpersonal effectiveness. People who excel in these skills do well at anything that relies on interacting smoothly with others.

Emotional Intelligence isn't some impress-people-at-a-cocktail-party topic. It's as important to your success as your "mental" intelligence is — and maybe even more so. Some very talented people self-destruct because they can't control their emotions as well as they control the technical requirements of their jobs. (You might even work with or for one of those individuals.)

If you want to increase your knowledge about EI, bookstores and Web sites offer a wealth of information. The more you know about EI — yours and others — the greater your success at reducing resistance and managing organizational change.

Avoiding the Pavlov's-dog syndrome

You may think that the five characteristics of EI read great on paper but prove unattainable in real-life and real-time situations. Just as with IQ, not everybody can have outstanding EI. However, we've met many a manager who has successfully developed all five of the EI characteristics. Of course, even high EI managers can't always stay calm and in control 24 hours a day. All human beings have their hot buttons, that when pushed, set them off on emotional roller coasters. But some people have a greater number of hot buttons with more volatile and violent reactions than others.

You can't totally stop losing your temper, becoming frustrated, or saying the wrong thing in the heat of a disagreement. You can, however, make sure that you minimize how often these emotional outbursts occur and the resulting damage to yourself and others.

Pavlov's dogs and Watson's child

Most organisms, including the human variety, have automatic, genetically programed responses to external stimuli called *reflexes*. If someone shines a bright light into your eyes or hands you a slice of pizza, you demonstrate predictable responses. In the first instance, your pupils contract, and in the second, you salivate. The same goes if you find yourself in a deserted parking lot late at night and hear footsteps behind you — your heart beat quickens, your breathing becomes shallower, and your body tenses with the fight-or-flight fear reflex. You came hard-wired with these stimuli/reflex relationships.

As life's experiences accumulate, people develop reflexes to external stimuli that were not preprogramed at birth. The scientist who discovered that natural reflexes can also become conditioned to, or elicited by, unusual events was Ivan Pavlov. Pavlov, a Russian physiologist accidentally discovered an interesting fact about the dogs in his laboratory. If he rang a bell a few seconds before giving his hungry dogs food, after a few times, they would salivate simply at the sound of the bell — even when no food was present. In his pioneering study, Pavlov showed that simple learning occurs by establishing a new connection between an unrelated stimulus and response — that is, a bell and salivation.

John Watson, an American psychologist applied Pavlov's finding to humans. Using his 11-month-old son, Watson, conditioned the child to fear a white rat that was initially his pet. Watson made a loud noise whenever the boy saw the white rat. Within a short time, just looking at his one-time pet — without any noise — caused fear in the child. Thankfully, Watson also demonstrated that his son's fear could be unlearned. In a short time, both boy and white rat were friends again.

Since the days of these two pioneering studies, the field of behavioral psychology has shown irrefutably that neutral conditions — objects, individuals, words, events — can trigger uncontrollable emotional responses in people. Just talking to someone who feels terror thinking about airplanes or the manager who hates the "whining" sound of an employee's voice demonstrates the power of Pavlov's discovery. Those two people weren't born fearing planes or disliking an employee. Their particular stimulus-response relationships developed over time — just as everyone else's does. But the good new is, these same relationships can also *undevelop* over time, freeing you and others from life's random conditioning.

The more hot buttons that you walk around with, the more vulnerable you become to the words and actions of other people. You never know when employees (unintentionally or intentionally) may push one, or two, or three of them. And when they do give a good push and you react in anger, you've given them control over your internal and external life.

It's like being one of Pavlov's dogs: Someone rings a bell, but instead of salivating like the dogs do, you lose your emotional cool — not a place that you or anyone else can afford to end up. (Read the sidebar "Pavlov's dogs and Watson's child" for additional explanation.)

Drawing on Your Skills for Reducing Resistance

You can triumph over resistance but not by overreacting — crushing it or stuffing it in the incinerator — because that only makes resistance rebound with a vengeance. Instead, you can win by rising above the struggle and by remaining in control of yourself.

When you face unhappy or bitter people struggling with disorder and disruption, you need your wits about you. The last thing you want is to let anger hijack you as it did this one manager: "I'm so mad, I can't think straight." Scientists have proven that anger overrides people's logic, making it nearly impossible to manage tough situations successfully. Instead, angry people often do the following:

- ✔ Focus exclusively on what is offending them and can't see the positive aspects of the situation in front of them.

- ✔ Have fewer ideas for solving problems and taint everything they do with hostility.

- ✔ Become less articulate and have difficulty expressing complex ideas or relieving employees' fears.

- ✔ Misconstrue or distort situations so that a neutral, or even positive comment, becomes an attack.

- ✔ Shoot from the hip without waiting to gather other pertinent and important information that might lead to a different response.

If you want to convince people that they should trust your judgment and unhook from their own anger, then you need your logical mind working at maximum capacity so that you can gain the greatest benefit from using the six resistance-reducing skills, which the rest of this section describes.

Skill 1: Seeing the problem from their eyes

Successfully managing change means getting people to buy into your ideas and follow you down the yellow brick road. But they only take that first step when they're certain that you have their best interest at heart and won't lead them to destruction. You also need employees to understand your ideas and help fix your problems along the way. And they will, but only after you first show them that you understand their concerns and plan to solve their problems.

"You've got it backwards. I'm the boss here. Not them. Their job's to worry about what I want, not the other way around." Spoken like a true manager from the gray-flannel-suit days, when the boss was boss and everyone else kept quiet and took orders. Times have changed. The title *manager* no longer gives the bearer priority over everyone else. The workplace has evolved into, "I can't get this new accounting system in without my employees. When they have problems, so do I. When I fix their problems, I'm also fixing mine."

Here's how to show employees that you're working with them and not against them.

- ✔ **Start by saying "Yes" to their view of the world.** That means withholding judgments until after you gather and digest all the facts — from *their* point of view. When you take the personal energy to understand and validate employees' needs, you not only know how to help them, you also validate them as valuable human beings.

- ✔ **Acknowledge that you don't have a patent on reality.** Your employees' view of the new organization structure are just as valid as your own (even if you disagree with their opinion). Remember, that from your lofty position in the organization, life looks mighty different than it does from where they're struggling. (Chapter 3 offers more information about how people create different "realities.")

- ✔ **Listen carefully and ask lots of questions.** While you can never "walk in another person's shoes" you can still get a good understanding of what's causing employees uncertainty and anxiety. Because words often mean different things to different people, make sure that you summarize what you think you heard (often times you'll find you missed important points), ask for clarification, request examples and details, and test trial solutions.

- ✔ **Suspend, temporarily, your own needs and problems.** No matter how many fires you've got burning, put them on hold — or if you're in the middle of a crisis, reschedule that meeting. When you walk into that room filled with employees, 101 percent of your attention must focus on them. They must see and feel your commitment to them. Anything less gives them the justification to stop listening when you start talking.

Skill 2: Finding common issues and concerns

Seeing where other people differ from you is easy. But when it comes to reducing employees' resistance toward your change, you need to balance the search for differences with a search for commonalties — common goals, common values, and common understanding of problems. Finding common ground provides the key for working together.

Look at the millions of chat rooms springing up on the Internet. Places that people can go to find others who have similar views and experiences. Whether it's a love of golden retrievers, surviving cancer, cooking Thai food, or hating your boss, there are human beings out there who are not so different from yourself. A place where trust has a chance to grow because people build upon shared interests. That's also the environment you want to create for your employees — where you see each other as allies working together, not enemies engaging in a power struggle.

Even in a resistance tug-of-war, you and your employees may actually be on the same side, if you can only turn the spotlight off of the differences and find the commonalties. So, along with your goals to "get this meeting over with," "have her stop complaining and just do it," or "walk out of there in one piece," consider:

- ✔ Finding three things (that's only three simple things) that you and your people have in common. (And if you should happen to find more, well, go for it.)

- ✔ Spending time talking about each shared interest to show employees that you and they are really on the same side.

- ✔ Reducing the "them" versus "me" mentality — that everyone hunkers down with.

When employees start considering you an ally, they begin listening to you, accepting some of your less popular ideas, and working with, not against you. And that certainly makes life easier for you, them, and the change initiative.

Skill 3: Focusing on the problem, not the person

Managers can easily let their feelings about an employee color their view of the situation. On the one hand, if managers like the person, then they're more flexible, forgiving, and tolerant of both the message and the messenger. On the other hand, if the employee is someone who pushes their buttons, then managers become less understanding, more judgmental, and give very little benefit of the doubt.

Focusing on the not-so-likeable characteristics of a person rather than the problem at hand not only causes you to lose valuable information but also intensifies your employee's already existing resistance.

When you treat one person with anything less then total respect, your other employees always wonder when they're next — and never totally trust you.

While it's not always easy, successful managers of organizational change consciously work to control their negative reactions to employees. This is when the five characteristics of EI come in handy. With practice and dedication, you can focus on the facts, not the annoying style of the person presenting them. You can listen to the information, ignoring the grating voice of the speaker. Above all, you can increase your own knowledge, while simultaneously reinforcing peoples' desire to follow you — even the ones who may not be on your list of favorites.

You might say, as one manager did, "That person never has anything of value to offer. They're a broken record — always harping on the same thing over and over again." Maybe so, but odds are that person does have value to offer. Rarely does only one person see a danger or experience a problem, Just maybe, your unpleasant messenger is telling you what others may be afraid to say. Think of that person as your canary in the mine: Before the days of high technology, miners had no way of knowing when invisible, odorless, deadly gas was silently seeping into the mine. So, they took canaries down with them into the bowels of the earth. When the bird collapsed, the miners knew the mineshaft was filling up with poisonous gas and that they had to quickly get out.

Okay, listening to the message, rather than focusing on the annoying messenger is easier to write about than actually do. And if you're tired and frustrated and in the middle of another crisis, then it's difficult to pull off. Your depleted energy won't always be able to control your conditioned responses to some one who rubs you the wrong way. However, with conscious effort and lots of practice, you can learn to focus on the problem instead of the person in all types of situations and come out the winner.

Skill 4: Promising only what you can deliver

Promising only what you can deliver sounds obvious enough. But you'd be surprised at the number of managers who fudge on it. When aggressive or obstinate employees confront you, it's tempting to promise them the moon to get them off your case and on to implementing the change. Or if you've got employees who've worked an 80-hour week and you want some way to show your appreciation, making big promises is easy. But the down side to promising (even with the best intentions) what you're not sure you can deliver is that you've set expectations that you might not meet. This breaks the fragile cord of trust.

Therefore, when you're faced with people who want more (and may indeed deserve more) than you have the power to deliver — tell them the truth — you can't do it. Tell them honestly that "Company policy won't let me give you time off for working overtime." If you can, explain the reasoning behind company decisions. Your employees may not like it, but they know the system as well as you do. Even if they're unhappy, they still understand. What they won't understand, or forgive, is being deceived.

Whatever you do, don't give dishonest excuses for avoiding employee requests that you don't want to fulfill. They have a pretty good idea what actions are and are not within your power. They may not like your honest explanations for refusing to do something, but at least they won't think you're a liar. Truthfulness is not always pleasant, but the alternative is much worse.

Skill 5: Using silence

While growing up, you might have heard the saying "Silence is golden." It is, but not exactly the way parents and teachers may have meant it. When used appropriately, silence is a great tool for facing unhappy, foot-dragging, and nonverbal employees.

You've probably been in meetings or presentations where speakers asked a question — only to immediately start answering it themselves. When presenters do this, listeners quickly learn that their opinions are irrelevant. Rather, speakers should ask their questions and then silently wait for people to respond — even if it feels like an eternity before the first person gives an answer.

Many human beings dislike silence. Have you noticed how gaps in conversations at a party cause people to stare at their feet or desperately gaze around the room? How about that awkward lull around the lunch table that gets filled immediately with comments about the weather or other trivia? Silence creates pressure to speak up, and someone will give in to the pressure.

When it comes to managing resistance, however, you can use peoples' discomfort with silence to your benefit. If you find that employees refuse to talk about what's causing them to oppose your change, let silence help by asking your audience or group where they see problems with the change and then immediately stop talking. Don't say a word. Just stand or sit quietly looking around the room — patiently waiting until the silence becomes uncomfortable enough for someone to speak up. We guarantee, someone always will.

When that happens it's like a dam breaking, a flood of comments follows — you'll get all the information you ever wanted and then some. When you've learned to make silence your friend, you've gained a powerful ally in working with resistance.

If you've never stood in front of a group letting silence drag on interminably, we should warn you, the first few times can be very uncomfortable — and even unnerving, especially if a large number of employees are staring back at you. Initially, people wait to see how long you're willing to tolerate their silence. If you've learned how to relax in silence, it's your audience that gets uncomfortable and eventually breaks the sound barrier. Should you be in a small room with only a few people staring back at you, then your wait isn't very long. The pressure on them to respond is much more immediate.

Understanding and managing employee resistance requires that your people, not you, do a lot of the talking. So, develop your skills of using silence to motivate I-won't-say-a-word employees to talk, talk, and talk.

Skill 6: Respecting people — even when you don't think they deserve it

Most of you reading this section probably agree that showing respect to other human beings, even in the workplace, should be standard operating procedures. You know, treating others with politeness, civility, good manners, kindness, tactfulness, diplomacy, consideration, and courtesy. But sadly, respect has often become the exception, not the rule.

Take a look at the way some people describe how their managers treat them or their co-workers:

- ✔ "It was supposed to be a brainstorming meeting, but our manager had his own ideas of what he wanted and if he didn't hear it, he'd sarcastically demolish your suggestions. You'd feel so humiliated that you'd stop talking."

- ✔ "He made my life very tough. What he would do is stand over my desk and really scream about why something wasn't done. Now, he didn't ask if it had been done and if he had, I could have shown him it was. But the impact in the room had been made already."

- ✔ "Every time we'd make a mistake, she'd laugh at us as if we were idiots. Now we're helping each other rather than asking her."

- ✔ "It became a big joke. We'd say good morning to him, but he'd never acknowledge it. He'd just keep walking to his office as if we were invisible. We've taken bets to see who gets the first 'hello' back."

- ✔ "Two cubes away from me, the supervisor very loudly said, 'Oh, I see you need an attitude adjustment meeting.' And I'm sitting there thinking, 'Oh, don't ever let her say that to me.'"

Not pleasant descriptions of managers' behavior, but then reality isn't all rainbows and lollipops. Most likely (and sadly), you could also add your own examples to the above list.

What causes decent people to treat others with disrespect? First, when people feel stressed out, frustrated, or unhappy, acting respectfully often gets lost in the chaos. Second, you also have managers with low EI who let their emotions rule them rather than the other way around. And third, there are individuals who firmly believe that employees are the enemy, making an aggressive offense their best defense. Really, the list of reasons could fill an entire book.

You can also fill an entire book with the resentment and resistance that disrespect generates. Every time managers damage an employee's self-worth by treating him or her rudely with contempt or scorn, they also damage their own fragile credibility. Unwittingly, managers destroy their ability to motivate and influence others — their opportunity to manage change successfully. You might say that treating others poorly is like picking up hot coals and throwing them at another. You may burn the other person, but you're still the first one to get hurt.

However, when employees' feel that you treat them with respect your payback is enormous. You get their loyalty, support, their willingness to defend and protect you, as well as their desire to make sure that you look successful. That's a pretty good return-on-your-investment for just treating others the same way that you, want to be treated — as a valuable and worthy human being.

Chapter 9

Assessment: How's Your Organization Doing with Resistance?

In This Chapter
▶ Checking how you and your managers work with resistance
▶ Interpreting your Resistance Score

*H*ere's your chance to evaluate how well you, your management team, and/or your own manager manage resistance. We've written this questionnaire so that you can answer it without reading all six chapters on resistance (though, of course we hope that you do). After you have responded to the 14 statements, get out your handy calculator to do some simple addition and division. Or if you want to keep your arithmetic skills from getting too rusty, grab a pencil and paper.

After you've calculated (electronically or manually) your Resistance Score, find the description that corresponds to your score. You can then judge how well your organization presently manages resistance to change, as well as what you can probably expect with future changes. And by examining your response to each of the individual statements, you can get a good clue of ways to improve how you manage resistance.

Here are five ways for you to use this assessment chapter. You can

✔ Keep your evaluation to yourself — as a way to validate intuitions and gut feelings about how well resistance is managed within your organization.

✔ Use it as a discussion topic with your own management or work team to help you improve how you manage resistance.

✔ Discuss your results with your manager (providing that he or she is open to discussions like this).

✔ Send your results to the people who manage the change you're presently struggling with, such as HR or a special taskforce. Or if you're part of the team managing a specific change, use the results as an evaluation and guide for improving resistance management.

✔ Give the assessment to every one in your organization (if you're a manager), asking that they honestly fill it out. And if you do want honest feedback, then make sure that you protect confidentiality!

No matter how you choose to use "Your Assessment" we hope that it provides you with useful information about working with resistance. If you find that your "Resistance Score" falls into the "danger," "caution," or even "optimistic" categories, Chapters 3 through 8 offer you tools for working more effectively with resistance and improving the opportunities for success.

Recording Your View

When it comes to resistance, do managers fight it or work with it? Do you work in an environment that sees only one way of solving problems or values diverse ways of thinking? Do managers force resistance underground or support it? Circle the number that best represents how your organization views and responds to resistance. Where **1 = never** and **6 = always.**

1.	My organization considers resistance an unavoidable and natural part of change.	1 2 3 4 5 6
2.	Because managers expect resistance to major changes, they're not defensive when it occurs.	1 2 3 4 5 6
3.	Managers continue to view people who resist change as valuable and loyal employees.	1 2 3 4 5 6
4.	Managers look beneath the surface of resistance to find the hidden solutions to current and potential problems.	1 2 3 4 5 6
5.	Management keeps me up-to-date about what is happening with our change efforts, which reduces my uncertainty and frustration.	1 2 3 4 5 6
6.	I have input into changes that effect my job, which helps me feel involved.	1 2 3 4 5 6
7.	When implementing changes, managers focus as much on the people issues as they do on the technical issues.	1 2 3 4 5 6

8.	All people are treated with respect and dignity, even when they express opinions different from management's.	1 2 3 4 5 6
9.	As an organization, we create solutions to problems by merging different and even conflicting ways of thinking.	1 2 3 4 5 6
10.	Managers encourage honest dialogue on sensitive and uncomfortable issues.	1 2 3 4 5 6
11.	In our change efforts, I have opportunities for open, meaningful and safe two-way communication with upper management.	1 2 3 4 5 6
12.	I have a formal way to anonymously communicate my opinions to leadership.	1 2 3 4 5 6
13.	Management listens to and promptly responds to our issues and concerns about changes.	1 2 3 4 5 6
14.	Managers put as much emphasis on protecting employees' self-worth as they do on their own.	1 2 3 4 5 6
TOTAL		_____

Tallying and interpreting your score

Total of responses is	_____
(Score is total divided by 14)	
Score is	_____

Your score is 1 — 1.9

Danger: Leaders probably still remain trapped in the myth that resistance is bad and that employees who resist are disloyal. Managers usually approach both resistance and disgruntled employees as the enemy, losing the benefits of people's insight and expertise. Furthermore, management sees little value in building upon and integrating the diverse ideas that fill the organization. There's usually only one way to do things — and that's their way. By not tapping into the knowledge, experience, and creativity, in all job levels, problems fester, landmines explode, and changes eventually self-destruct.

Your score is 2.0 — 3.5

Concern: While leaders still operate from the myth that resistance is bad, they're gradually realizing that opposition may also have some value — and that not all unhappy employees are disloyal. On those occasions when they listen to people who bring unpleasant messages, managers minimize, or even avoid disasters. But more often, they shoot messengers and struggle with respecting diverse opinions, which keeps many problems hidden and solutions elusive. Not all your changes end in disaster, however, some do fail and many just hobble along.

Your score is 3.6 — 5.0

Optimism: Leaders are transitioning from the myth that resistance is bad to the reality that it has value. In your organization, many changes are implemented well. Most likely, managers unconsciously recognize and often use the valuable knowledge hidden in resistance — and work with disgruntled employees, rather than against them. But, because managers do not consciously and consistently leverage employees' diverse experiences, a few problems still remain unresolved making success sometimes difficult to duplicate. Occasionally, a few changes may fall short of your expectations.

Your score is 5.1 — 6.0

Celebration: Your organization's leaders see resistance as an ally, not the enemy. Managers consciously look for and consistently use the wealth of information that lies hidden in employees' opposition. When implementing change, they're comfortable working with diverse experience and knowledge. Consequently, managers avoid, quickly resolve, or minimize the majority of obstacles that sabotage change efforts in other organizations. Tell your managers what a great job they're doing!

Part III
Planning Your Change — From Calamari to Tiramisu

The 5th Wave   By Rich Tennant

SETTING UP AN INTRANET HAS REALLY HELPED OUR BUSINESS.

MUSTARD

HOT DOGS

RELISH

BUNS

In this part . . .

Change doesn't happen overnight. That's why it's important to first of all determine whether your change initiative is really necessary and then create an action plan for success. This part takes you through all the steps that lead to implementation of a change success story.

Chapter 10

Making Sure That Your First Step Is The Right One

"Now we're on a Six Sigma kick. I think [the president] read about it in one of those in-flight magazines and decided it would be a nice thing for us to do. It'll disappear like all the others."

Controller
Private Company

In today's crowded skies and overstuffed supermarket shelves, you can't afford miscalculations and missteps. They're deadly. Eager suppliers batter down your customers' doors to prove how they can do it better, cheaper, and faster than you can. Blossoming home schooling and charter schools steal students from floundering public schools. Struggling hospitals build state-of-the-art health clubs in their fight for patients. If you don't want to end up like the Tyrannosaurus, then obviously you must keep evolving — adapting. That means nothing short of continuous innovation and improvement, as well as maintaining highly motivated employees who willingly make the sacrifices demanded by ongoing transformations.

Some organizations carefully and systematically select changes and then diligently work to make them succeed. For others, it's grasping onto the latest management fad with the hope that something eventually works. In the first scenario, change winners get a high return on the time, effort, and money they spend to do it right the first time. In the second scenario, these organizations pay a steep price for their grasp-it-try-it-discard-it cycle — never finding their miracle fix-it cure. In this chapter, you see that the difference between those that succeed at change management and those that fail isn't so much about the changes they select, but the way and reasons for making their choices. Even before they actually start their change journey, some organizations have already set themselves up for failure.

Getting Trapped in the Loser's Circle

With studies showing that at least two-thirds of organizational changes end up discarded, what makes organizational changes so vulnerable to failures? Analyzing organizations in various stages of their change efforts, we discovered the following seven-phase cycle in which many managers get ensnared — a cycle of great hopes and disappointing failures.

- **Phase I: A new change.** Here's where the leaders feel all the enthusiasm for a new beginning. It's a time of believing that anything and everything is possible — for the leaders, that is the case. But for employees who have experienced the "flavor of the month" club, they usually skip phase I and move right into phase II.

- **Phase II: Watchful cynicism.** People who know that new marketing plans and process teams don't magically appear like Cinderella's carriage hold back their feelings of enthusiasm. It's a time of wait-and-see whether leaders continue down the road or, as with so many other efforts, abandon this one, too.

- **Phase III: Reinforced pessimism.** Problems happen — even in the best-planned change initiatives. You get delays, mistakes, and surprises. If employees have already been burned by past failures and have shaky trust in their leaders skill to implement changes successfully, even the smallest mishap feeds feelings of future doom. For many leaders, the normal adversities of change plant the seeds of disillusionment — things were suppose to get better, not worse.

- **Phase IV: Protective resistance.** Armed with cynicism from past failures and experiencing naturally occurring snarl-ups, employees begin protecting themselves from one more failure. They do so by either making inconsequential, superficial changes or giving lip service while doing nothing. Either way, leaders, eager to believe that things are improving, lull themselves into believing that everything's just moving along famously. They can now breathe a deep sigh of relief and go off to do their "real" work (or the next change effort), letting their new benefits program take care of itself.

- **Phase V: Active resistance.** Without leaders' active assistance and monitoring of their change, confusion and chaos mount. Passive resistance by employees turns into aggressive opposition. Now, the change's struggle for life becomes a losing battle. People have clear messages not to waste their time — another change is about to bite the dust.

✔ **Phase VI: Escalating disillusionment.** Leaders also have a clear message, what they thought was taking care of itself was really self-destructing. No longer can they pretend that their new culture is working great. Leaders begin waking up to the reality of resistance gridlock. As active opposition permeates all aspects of the change, they can no longer rationalize that problems came from natural growing pains. Now, their own interest in getting that new culture gets replaced with frustration and discouragement.

✔ **Phase VII: Abandonment**. Admitting failure, leaders abandon their changes to the fates. Potentially valuable innovations disappear, and employees have yet another failure to add to their growing list.

And this brings you back to Phase I — looking for that next great solution to provide what the previous quick fixes didn't (see Figure 10-1).

Don't despair. Remember, at least one-third of organizational changes do succeed. They manage to break out of or even avoid the loser's circle. Their success comes because of the way they start their journey — selecting the changes they implement.

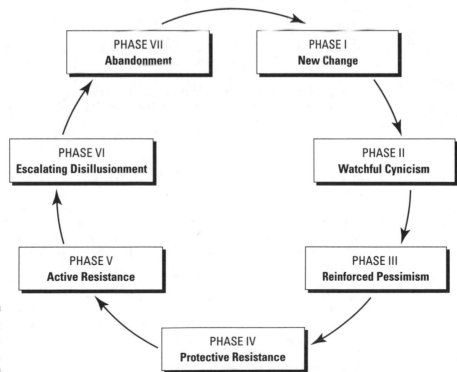

Figure 10-1: The loser's circle.

Packing the Two Ps — Purpose and Prioritization

In an ancient Chinese saying, a journey of 1,000 miles begins with the first step. True, yet before travelers take that first step, they must have made a few vital decisions, such as where they're going, why they want to go there, and how they plan to get there. Reasonable questions to ask one's self before starting on a voyage, but imperative for you to thoroughly answer if you're leading others on a journey. Guides of organizational change must logically and completely answer these questions before expecting others to follow. However, you'd be surprised how many managers reorganize, create new positions, form processes teams, or redesign distribution systems without clearly answering these three most basic questions. (Or maybe it wouldn't surprise you.)

You can find many reasons for embarking on a change effort. Most changes you would like to do are undoubtedly good ones — some more critical than others to your survival. That means your change journey begins with you answering the following two questions:

- Why am I doing this change?

- Of all the changes that I'd like to do, is this the most important for the organization, employees, and me?

The chance of failure is so great and the price of failure so high, examine your reasons and priorities carefully to minimize your risk and maximize your investment.

The reasons for taking your journey

The following are some of the reasons that motivate managers to embark on their change journey. A couple of those reasons may seem "illogical" to you, but then, being logical 100 percent of the time isn't part of the human race's operating system. (In fact, even computers, designed to be logical, don't act that way all the time either.)

- **Boredom.** In the not-so-distant past, physicians would advise patients who seemed discontented or melancholy that they should change their routine, get out of the rut, and even take a long ocean voyage. Today, some managers, especially those with an entrepreneurial bent, get easily bored with day-to-day routines and decide that things need shaking up. Instigating change when you feel that professional "seven-year itch," but don't have a clear problem to solve, only throws your organization into unnecessary disruption and into the circle of failure. Rather than throw your organization into turmoil, you should try changing your job.

✔ **Gut reaction.** Some people have and use more intuition than others. On the one hand, intuition is a great thing — it allows you to implement many good decisions quickly. On the other hand, using intuition makes it difficult for you to explain logically and specifically to employees your reasons for making a particular decision. And when you run into all the natural detours that accompany any journey, gut feelings, without hard data, won't sustain you through the frustrations. Therefore, use your intuition to open new doors, but make sure that you also do your homework so that you understand your reasons for opening that door and what lies behind it.

✔ **Sounds good.** If it's gotten another company on the cover of *Business Week,* then that change effort must also work wonders for your organization. You're not yet desperate, but your organization isn't performing the way you'd like — you might say it's having a "bad hair day" or quarter. Instead of a major change effort, you may want to try something far less ambitious than a culture change. Minor improvements may be all you need to deal with some of the concerns facing you. It's amazing how whittling away at the smaller issues can solve, what looks like, one gigantic problem.

✔ **Quick fix.** When the ship feels like it's sinking, any lifeboat (or jacket) will do. Not so with organizations. When you've got discontented customers, disgruntled employees, and disenchanted investors, it's tempting to latch onto an idea that's being heralded as the next-best-thing-to-sliced-bread. Introducing reengineering or redesigning your internal network may fix some problems, but they also give you gobs more. So, before you grab something that has saved others, make sure that it's really, really the best solution for your problems and your unique organization. Don't get caught grasping another quick fix to repair the one that didn't work.

✔ **Best alternative.** The managers that succeed in managing change do so because they carefully analyze their organizations' needs, analyze the various solutions, and then select the best fit. And even when they have found a "cure" for what ails them, they don't send everyone madly dashing off into that new direction. Change winners usually launch trial balloons in single departments to see what works and what causes even greater headaches. Carefully and systematically, these managers altered the change to match the needs of their employees and organizations. No cookie-cutter approach for them. With lots of careful planning, hard work, patience, and determination they arrived safely, soundly, and successfully.

You may find your organization facing a life-threatening situation. This type of danger eliminates the luxury of normal trial runs. Follow your common sense. How can you get a sanity check with the time you do have available? Do you have a week for a team of knowledgeable people to do a mock run-through of the process redesign? If not a week, can you get technical people in a room for a day to talk through this with you? Remember, any input that helps you avoid surprises increases your probability of success.

The prioritization of where to go

You can't escape priorities. Every day you're forced to choose between multiple demands, such as pressing job and personal commitments, competing work projects, tugging family members, exacting customers, and insisting employees (and all of them simultaneously). You're even forced to make priorities when you take a simple one-week vacation — is it camping with the kids, hiking the Himalayas, repairing the garage, exploring Roman ruins in Morocco, having your wisdom teeth extracted or diving on the Great Barrier Reef?

So too, must you prioritize the change efforts you implement from the never-ending list of ones clamoring for your attention. Given how you're bombarded with do-this-immediately-or-perish ideas from recent business articles and by the latest business gurus, prioritization isn't such a simple process. How do you select what new endeavors give your organization, your employees, and yourself the most improvement for the time and money spent?

Here's a basic process for helping you prioritize potential change initiatives. We leave the specific details for you to customize according to your specific needs. Your key to the prioritization process is creating criteria for evaluating what to do and not do.

The change prioritization process includes

✔ **Creating a wish list of all the changes that you would like.** Make sure that you include both the big ones (such as reorganizations or culture change) and the less "important" ones (such as a new expense reporting system or new benefits package). We show you in Chapter 5, how all change efforts drain employees' time and energy eventually causing them to oppose you and your efforts — even the changes that you consider "little ones."

✔ **Agreeing with your team about what criteria you use for evaluating your change-list items.** You don't have the resources to do everything on the list immediately (or in some cases, ever). Therefore, be sure that the ones you do select solve your most serious problems and give you the most benefit for the buck. Types of criteria you might choose include items that:

- Solve a major productivity, customer, cost, or employee problem — poor results on customer surveys or high loss rate of skilled people.

- Stay within available resources — you can afford to commit five people full time for six months on a new process design, but then you can't commit those same people to the other projects that you promised your customers they would receive within the next four months.

- Can be accomplished within a desired time frame — you must cut costs 10 percent within three months or defect rate 25 percent within two months.

- Will produce significant benefit across a large number of departments or people — need to reduce the high levels of overtime or improve peoples' morale that was very low in the latest employee survey.

✔ **Evaluating each change effort according to your pre-determined criteria.** This step is where you carefully examine each of the changes on your wish list — critically judging them according to your agreed upon criteria. By scrutinizing all desired changes according to specific criteria, you are making your selection based on an impartial analysis rather than "that feels good to me" approach. Some managers use a numbering system, others simply a matrix.

✔ **Ranking changes based upon how they meet your criteria.** Whether you use numerical scoring or just count check marks on a matrix, you quickly see which changes most successfully meet your needs. Start writing your ranking list with the change that gives you the most benefit and then continue with the others according to their ratings. If you've got ties, just list them together on the same line.

✔ **Making your selection and eliminating all the rest.** Here's where you've got to have the guts to say "no" to great ideas that just don't do a good job meeting your criteria — solving your organization's issues and concerns. You may have the people and money to implement the first three or four of your major efforts, or just your top one. How many you do isn't important. What is important is that you and your employees know that you're making the best use of their time and the organization's resources.

Paying the High Price of Failure

Many managers moan and groan when we walk them through the prioritization process: "It's a waste of time" or "We know what needs to be done, and it's my job to do it." Yet, it's these same managers that find themselves caught up in the Loser's Cycle. They selected change efforts that seemed well meaning, but ones that employees didn't consider worth their time and effort. It's also these same managers that get the reputation of looking for that "next quick fix."

No question about it, decentralizing, implementing a new e-mail system, using customer satisfaction surveys, or creating a new benefit package (not all at once, please) can give you great payback. But each of these changes arrives as a double-edge sword because if they crater, you usually pay an enormous price. The following sections describe the five costs of failure facing you when your change efforts strikeout.

The five costs of failure frequently occur together, and their cumulative impact creates a devastatingly lethal legacy.

Wasted money and time

Every change has a financial price tag. Whether an organization begins a new initiative entirely in-house or buys a product from an outside vendor, management spends large amounts of money on that change package. You spend this money on program design, materials, and trainers. In addition, a company may rollout the new direction with expensive multimedia events at worldwide locations, handouts for employees, posters, and even new recognition and reward programs.

Add to this expense the time that managers spend in change-related meetings, as well as the hours lost when employees spend time away from their day-to-day responsibilities attending training sessions and/or special communications meetings. Finally, you must enter into the equation the massive hours spent in actual implementation.

If the change fails, managers lose not only money, but also precious time and productivity with little or nothing to show for their wasted resources.

Missed opportunities

Sadly, those organizations whose change efforts falter miss opportunities for financial savings, process cycle-time reductions, and customer retention.

In the first year of their TQM effort, a private company trained nine quality-improvement teams (with 4 to 12 people on a team). The second year, it trained 38 additional teams; and in the third year, it added 36 more. Of these 83 teams, only seven provided significant financial payoffs. However, over the first five years, those seven teams produced more than enough savings to cover the costs of the other 76 teams.

Those seven teams had immediate supervisors who provided the leadership and support needed to make the changes, even though middle and upper management did not provide ongoing support. Without strong leadership involvement, the other 76 teams failed.

What would the savings have been if all 76 teams had results similar to the successful seven? Savings would have probably been at least ten times the cumulative cost of all 83 teams! Just think of the money that could have been made, but instead was poured down the drain; the customers that employees could have delighted, but instead left unsatisfied; and the high morale managers could have built upon, but instead squandered.

Destroyed confidence in leaders

When change fails, it causes employees to lose confidence, respect, and trust in the judgment of their leaders. Employees become convinced that either the "programs" were poor business decisions that leaders should never have implemented or that they were good ideas but leaders lacked the skills necessary for successful implementation. Either way, in employees' eyes, leaders failed — and their leaders are failures.

Confidence, respect, and trust are hard to win, easy to lose, and, once lost, even more difficult to regain. True, one failure doesn't automatically destroy employees' willingness to follow you, but "programs of the month" do. (If you want to understand more about how failed changes damage your credibility, you can turn to Chapter 5.)

As a "fast-track" first level manager at a Fortune 500 company put it: "Funny how life and all these management programs are so much alike — they both give you great expectations and promises and even greater disappointments. For me, the greatest disappointment was realizing that our CEO wasn't so wonderful after all. How do you believe in someone, no matter how brilliant, who can't get a simple change right?"

Reduced morale and productivity

If you're in an organization brimming with enthusiasm, a can-do attitude, and team synergy, there's little that you or others can't accomplish. It's an energized work world that paychecks can't create and fancy titles can't coerce. It's an organization fueled by success.

However, a work environment characterized by defeatism, distrust, and disrespect for leadership negatively impacts employee morale and productivity. It's hard to keep your spirits up and struggle long hours if you feel that you don't work with a winning organization.

The following comments come from employees who work in different companies where change failures, not successes, are the norm. Even on a piece of paper, you can still "hear" their feelings of defeat.

- ✔ "We're all only doing just enough to get our paycheck and get by. No reason to give them any more."

- ✔ "Have management tell me what they want me to do, and I'll do it, but that's it. I'm through jumping through hoops for them."

- ✔ "When I came to this department, I was told, 'Forget about TQM. Just do your job and hang it all up at five.' They were right."

- ✔ "I'm tired of beating my head against a wall trying to make this reorganization work. It's about time that I accepted reality and got on with my life."

Increased resistance to future changes

Resistance — employees' resistance and managers response — is one of the most important variables in determining the success or failure of your change efforts. So much so, that we've dedicated Chapters 3 through 9 to this area. Briefly, once people experience a series of failures, they expect future ones and build defenses against the pain of more failures to come.

Another way of describing the Losers Circle (discussed in the beginning of this chapter) is that failure, frustration, anger, and resistance feed on each other. Expecting another failure, employees prepare for conflict with management and dig in for another round of resistance. Leaders, reeling from past failures, approach future change efforts expecting to do battle with uncooperative employees. Inevitably, each side's expectations become self-fulfilling prophecies — negative ones. When changes become losing battles like this, everyone is the loser.

Paying the high costs of failure isn't inevitable – you can also reap the great benefits of success. You have choices about how you plan for and implement your changes. When you do these wisely, you protect your organization, employees, and yourself.

Staying the Course

Whether you're implementing a change to prevent your organization from becoming the next Titanic, or just fine-tuning a specific area to become even better, don't take your first step unless you're willing to persevere through thick and thin. That means you must not only select the most appropriate change for your needs, but also answer one more question. Do you have the dedication and determination to cross the finish line?

As chance, circumstances, and the fates play havoc with your journey (nobody promised you a rose garden, let alone one without thorns), you'll need to keep persevering during the never-ending adjustments and detours. So, before you take that first step and ask your people to trust you as their change guide, make sure that you're personally committed to making your change successful. Anything less and you're right back to dishing out "flavors of the month."

Jesse Jackson, clergyman and civil rights leader, summed it up by paraphrasing Napoleon Hill when he said, "If I can conceive it and believe it, I can achieve it. It's not my *ap*titude but my *att*itude that will determine my *alt*itude — *with a little intestinal fortitude!*" Successfully completing any change journey demands that you have both the winner's "attitude" and "fortitude."

Chapter 11

Getting Your Act Together

· ·

In This Chapter

▶ Understanding why planning is so important

▶ Forming change management teams

▶ Getting to know the six steps in the planning process

· ·

"I didn't want to waste valuable time going through some bureaucratic exercise. Now I'm glad that we did. Rather than feeling out of control [merging these two departments], I feel as if I've finally got a handle on what we've got to do."

Vice President
Fortune 100 company

*I*f you analyze the reasons why many companies go out of business, you probably end up with a very brief but highly descriptive epitaph: "They didn't plan to fail; they simply failed to plan." The same epitaph works for any organization whose change efforts fail.

Planning is often the difference between victory and defeat (if you hold luck constant): One university raises far more money than another because it devotes more energy to analyzing its alumni and figuring out an effective approach to soliciting funds from them. One hospital grows, while others get bought out, because administrators spends more time strategizing ways to retain respected doctors, recruit high quality medical personnel, and attract patients. Similarly, one company brings a product to market much more readily than the competition because management has carefully developed a step-by-step process for getting new ideas out of Research and Development, into manufacturing, and out the door to customers. Do you see a theme developing here? The same theme fits for merging departments, creating an employee survey, or reengineering processes.

Every successful undertaking starts with good planning: No matter how hard you work on your change, you can't overcome inadequate or faulty planning.

This chapter focuses on the planning process — what you need to have in place before you actually create your implementation plan. Initially, this may sound like one more bureaucratic, paper-pushing activity. It isn't. If you want a strong building, you need a solid foundation. The same holds true for implementing a successful change — you need to build a solid plan, or foundation.

Skimping on Planning: Tempting but Deadly

As important as planning may be to the success of change efforts, managers seem to skimp on it. What makes them resist taking the time up front to plan well? Here's what we've discovered from working with many managers:

- ✔ In today's culture, the emphasis is on the doing. (Indeed, some managers seem to subscribe to the maxim that those who can, do, while those who can't, sit around and talk about it.) The increasing rate of change in areas like technology adds a sense of urgency that seems to support this culture with tools like laptops, cell phones, and e-mail.

- ✔ Customers (inside and outside the business) have developed less tolerance for deferred gratification. It's becoming a "give-it-to-me-now" society. Here again, technology reinforces this mentality with faster fax machines (do you remember thermal paper?), extra-priority overnight mail, and we'll-immediately-notify-you e-mail systems.

- ✔ Planning doesn't appear very exciting. It's hard work, and it takes valuable time. There isn't much positive and immediate feedback for planning. The big applause comes with the successful implementation. And even then, people have usually forgotten about all the planning that made everything run smoothly.

- ✔ Managers easily find excuses to avoid getting involved in the planning stage. Their excuses range from "everyone understands what we need to do" to "I've got my real work to do," to "I made the decision, now someone else can figure out the details."

While life makes short-changing the planning process easy, it doesn't give you a natural safety net when you plummet to reality. What do you lose when you sacrifice the planning stage of change management?

First, you lose the coordination and synergy of having all employees reading from the same sheet of music or rowing in the same direction. Some managers believe that because the pieces and parts of the change appear clear to them, they must also be obvious to all others. But that's not the case. Instead, constant disagreements erupt over what should be done and who does what. Now rather than everyone working together, employees waste time in conflict and rework. No wonder everything slows down and gets bogged down.

Second, managers begin looking incompetent. "Who's in charge here?" becomes a common refrain. Even though no one wants to do the planning, employees still expect to see their new marketing plan roll out with clearly defined actions, responsibilities, and dates. But, if they see confusion and chaos, people know where to look — management's ineptitude and bungling.

Third, managers abdicate all ability to track progress and quickly fix minor issues before they become overwhelming catastrophes. No tracking mechanism means no way to know how far you've fallen behind schedule (what schedule?), who's not doing what they were assigned (what assignments?), and how all the different processes fit together (what processes?).

Lastly, employees lose valuable opportunities to quickly get involved with the new direction. Without an actual implementation plan in their hands, they don't have a map of where management is leading them, how the organization will get there and when everybody is supposed to arrive. Left operating in the dark, frustrated, uncertain, distrusting employees hold back their support.

After you decide upon implementing a change, immediately jump into the planning process — the stronger your plan, the stronger your foundation for success.

Forming the Change Management Team

You may be a "do-it-myself" person. And that's fine, but leading an organization through change is not one of those times that you want to drive around in circles before asking for help. You've got too much at stake to make mistakes. Therefore, create a team to spearhead your initiative and to help take on day-to-day responsibilities. You're still in charge; you just have a support system to reduce the demands on your time and warn you when you're about to step on a landmine.

You can select one of two approaches in forming your Change Management Team (CMT). You and your direct reports can form the CMT, or you can select employees from around your organization to form the CMT. Both ways have their pluses and minuses, so you need to decide what fits your needs and style best.

Using your leadership team

With this approach, you and your direct reports form the CMT. If you and your leadership team function as the CMT, there's no doubt about your commitment to your change effort. In addition, you and your team probably have the power and authority to quickly resolve difficulties as they arise. If you find yourself involved in multiple changes, then you need the CMT to integrate the various efforts so that employees don't feel like taffy being pulled in different directions. You and your leadership team are in the best position for providing this coordination.

However, the leadership team may not have all the information that's available to the rank-and-file employees. So with a leadership CMT, you are risking problems that fester until they get too big to remain hidden. Or people may become suspicious of what the "big bosses" are doing behind closed doors. Furthermore, closed out from the CMT meeting, employees may feel that their ideas aren't important, reducing their commitment to your undertaking. Finally, when you and your leadership team function as the CMT, it requires a major time commitment — time that may be better spent elsewhere.

Using an employee team

In this method, the CMT is made up of employees (8 to 12 people) from across your organization, while you and your leadership group function in an oversight and approval role. Obviously, employee representatives on the CMT possess more knowledge relating to employees' perceptions and problems. Employees also feel more involved in the change process and have a stronger sense of ownership in the resulting implementation plan. If you have specific, well-focused changes, then you might want to consider an employee comprised CMT.

On the down side, employees may not possess an overview of the entire organization or business. They may also need extra training in understanding the change process. Plus, you don't get off scot-free: The CMT definitely depends upon your guidance, decision-making, and problem-fixing powers. Finally, there's the question of who will be on the CMT, who leads the team, and who will be the facilitator to help with all the messy team dynamics (in which people may lack sufficient skills).

You must stay personally involved. It's still your plan.

If you choose to go this route, we offer just one caution: You need to learn to trust your CMT. The members of the CMT might not come up with the same solutions that you would or would like them to. But if the CMT members are to feel empowered and provide valuable input, you have to give them the latitude to make their own mistakes. If you can do that, you'd be amazed at how productive and creative they are.

Regardless of which way you choose to build your CMT, you must maintain ownership of the team's products and ideas. That's easy to do if you're on the team, but more difficult if you're viewed as an outsider — not really involved with the team.

Understanding the Process of Change

Every organizational change is a process. Some processes work, while others don't — which means, some changes succeed while others fail. There's no silver bullet — no single way of designing the process that fits in every situation. Types of changes, cultures, CMTs, and employees all mix together differently. While the six general process steps remain constant, each manager must customize them to fit his or her unique situation.

The process model

Figure 11-1 shows a diagram of the change management process that guides your CMT in its planning. We borrowed and modified a model developed by the social psychologist Kurt Lewin almost 50 years ago.

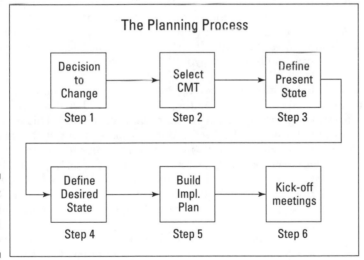

Figure 11-1:
The change planning process.

The process sequence

The following numbered list presents the planning process linearly. As you read the following six steps, please remember that this isn't a cookie cutter, one-size-fits-all approach. Your CMT must customize each step to meet your specific circumstances and changes.

1. Decide upon a change. In Chapter 10, you read about the need to clearly understand your reasons for making a change and how to prioritize and select the changes to implement. (If you haven't read that chapter yet, you might find it very helpful.)

2. Select your CMT. You need a team of qualified people to oversee the planning and implementation of your change. To survive, every change needs planning, monitoring, and nurturing, and that's what the CMT does.

3. Define your present state. This step has three parts: developing a "what's going well" list, creating an "issues and concern" list, and reconfirming, in the CMT's collective mind, that a change is indeed needed. All of this information is in Chapter 12 for you.

4. Define your desired state. The CMT creates a detailed description of the target or goal that you want your employees to meet. You all need to be heading in the same direction. Chapter 13 guides your CMT in this step.

5. Develop your implementation plan. Here are the nuts and bolts of your change effort. You need to include the human side as well as the technical side of change. And don't forget your score card for tracking how well you're meeting your goals. Your CMT can use Chapter 14 as a template for its implementation plan.

6. Hold your kickoff meetings. How you tell employees about your new direction sets the stage for how they think about and react to it. This isn't the time for fancy multimedia shows, but rather it's where you and your CMT logically present your case for asking others to disrupt their lives. In Chapter 15, the CMT can find clear and easy-to-use suggestions for creating and presenting your kickoff meeting.

And what happens after the kickoff? This is when you put all your planning to work. You actually start implementing your improved customer care program, your after-tax-reporting process, or your plant renovation. This is also where your implementation plan becomes your roadmap and project management tool rolled into one document. However often you use it, please have the CMT review the plan's scorecard at least monthly. If you're falling behind schedule or run into roadblocks, your CMT knows it and can take corrective action quickly. Whatever you do, please don't shove the implementation plan into a desk drawer or some dust-gathering pile of papers — like "change losers" do.

Your implementation plan isn't written in stone. It's a living document. No matter how well you prepare it, unforeseen events make parts of any plan out-of-date, so you make modifications as needed during the year. At least once a year, you and the CMT should refresh and totally up-date your plan (recycle through the full six-step process).

Creating a Winning Process

The CMT members don't operate in a vacuum. They have a roller-coaster life just like all the other employees who work with and for them. When a person adds membership on the CMT to an already over-packed and out-of-balance work life, it's an act of dedication to and belief in an organization. In fact at times, working on a CMT can be a hardship and a thankless job. But it can also be an exhilarating experience when you watch a change effort unfold successfully.

To help your CMT experience the joys and pride of success, members must always keep in focus the extraordinary diversity of people and the never-ending need to market their change plan and process.

Managing a diverse organization

Diversity is simultaneously good and bad. It's good because it brings multiple viewpoints, ideas, and alternatives to the planning and problem-solving process. It's bad because this variety of viewpoints, ideas, and alternatives also brings debate, tensions, and conflict to your meetings and work place. The CMT can't avoid the downsides of diversity, but the CMT can minimize it and make the upsides work.

Two plans — one a failure and the other a success

The angel of death to any team is *groupthink*, which means the loss of creative, out-of-the-box thinking and problem-solving ability because members feel pressured by the group to conform to one way of thinking. This usually occurs when team members become insulated from others, new ideas get rejected without consideration, and leaders force their own personal agenda on the team.

An often-used example of groupthink is the Bay of Pigs fiasco. On April 17, 1961, the Kennedy administration backed a disastrous attempt by Cuban exiles to overthrow the government of Fidel Castro. Two CIA leaders and a small group of advisers dominated the planning sessions for the invasion. Shutting out all objections and criticism, they created a plan containing operational mistakes due to bad or missing information. Even with outstanding individuals working long hours behind the scenes to prepare for the invasion, the negative effects from bad planning couldn't be overcome. As a side note, no one planned for the survival or rescue of the 1,500-man brigade that invaded the island.

About 18 months later, another crisis occurred, this time with Russian missiles in Cuba, but the results were just the opposite. On October 16, 1962, the U.S. obtained photographs showing nuclear missile bases under construction. All major cities including, New York, Chicago, and Los Angles were vulnerable to nuclear attack. To prevent groupthink from destroying how it handled this crisis, the Kennedy administration consciously worked to reinforce diverse thinking. Outsiders, deliberately brought into the Executive Committee's meetings, openly expressed objections to any and all initial ideas. The Attorney General, Robert Kennedy, played the role of devil's advocate — consciously attacking premature consensus making. With the Administration's outstanding planning, the U.S. averted a nuclear catastrophe.

This isn't a short course on diversity. We just want to stress how important it is for people on the CMT to create an environment where conflicting ideas can flourish with respect and dignity. Members must realize that they will often be looking at the same issue from different perspectives. And, just as important, what appears crystal clear to the CMT, may actually appear muddy or even dangerous to others not on their team. The success of the CMT depends upon expanding their options and solutions, not narrowing them.

Here are some suggestions for creating an environment that encourages and rewards diverse thinking:

- **Agree upon a set of meeting "norms" that govern how people work together.** You want CMT meetings where everyone feels heard and all ideas get equal time. What you don't want is to end up with a "Bay of Pigs" scenario because groupthink shuts out controversial ideas.

- **Agree upon a process for managing conflict when it arises.** The Harvard Negotiation Project has written a wonderful series of books to help the CMT in this area: *Getting to Yes, Getting Together,* and *Getting Past No.* The power of the CMT comes from building on the wealth of experiences and knowledge of the people sitting in the room. And that means successfully resolving the ever-present conflicts that naturally occur between multiple opposing opinions with minimal residual bitterness and hurt feelings.

- **Reward people who rock the boat.** That's difficult to do if you work in a culture that avoids conflict. However, you'll often find that dissenters usually have a seed of truth in their dissension. (Besides, if they can do it in the CMT, members will be more likely to work skillfully with resistance coming from outside the CMT.)

- **Create values that reinforce and protect different frames of reference.** No matter how well you or the CMT think you understand something, life always manages to prove the opposite. You might want to write down a value list that you read before each meeting. And as you craft your plan (or anything else), always leave a little room for changes and modifications that naturally occur.

- **Go outside the CMT and ask for others' opinions.** Do test runs and trial balloons, then come back and update your plans based upon your new knowledge. Even if everyone on the CMT has finally reached consensus, you still need a reality check. And the best people to give you that dose of reality are the employees who do the day-to-day work.

If you're an observer of human behavior and want to read more about what makes individual's so different, check out Chapter 3.

Getting buy-in

With the baby-boomer generation having grown up listening to Bob Dylan's words, "The first one now will later be last for the times they are a-changing," and the following Generation Xers developing their own unique culture, it's not surprising that many employees have stopped seeing managers as god-like. The leader and the CMT can create the most brilliant and detailed plan in the history of organizational change, but they can't force employees to accept or follow it. The power of the CMT lies, not in fancy titles, but in its members' ability to sell. Procter and Gamble must still encourage consumers to buy their disposable diapers and General Mills still fights for shelf space. So, too must the leader and CMT encourage employees to accept a new distribution system, as well as take on additional demands.

At every step along the process, remind yourself that you're trying to persuade individuals to do something that may not fit in with their priorities. CMT members must turn themselves into super salespeople. They must become the same kind of salesperson from which you willingly buy. And because you probably don't like the high pressure, push-it-down-their-throat type of people, you can bet your employees won't either. That means you and the CMT must

- ✔ Listen to employee needs and requirements.
- ✔ Answer questions honestly.
- ✔ Provide clear and relevant information.
- ✔ Create opportunity of two-way dialogue.
- ✔ Focus on fixing their problems.
- ✔ Know your product thoroughly.
- ✔ Believe in your product.
- ✔ Show enthusiasm.
- ✔ Create an atmosphere that encourages buying.

Granted, there are times of supreme crisis when you don't have a lot of time for dialogue and handholding. However, the leader and the CMT can still provide the facts, share their plan, and demonstrate the urgency through their own commitment.

Even when you sell ideas within your own organization, never forget that you're marketing to a diverse world.

Chapter 12

Describing Your Present World

· ·

In This Chapter

▶ Creating a balanced perspective of where you are now

▶ Describing what's going right

▶ Defining critical issues and concerns

· ·

> *"Things aren't perfect, but things aren't that terrible around here either. We don't need change for change's sake. They [leadership] haven't given me one good reason why we now need to do all this extra 'quality' work. What do they think I've been doing the past 12 years? Garbage?"*

> Middle manager
> Fortune 100 company

When planning for a change, most managers typically focus on the technical side: the budget, training needs, time tables, who does what, and deadlines. The human side gets lost amongst all the technical details. Morale, motivating employees, the need to protect one's job and self-worth, the importance of two-way communication, territorial power struggles, and resistance all fade from view.

If your employees were robots, you could safely focus on only their technical tasks. But, alas, people are emotional human beings. So, focus on the human side of your change effort as diligently as you do the technical requirements.

This chapter tells you how to talk to your employees about upcoming changes. When you ask people to turn their lives upside down and inside out for you, you'd better be able to explain the reasons for the changes clearly and logically. Explain what's not working right, but be sure that you don't antagonize the very people you're asking to support you. So protect their self-worth by letting them know that they aren't the reason that changes are taking place.

Creating a Balanced Perspective

There's an old rule that coaches follow — at least, those who want to achieve impressive results. A good coach (any coach, whether he or she coaches volleyball or voice) always begins by describing what is going right, before focusing on what's going wrong and what needs improvement. On the one hand, coaches who give only criticism find themselves out of work — no one's self-worth can stand a barrage of negativity for too long. On the other hand, coaches who give only positive feedback also end up unemployed. Their teams or students don't succeed because they never improve. Balance is the key.

Managers have often been compared to coaches, and the act of giving feedback to employees has been compared to coaching. Whether it's improving a volleyball serve, singing *Madam Butterfly,* or accepting reengineering, coaches and managers must build similar relationships with the individuals they coach or manage. Managers and coaches must ensure that people:

- ✔ Believe that they know what they are doing.
- ✔ Feel that they have their best interest at heart.
- ✔ Feel good about themselves so that they're secure enough to take risks and try new ways of doing things.
- ✔ Trust them enough to follow their advice.

Managing/coaching is all about understanding people. You're balancing the positive with the negative — blending what's going right with what needs improvement. (For more about managers as coaches, turn to Chapter 17.)

The winning power of a coach

In Sydney, Australia, on Wednesday, September 27, 2000, the United States unexpectedly destroyed Cuba's 20-year global dominance of international baseball. Consisting of only over-the-hill and young minor leaguers, this U.S. team did the impossible.

After losing a bitterly fought game to Cuba four-days earlier, the players didn't give up. Sports writers attribute a portion of this stunning upset to the team's coach, Tommy Lasorda. As sports writer, Hal Bodley, wrote in *USA Today,* "He was a perfect choice. His daily sermon to this group of no-names was that they could win the gold medal. They believed him."

Obviously, he wasn't just a Pollyanna-ish cheerleader. Lasorda, who celebrated his 73rd birthday in Sydney, had only a few months to make a team out of people who had never played together — many who had not even met — before. Using his vast coaching experience, Lasorda built on players' strength and eliminated their weaknesses.

As you travel down the road of change, painting a balanced picture of the *present state* is essential. (Present state is a shorthand term that includes any technical or human condition that exists in the organization at the present time.) Before you launch into the negative — what's wrong that needs to be changed — remember to accentuate the positive. Most employees can easily tell you "what's wrong around here," but they also have their pride to protect.

Use your Change Management Team (CMT) to help you gather and sort out the critical data on your company's present state. (Chapter 11 tells you more about the CMT and how understanding the present state fits into the overall change process.) Take advantage of the CMT members' diverse backgrounds, experience, knowledge, and viewpoints. After you have all the issues in front of you, then you and the CMT can package the data for public consumption — in other words, determining what you are going to tell employees about the need for them to change and how you are going to tell them.

The next section discusses how you can collect your data.

Acknowledging What's Going Right

You know, most employees are basically good people. They don't get up in the morning telling themselves, "Today, I'm going to make four mistakes before noon." In fact, much of their self-image is wrapped up in doing a good job. Therefore, when you announce that you're going to shake things up, people consciously, or subconsciously interpret that as meaning that they've been doing something wrong — or you wouldn't be asking them to change. It's a natural knee-jerk reaction. It is difficult to announce changes without hurting employees' self-image or self-worth. This problem of self worth is discussed in greater detail in Chapter 5.

What's the payoff?

Change effort is never easy; it requires long hours of hard work, patience, and persistence. Employees must willingly stay the course, often for months or even years before they obtain major goals. All these things require a can-do attitude — a feeling that you really can succeed. Creating and sharing a what's-going-right list sets that stage.

No question about it, documenting what's going right takes time, but it will reduce the time you spend pushing, pulling, and pleading with people to support you and to start doing their jobs differently. As a result of spending the time to develop a what's-going-right summary, you do the following:

✔ **Reinforce morale.** How employees feel about coming to work influences how they perform when they show up. You want people who feel good about the organization, their job, their peers, and their manager. It makes them more creative and productive. Telling employees, honestly, the great things they've done and are doing gives every one a little morale boost — even you.

✔ **Protect other's self-worth.** How individuals feel about themselves also impacts how they feel about their jobs. If they have a more positive self-worth, they will have more energy, a greater willingness to try new things, and a higher tolerance for frustration. These are characteristics that you need to successfully implement changes.

✔ **Build your credibility.** Your ability to lead others depends upon not only your technical skills, but also how well you motivate your employees. Don't worry, you're not out to win the Ms. or Mr. Congeniality award. But you can't succeed if you fill a room full of distrusting, discouraged, and disgruntled people. You want a room that contains trust and optimism.

✔ **Reduce resistance.** Resistance is your change effort's shadow — always following you around. You can't escape resistance, but you can minimize the amount and how tenaciously it clings to your change. Obviously, the more positive people feel about something, the more they support it — with the reverse being just as true. For more information about resistance, see Chapters 3 through 9. (Yes, it's so important that this book dedicates seven chapters to resistance.)

Once you have your what's-going-right list, use it in meetings and speeches. Every chance you get, remind employees that they have been *and* are doing a great job. Especially during the frustrating, dark-days of transitioning from the old ways to the new ways, you want to keep reminding yourself and others that success is possible — you did it before and you'll do it again. And, at least annually, update your list. You'll find that you add significantly more items than you ever take away.

Who creates your list?

Please do not create the list sitting isolated behind closed doors. You need all the input you can get — both in volume and variety. You have four options for creating your what's-going-right list:

✔ **Work with your CMT to create your list.** These people come from a variety of areas and have a broad view about how your organization functions.

✔ **Pull together a cross-section of employees to share their ideas.** The farther down in the trenches you go, the more day-to-day, real life examples surface.

> ✔ **Canvas customers and suppliers.** Or if you have recent customer or supplier surveys, you can use them. External people look at your organization from a different perspective.

> ✔ **Do all three of the items in this list.** The more data you collect, the more credible you sound, and the more solid case you can present.

Which and how many of these options you chose depends on how much time you can spend collecting data.

How do you create your list?

Before you start the brainstorming process, grab a facilitator to guide and record the session. You can chose a trained team member, a HR person, or an outside consultant. Make sure that your room has lots of flipchart paper, markers, and masking tape to attach the paper to the walls as you fill each page. If you're mindmapping (which we explain in the next section), you need blank 8½ by-11 sheets of paper to give each person. You're now ready to begin your basic two-step process — data collection followed by data analysis.

Step 1: Getting it all down on paper

You've pulled 8 to 12 people off their jobs, and you need to get their ideas (some of them very fuzzy) out of their heads and onto paper. How? You have two options: traditional brainstorming and nontraditional brainstorming, called *mindmapping*.

For most organizations, traditional brainstorming is the problem-solving technique of choice — because it's all they know. Basically, you have a facilitator who stands in front of the room recording ideas that people call out and who makes sure that everyone follows the rules. The rules are

> ✔ All ideas are good.

> ✔ Discussions can only take place after the brainstorming session.

> ✔ No one can criticize or evaluate other people's ideas.

> ✔ Brainstorming stops when no one has any more ideas.

Mindmapping, less familiar to the business community, exceeds the volume and creativity that traditional brainstorming produces. Back in the late 1960s, Tony Buzan, creativity specialist, *Mensa International Journal* editor, and host of a ten-part BBC series called *Use Your Head,* designed mindmapping. He wanted to find a way to quickly produce a large number of diverse ideas on a given subject. And he did.

Traditional brainstorming and list-making techniques use your left brain (strong language ability and analytical, logical, and sequential functions), ignoring your right brain (limited language ability, but holistic concepts, artistic endeavors, and inter-relationships). Buzan's mindmap integrates both sides of the brain and jump-starts the creative process. Using mindmaps, teams produce a broader range of ideas more quickly than with any other technique we know.

If you're new to mindmapping, we recommend that you visit Web sites and pick up a book or two for more in-depth information. (If you're not sure what book to buy or to check out from your local library, look for reader reviews on the Web sites. You'll see what worked or didn't work for other people and have a better idea of what you might like.)

Note: For those of you (and you're a rapidly growing number) who attend multicultural meetings where attendees speak different languages, conducting a brainstorming session in English isn't totally successful, but mindmapping works beautifully. In one meeting we facilitated, employees came from Germany, Brazil, America, and Malaysia. When it came time for brainstorming, individuals created their mindmaps in their native language and then switched to English for the read-out. This way the team didn't forfeit valuable knowledge, creativity, and insight by forcing people to brainstorm in a "foreign" language.

Just as each person has his own style for traditional brainstorming, so, too, do people have their own mindmapping techniques. One of the things that experts agree on is that you must customize the process to meet your needs. Therefore, we provide you with basic guidelines, which you can then build on.

1. **In the center of a blank piece of paper (8½-by-11 is optimal), draw a circle, elliptical ring, square, or any other shape you would like.**

2. **Inside your circle (or other shape), write the topic you're brainstorming.**

   For this chapter, the topic can be "going well, "what's right," "issues & concerns," or "problems." As long as everybody in the room agrees upon the topic or subject under discussion, the words written inside the circle should be meaningful to each individual.

3. **Draw lines coming out from your circle or other shape — if you're using a circle, it looks like a sun that most children typically draw.**

   Ten lines are fine, but the number isn't important because usually you'll add more lines once you start writing.

4. **Begin thinking about ideas that relate to the topic, and as each idea comes to you, *quickly* write it down on one of the lines.**

   If you think of a related topic, then you can add subbranches to your main line. Limit the number of words on each line to one word or a simple phrase. Don't get caught-up with getting your thoughts just right — that comes later. Just generate as many ideas as fast as you can. And above all, don't judge your ideas as "good" or "bad." Write down even the dumbest, irrelevant ones as they come to you.

5. **At the end of three to five minutes, stop.**

   If you find that ideas stop flowing before that time, then just trace the outline of the circle in the center of your page. After a few times around with your pencil or pen, other ideas start flowing again.

If you want to sample this technique, here's a quick way to do it. Get one or two other people together. Pick a simple word such as "work" or "car" as your topic. Draw your circle, put in the word, and then add the lines. For about two minutes, list every word that you think of associated with your subject. At the end of the time, compare your lists — count up the number of words that are exactly identical and those that differ. You'll be surprised by the quantitative and qualitative differences that you discover.

Step 2: Organizing it

In the traditional brainstorming sessions, facilitators record ideas as individuals call them out. However, with mindmapping, individuals complete their own mini-brainstorm page. To combine the results from everyone's mindmapping, the facilitator has participants informally read aloud what they've put on their paper. Once everyone has read his or her ideas, then mindmapping continues the same way as traditional brainstorming.

Now you've got to make sense of walls covered with flipchart paper. As a team, go through items making sure that people agree, clarifying any confusion between interpretations and eliminating redundancies. You can also create categories that bundle similar concepts. When it comes to what's-going-right, more on your list is better, so don't spend time weeding out ideas that aren't "heavy hitters." On a new sheet of paper, put your revised list into some kind of order or sequence.

What does a typical list look like?

Each what's-going-right list is unique and specific to the organization producing it — customized to its particular world. Because people's experiences differ, employees' perceptions will differ as to what they think is going well. Your lists include all types of items — financial information, customer attitudes, product quality, leaders' skills, company policies, managers' skills, as well as employee relationships and feelings.

The following are two distinctly different what's-going-right lists from two very different companies.

A 50-person European start-up company

An employee-formed and lead CMT created this list. At the time, the organization was only in its third year of existence. Here's a portion of what the CMT created using mindmapping:

- ✔ Caring bosses
- ✔ Exciting work
- ✔ Freedom to be creative
- ✔ Friendly, fun place to work
- ✔ Good pay
- ✔ Rapid growth
- ✔ Hiring good people
- ✔ Leading edge technology
- ✔ Lots of responsibility
- ✔ Right business/right time
- ✔ Selling to large clients
- ✔ Starting to make a profit
- ✔ Successful company
- ✔ Teamwork among people
- ✔ Variety of work

A large traditional U.S. company

This company has been around for decades and was in the midst of a major culture change and implementing quality/process management when a division created the what's-going-right list. The division's CMT consisted of the vice-president and his leadership team (direct reports). They also used mindmapping to develop this list:

- ✔ Communication starting to improve
- ✔ Good people
- ✔ Improving teamwork
- ✔ Improving focus on customers
- ✔ Outsourced billing performance is improving
- ✔ Pursuing new products
- ✔ Reducing operating costs
- ✔ Reducing the number of suppliers
- ✔ Starting to reduce paperwork/bureaucracy

- ✔ Steadily growing profits
- ✔ Strong growing market
- ✔ Quality, technically up-to-date tools

In the next section, you see the flip side of these glowing words — on an issues-and-concerns list.

Understanding the Issues and Concerns

Creating your issues-and-concerns list is another way to describe the present state of your organization, but this time without the pretty pictures. It's the other half of the balanced perspective that everyone must understand. You usually do this piece right after the what's-going-right activity.

We'll be honest with you. Sometimes creating your issues-and-concerns list isn't an uplifting experience — and sometimes it's downright painful. You're asking others and yourself to open up old wounds and face problems that some people would rather not acknowledge. But you need to identify *specifically* your reasons for asking employees to follow you into disruption and dislocation. In addition, the issues-and-concern's list may help you to spot implementation problems before they derail your change.

What's the pay-off?

You won't get the same positive response sharing this issues and concerns list with your employees as you did when you told them what great things they were doing. In fact, you'll probably leave people feeling emotionally down and even depressed. Nobody likes looking in the mirror and seeing all the wrinkles, blemishes, and bulges. But at the same time, employees must honestly hear why they need an organizational face-lift.

Sharing your issues-and-concerns list helps shield you and your change effort against protests of "I don't know why we need to do this" and "this is just another flavor of the month." It helps you to:

- ✔ **Build your credibility.** Your employees need to know that you aren't wasting time and money on a whim, that you have legitimate problems that need fixing, and that you've carefully thought through the variables and looked at alternatives. Based upon the CMT's analysis, you believe that reorganizing the department, developing a new benefits package, or creating a customer care center best meets the needs of your organization. People see that you've done your homework and that you also understand the problems they're facing.

✔ **Reduce resistance.** When you present an accurate analysis of the challenges facing your organization (don't cry wolf pretending that there's a problem when there isn't one), most employees aren't surprised — they may face those same problems day after day. Individuals may not agree with your solutions, process, or timetable, but few items on your list come as a complete shock. Once you get employees agreeing, even grudgingly, that this is their "present world," then you remove a major justification for them opposing you. After your presentation, it's hard for people to keep proclaiming that everything's fine and that there's no need to change.

✔ **Increase commitment.** At the same time that you reduce employees' reasons for resisting, you also want to increase their willingness to support you and your new direction. By discussing how present problems make their jobs tougher and soon-to-be difficulties threaten their job security, you build a case for acceptance of change. You've shown people that it's in their best interest for everyone to pull together in the same direction.

Who creates your list?

The same team that created your what's-going-right list creates the issues-and-concerns list. Most CMTs do both lists the same day. That way, they maintain their own balanced perspective. Plus, they can see how some of their positive issues remain vulnerable to existing problems. Finally, analyzing both sides of the coin at the same time makes the CMT's task of creating their presentation to employees easier.

For this activity, along with the flipcharts, markers, and masking tape, make sure that you also have sheets of colored, half-inch stick-on dots. You need them for the multivoting process.

How do you create your list?

You and your CMT use the same brainstorming technique for this activity as you did with the what's-going-right list. (See the "Acknowledging What's Going Right" section earlier in this chapter.) If you used the traditional brainstorming, then use it here. And if you used mindmapping, then that is how you create your needs-and-concerns list.

After the facilitator has recorded all the responses, the CMT makes sure that everyone understands each other's items and eliminates duplications. (So far so good.)

Your next step, however, is different from your what's-going-right session. Again, you have lots of paper taped to the wall, but now you can't use all the problems that people have identified. You need to focus on the most critical difficulties facing your organization — prioritize where you spend your limited resources. This is where *multivoting* comes in.

In multivoting, a team quickly and easily reduces a list containing a large number of items to a smaller number — a list on which everyone agrees (maybe some more than others). Here's how you do it:

1. **Tell people to pick the issues that they think leave the organization the most vulnerable.**

   The number that each person gets to select depends upon how large your original list is. There isn't a hard and fast rule. Usually, the range is between four and eight items per person. Obviously, your CMT can have people select fewer or more items.

2. **Give people the agreed-upon number of stick-on dots for them to use for "voting" on their items.**

3. **Let people vote for their top problem areas by sticking one dot on each of their selected items.**

   Yes, we've known individuals who have felt so strongly about an issue that they applied two or three of their votes to that issue. But it should not happen. The facilitator should emphasize "only one vote per issue" and announce that everyone is on the honor system.

4. **Count the votes for every item.**

   Some may not get selected and others may only have one vote. But you will also find some on your list for which almost everyone votes.

5. **Identify your top priority items and then the next tier or two, based upon the number of votes received.**

   Sometimes that division occurs naturally, other times the CMT has to select an arbitrary cut-off number between the two categories.

What does a typical list look like?

Here's the other face of your organization's present world. Again, there aren't any right or wrong answers, nor are there any correct ways to write out the topics you put on your list. It's what the CMT agrees on that counts. Earlier in the chapter, we show you the what's-going-right lists for two companies; here you can see the issues-and-concerns lists.

A 50-person European start-up company

As you would expect, a new company faces some very unique problems, but many of their difficulties are typical for any organization. Here is the partial list of the issues that CMT members created with mindmapping followed by multivoting:

- Client not bound to initial specs — keeps changing mind on requirements
- Conflict and finger-pointing between groups when something doesn't work
- Don't know what's expected of me and don't know how I'm doing — nothing is ever said to me
- Government regulations — particularly tax processes and rules regarding employee hiring and lay-offs
- Lack of communication with employees before commitments are made to customers (coordination of project workload versus resources versus committed delivery date)
- Lack of resources
- Need better project management
- Need separate client demonstration area — bringing clients into work area disrupts everyone's work
- Need receptionist to answer phones — having to answer all in-coming calls breaks concentration
- No defined workday — people wander in at all hours
- No space for research and experimentation
- Office space too cramped — distracting to have people on top of each other
- Receivable and cash flow problems — need cash to pay wages and bills
- Use of temporary programmers who don't conform to company standards, have no loyalty, some poorly skilled, and no consequences for poor work

A large traditional U.S. company

Responding to a more competitive marketplace, this company had to make multiple, simultaneous changes to remain competitive. The issues-and-concerns list consisted of both technical and people topics. Because of the need for confidentiality, we're only sharing the "human" items on the list.

- Authority for decision making not clear
- Competitors reducing prices of products
- Danger of competitors making technical breakthroughs

- ✔ Dependence on outside vendors to get work done

- ✔ Industry and markets changing rapidly

- ✔ Job security

- ✔ Lack of support from other departments

- ✔ Long-term picture of industry and markets unclear so the company doesn't know what direction to move in

- ✔ Need for new products and services

- ✔ Need better communication on what's happening both on projects and with changes

- ✔ New competitors that move faster (have less bureaucracy)

- ✔ Roles and responsibilities not clear — overlaps between people and departments causing conflict

- ✔ Skill expertise loss; need to update technical skills

Crafting the Need for Change — in Ten-Cent Words

You can use the what's-going-right and issues-and-concerns lists as the foundation for talking with your employees — to explain the reasons you're putting them through all the stress and strain. Preparing for your initial announcement of the change is the time for you to personally customize what you say and how you say it. Make sure that you logically pull together all the information in a way that clearly shows how their organization exists today. You're thanking them for all their hard work, while simultaneously building a case that shows the dangers ahead if they don't change. These dangers may cover a broad range of areas.

Don't get trapped into describing your composite view of the world with the vocabulary and focus of a stock analyst. In order to buy into your picture, employees must see a realistic and reasonable representation. So talk to them in direct, everyday language. Give them enough detail so that they can start seeing the organization as it appears to you and why change is necessary. How you actually present this information to your employees is discussed in Chapter 15.

Chapter 13

What Does Your Brave New World Look Like?

In This Chapter

▶ Deciding the content of your Desired State

▶ Keeping your Desired State realistic

▶ Making the Desired State meaningful to employees

"I don't think he knows what he wants from reengineering. And if he doesn't, how does he expect us to know?"

Supervisor
Private company

You're certainly not foolish enough to follow people who don't know where they're going. Neither are your employees. Put yourself in their shoes. If you want them to join your march into the future, then they need an easily understood and realistically drawn picture of where you want to take them. And they need to feel that your picture is achievable — the very same things that you expect from your manager.

If you consider the three questions "where are we," "where do we want to go," and "how do we get there," this chapter helps you answer the second question. In Chapter 12, you read about describing your present world, and in Chapter 14, you read how to get there — creating your implementation plan. In this chapter, you find how to craft a written description of your Desired State that reinforces employees' buy-in to your change.

The Desired State is similar to a vision of what you want your school district, company, health care center, or partnership to evolve into. Traditionally, a *vision* is a high-level, overarching view of where you're headed, while your Desired State specifically zeros in on your change effort. The Desired State may be very specific such as a new eighth-grade math curriculum or a move into e-retailing; or it could be more abstract such as a culture change or a merger between two hospitals. Regardless of the organizational breadth of your change initiatives, you need a clear, written description, shared with the employees, of how you expect the world to look after the change. This Desired State description helps build a common understanding among all employees of where you are going and what is expected of them.

This chapter provides a menu from which you can select the items you want to include in your Desired State document. Because every organization and the changes within organizations present different opportunities, we can't give you a paint-by-numbers kit. What you do find, however, is a guide to help you in creating a Desired State specific to your needs.

Before you jump into this chapter, you need to know that constructing your Desired State takes time and hard work. It's tough turning gut feelings, insights, and intuition into detailed, true-to-life, word-drawn images. But when you carefully create your Desired State and communicate it well to employees, you reap big dividends.

Two Important Do's

People have written numerous books and business articles about creating visions that capture the hearts and minds of employees (or the voting public). Rather than overwhelming you with all the do's and don'ts for writing your Desired State document, we recommend two principles that you and your CMT (Change Management Team) must safeguard (that's a positive way for saying "never violate"): Keep it realistic and make it personal. (See Chapter 11 for more information on forming your CMT.)

Keeping your Desired State realistic

Creating your Desired State is similar to building a house. You have a long wish list and a certain budget. So you balance your wants with your pocket book and realistically build a home that, while not totally perfect, still meets your physical and emotional requirements. With the Desired State, you're creating a future. As much as you might like to make it "perfect," it must also appear credible and doable to your employees. Anything less, and you've lost their trust and gained their opposition.

You're actually setting long-term goals for your organization. Like any other goal, your Desired State must be specific, attainable, measurable, and focused on the need of your organization.

Don't fall into the trap of describing things that sound good but that you and your people have no control over. You can't control the next technological breakthroughs, or your competitors, or the world economy, or the changing needs of employees.

However, there is plenty that you do control. You can move your organization into a more competitive position and state of readiness so that employees can quickly respond to current and future challenges. You can create a team of people that see the competition as the enemy — not each other as the competition. You can nurture customer loyalty by exceeding their expectations. You can build alliances with your suppliers. You can encourage a work environment where diversity and creativity flourish. Or you can design millions of other achievable goals for your organization's future.

Your employees won't pour their hearts and souls (or even put 10 minutes) into something too idealistic to be reached. Just as important, they won't follow someone who asks for the moon and seems to be setting the team up to fail.

Perhaps your motto for this step in your change process should be, "Be bold, but be real."

Making your Desired State personal

A theme is interwoven throughout a successful change project: If you want to convince, motivate, guide, and lead employees to change, then talk to them in everyday, job-related words.

Employees can't buy into your process management teams, new time reporting system, or customer call center unless they understand what all the fancy ideas mean to them — personally. Here are some ways that you can personalize your Desired State to your audience:

- ✔ **Tell your employees whether the way they work is going to change.** If it won't, tell them. If it will, then prepare employees by telling them when and how (as much as you know). And let them know that, as time goes by, you will continue updating them.

- ✔ **Tell your employees what new skills they need and how they get them.** Give people as much information about what set of new work skills they must have and what training provisions you've made to support them. If they won't have to develop new skills, then tell employees up front so that they can rest easy.

- ✔ **Tell your employees whether they have to act differently.** Modifying work place behaviors — requiring people to think and behave in new ways — usually occurs with major changes such as creating a new culture or a move to improve customer retention. Share what you know, but also acknowledge that only time and experience will show what new behaviors they need.

- ✔ **Tell your employees whether this is a great opportunity for them or a kick in the pants.** If it's a great opportunity, tell employees but don't go overboard and set up unrealistic expectations. If people will be hurt in this effort, let them know what some of the negative consequences might be — even in your overview presentations. (Don't let your people get blind-sided.) Save specific details however, for one-on-ones.

Obviously, you can't answer all of the questions that employees might have and relieve all their concerns in one presentation. But you can make a good start at creating a user-friendly change by tailoring your presentation to the audience in front of you.

If you don't take the time to translate your Desired State into employees' day-to-day language, you lose their willingness to support you.

Put on your marketing hat. You want employees to buy into your change; therefore, they must see how it meets their needs. You do this by using examples from their jobs and discussing problems that they struggle with daily. You can't expect people to sign on without understanding what you're doing and how that improves or protects their work world.

Creating Your Desired State — What's in It?

How do you decide what subjects to include in your Desired State?

We offer a menu from which you can select topics for your Desired State. You and your CMT want to focus on only those areas that are the most relevant to the needs of your organization and directly relate to your current change effort. Forget about all the rest for now. You will need to create additional segments of your Desired State when you plan your next change(s) sometime in the not too distant future — and you will because the world, your competitors, and your employees keep shifting on you. Expect more changes ahead.

Don't spend the next six months developing the perfect picture — kitchen sink and all. The world might have changed by the time you come up with the perfect design, making it irrelevant.

The three categories in your Desired State

The content of your Desired State contains three main categories. Each provides employees with a specific reason to say, "Yes, this is the way we should go;" or "I can buy into this. It makes sense to me."

✔ **The first category includes broad general items that link your change with the overall direction of the larger organization.** You don't want people to think that you're going down some obscure path or leading them into conflict with basic corporate goals and strategies. Even if you're reorganizing your department or introducing a new appraisal process, people need to know that supporting you simultaneously supports the company. In this category, you include items like company mission, vision, and values.

✔ **The second category includes those segments of the Desired State that relate to products, services, finances, and markets.** You need to show employees how a focus on legal entities, a merger of two departments, or centralization is consistent with and supports the business direction. In this category you can include such things as long-term revenue growth targets, process improvement, customer loyalty, financial accuracy, and government compliance.

✔ **The third category focuses on people.** What do employees need to do to improve productivity, work more creatively, and reduce conflict within and between groups? What motivates them, reduces turnover, and helps them do their jobs more effectively? Typically, when managers plan a change, they usually emphasize the technical requirements and overlook the human requirements. People need to feel valued and included before they're willing to sign on.

When you create your Desired State consider items from each category. How many items you include is up to you, but make sure that you cover enough areas to address people's issues and fears. The more information you give them, the less likely they'll complain that they don't understand and the fewer reasons they have for resisting you.

The menu

If chefs included in their menus all the meals that they know how to prepare, diners would spend hours reading lists of options. Therefore, chefs select dishes according to such things as the season, popularity, cost, ease of preparation, personal interest, and the type of restaurant in which they work.

Similarly, the lists of possible topics that you can include in your Desired State could run for pages, but employees probably wouldn't read them. So, we're giving you a short list to help you get started. If you discover that we don't mention an area important to you, by all means add it. This list represents a sample of what's available. Also, you'll find some items that don't apply to you, your organization, or your change — ignore them. What's important is that you create a Desired State for your change that is meaningful to employees — that gets them to buy into it.

Items to consider for your Desired State:

- ✔ Company vision and mission
- ✔ Your organization's/department's vision and mission
- ✔ Company values and ethics
- ✔ Your organization's/department's values
- ✔ Products and services that you want to emphasize or create
- ✔ New markets you want to enter and old ones that you want to expand
- ✔ Competitive position in the market
- ✔ Policy toward quality
- ✔ Kind of culture needed to support your change
- ✔ Ways you want people to work together and treat each other
- ✔ Ways you want people to treat customers and suppliers (both internal and external)
- ✔ Technical skills that employees need
- ✔ People skills that employees need
- ✔ Policy toward professional and personal development

Once you and the CMT have decided which areas you want to include in your Desired State, your next job is determining how to present it to employees. On the one hand, a corporate mission doesn't require much effort — just reproduce it. But on the other hand, if you want to improve teamwork, then you need to specifically describe the ways you want employees to interact. The next section provides examples of how other managers tackled this task.

Linking Your Desired State to Issues and Concerns

If you're implementing a change, you're probably doing so because something needs fixing or opportunities have come a-knocking.

If you are facing legitimate problems, however, then your goal is to create a clear and strong linkage between those problems and your Desired State.

In Chapter 12, you create your issues-and-concerns list, and you should use that list to explain, support, and justify your new direction.

Large problems, such as turf battles and back stabbing between employees, are critical enough to be addressed as part of your Desired State description (see Example 1 in the following section). Other smaller issues, such as cramped office space for programmers, can be handled off-line — not as part of your brave-new-world description. There's no one-shoe-fits-all rule. You're the manager, you know your organization and your people, you select what issues and concerns need addressing in your Desired State.

To help you, we provide three real-life examples from three different organizations that created a Desired State for their change efforts.

Example 1: Improving teamwork

The following example comes from a company that experienced a merger — two departments were shoved into one. On their issues and-concerns list, one of the problems identified by the CMT included conflict, mistrust, and lack of cooperation between employees, as well as constant finger pointing when problems occurred (which they did, frequently). As part of their Desired State, one of the items that the leadership team/CMT selected from the menu was how people work together and treat each other. Using the mindmapping technique (which we describe in Chapter 12), the CMT added the following information to their Desired State:

We need a work place environment that maximizes the talents and creativity of each of us; a work place that fosters team synergy and a winning team.

People who demonstrate our desired behaviors

- Are team players
- Show respect for others
- Are trusting and trustworthy
- Use common sense
- Strive to personally improve
- Possess a sense of humor
- Maintain a positive attitude
- Respect personal privacy
- Take ownership of results and challenges
- Practice open communication
- Are civil and courteous

> ✔ Meet commitments to fellow team members
>
> ✔ Are supportive of others

This list is a bit longer than the average, but the CMT wanted to explicitly state the behaviors required in its new organization and respond to specific behavior problems. You can customize your list, just as this CMT did.

Example 2: Improving relationships with customers

The example shown here comes from a company that desperately needed to improve its image with customers. One of their selections from the menu focused on the customer:

Quality products priced competitively are obvious requirements for acquiring new business. Beyond that, however, the initial customer decision to use our product and our ability to retain that customer depend heavily on the relationships we build with each customer.

All employees will

> ✔ Be knowledgeable of customer's business
>
> ✔ Listen to the customer
>
> ✔ Understand and focus on the customer's needs
>
> ✔ Ensure that customers know they are heard
>
> ✔ Help customers to be successful
>
> ✔ Meet our commitments to the customer
>
> ✔ Be frugal with customer's resources
>
> ✔ Protect customer's confidentiality
>
> ✔ Own any customer problem until handed off to an appropriate team member
>
> ✔ Be proactive
>
> ✔ Treat the customer with courtesy and respect
>
> ✔ Be honest and trustworthy

The CMT followed this segment of their Desired State with action items in their implementation plan.

Example 3: Creating a workforce for the 21st century

To remain competitive in today's market, companies realize that they need employee skill sets that go beyond just technical competency. The all-employee CMT of this company included continuing education and employee development as a segment in their Desired State. They used mindmapping to create their list:

Our success in the future requires that we have a "continuous learning" culture where employees constantly upgrade their technical, business, and personal skills. We need employees who are

- Technically proficient

- Communicators (oral and written)

- Listeners

- Mentors

- Students

- Researchers

- Achievers

- Decision makers

- Clear and logical thinkers

- Organizers and planners

- Problem solvers

- Business savvy (understanding financial statements)

- Socially polished

To support their Desired State, the company created an employee development policy, a guide for company-approved continuing education, and a flexible work schedule to accommodate employees' time off for educational programs.

Customizing Your Future

No two Desired States read alike, cover the same territory, or use the same volume of paper. Issues and concerns differ greatly from organization to organization. But so too does the make up and personality of each CMT. Therefore, when you and your CMT sit down to create a Desired State for moving into opening an overseas market, creating an electronic employee feedback system, or developing a new patient care program you always begin with a blank piece of paper.

There are as many different versions of the "perfect" future as individuals sitting in your conference room. That means that you need to create an environment where people respect diversity, trust each other enough to share unpopular ideas, quickly resolve conflict, and easily synthesize diverse opinions. That in itself is a Desired State.

Chapter 14

Creating Your Implementation Plan — Even When You Don't Want To

> "If she knows how we're going to create this new customer care center, she hasn't told us. It might all be in her head, but what good does that do anyone else? We need to know what she's planning and what we're supposed to do. I don't think that's asking for too much. Do you?"
>
> Middle manager
> Fortune 500 company

*W*hen it comes to getting managers to create an implementation plan, most of them would rather sit in a dentist's chair. What makes crafting plans such a negative experience? We'll let them tell you in their own words:

- ✔ "I get antsy wasting days here when I should be out there working. I'm not paid for planning; I'm paid for doing."

- ✔ "We live in a society that keeps telling us to get it now — don't wait, don't save, don't plan, but go for the gold . . . today . . . right this instant."

- ✔ "I don't have the patience it takes to put a plan together. My staff can do it. That's why I've got them."

- ✔ "This is a very competitive environment. If you can't show results, you're out of here. There's no second chance."

> ✔ "Nobody reads them [plans] anyway, so why should I waste time doing them?"
>
> ✔ "I'm already spending my nights and weekends working at home. If I have to sit in that planning meeting, I'll never get caught up."
>
> ✔ "I love seeing results. Not dreaming about them."

Every one of those managers had a valid reason for not wanting to develop an implementation plan. But each one also came to realize that they and their changes would fail without a well-constructed plan. (In fact, a couple were on the brink of failure.)

We don't expect you to become a planning junky after reading this chapter. But hopefully you'll consider the ROI (return-on-investment) worth the time and effort you spend planning — and give it a try. To ease you into creating your implementation plan, we offer a model and present examples from actual plans.

Going through this chapter, you can see that we divide the implementation plan into two components: the technical and the human. Unfortunately, most managers create plans focused primarily on the mechanics of getting their change implemented and overlook the people who actually get the job done. When we analyze successful and failed change efforts, we consistently find that the winners *always* focus heavily on the human side, while losers skimp on or actually ignore it.

Understanding the Power of Your Implementation Plan

Have we got a deal for you! Just for the price of one document, you receive seven (count them), seven, valuable tools. Of course, your seven-in-one-plan-o-matic won't chop, slice, dice, or peel, but who cares when you now own your own customized, change-specific implementation plan? You can now show skeptical employees that you're determined to succeed. And that they'd better be just as determined, too.

Seriously, without an implementation plan, your chance for success is slim (in fact, very slim). So don't head off into the wild blue yonder "guideless." You'll just end up being viewed as another flavor-of-the-month manager who can't seem to "get it right."

And now, here's what you get with your one document:

✔ **A roadmap.** It tells you specifically where you want to go, how to get there, and when you've arrived. It keeps you from driving around in circles and eliminates that humiliating need to stop and ask for directions. But like any other map, it's only useful if you look at it.

✔ **A communication tool.** You've got something tangible to share with employees. Talking people through your plan shows them what you want, what they need to do, and what they can expect from you. It's also a great way to stimulate discussions and discover what's lurking in employees' minds.

✔ **A marketing tool.** Over and over again, you must sell your customer care program, new accounting system, or redesigned product line. (Those days of managers being mighty kings and employees being compliant subjects are gone.) Your plan helps make concrete what often sounds loosey-goosey and insubstantial. And the more that employees understand and can "touch" your change, the easier it is for them to buy in.

✔ **A consolidator of multiple changes.** Employees need to know that everything you're asking them to do is part of an overall design that moves them in a consistent direction. Having one implementation plan that encompasses changes as they occur tells people that you have everything under control and that it all fits together.

✔ **A quality assurance tool.** Not even the most carefully crafted plan provides mistake-free implementation. But if you don't have a plan, your change efforts remain far more vulnerable to misjudgments, misunderstandings, misalignments, miscalculations, and miscellaneous errors. Even though your reorganization won't ever be defect free, a well-constructed plan provides substantial quality control.

✔ **A credibility enhancement.** With an implementation plan in hand, employees see that you're in charge and in control. While their support may build slowly over time, the foundation for success is laid — they know that you're committed, or you wouldn't have invested all that time and money. Of course, as the change unfolds, they'll keep you under a microscope to see whether you actually do carry out the action items and meet your proposed commitments — so you're not home free.

✔ **A resistance reducer.** You can never eliminate resistance, but you can significantly decrease its power by planning well. Of course, no plan magically turns naysayers into fervent supporters, but it does reduce the number of employees opposing you for legitimate reasons. In their minds the equation reads: poor planning = no plan = failure. Instead, you want people to think: good planning = solid plan = success.

With all the wonderful benefits you get from an implementation plan, shouldn't you give it a try? Well, more than just a try. All these advantages only result when managers systematically and thoroughly construct their plans. Like most things worth having, plans don't come free.

Designing Your Plan's Design

If you've read the previous four chapters, you know that a one-change-planning shoe doesn't fit all organizations, or even two. You probably don't want to look like one of Cinderella's nasty stepsisters foolishly trying to force an over-sized foot into an undersized glass slipper. Therefore, customize your plan. But never fear, we won't leave you reinventing the wheel (or shoe). The rest of this chapter provides a template and examples to speed up your creation process.

The domino effect

Your implementation plan is created by you and your CMT (change management team — see Chapter 11). Your plan is really a set of related, interdependent action items that need to be accomplished to implement your change. The plan contains those technical action items that we logically know must be done, such as budgets, time tables, and training. (See the following section entitled "Focusing on the Technical Side.") The plan also contains those human side action items that change winners know must be done to support the change, such as communication, culture, and appraisal forms. (See the section entitled "Focusing on the Human Side.")

The action items in your plan are two- or three-sentence descriptions of the work to be done. You and the CMT then charter a team for each action item to do the necessary detailed planning, accomplish the assigned work, and come back to the CMT with appropriate recommendations. If you have ten action items, you will typically have ten teams involved in completing the items. So, there are two layers of planning to be done for a successful change: the first by you and your CMT, and the second layer by those chartered teams providing the detail required for your overall plan. Remember that the success of your change really depends on the detail planning and commitment of these chartered teams.

Okay, this sounds bureaucratic and level upon level of make-do work. But it isn't. Any major change produces a ripple (or tidal wave) effect throughout your entire organization, requiring parallel changes in a variety of areas. And you must plan each of those modifications just as carefully as you did the primary one that started the whole process.

You're beginning to see why two-thirds of change efforts fail. Most managers stay focused on only their high-level changes, ignoring all the day-to-day details that also call for alterations. An updated culture, another acquisition, or a newly designed customer feedback process requires more than great kick-off meetings, training sessions, and glossy posters. They require a systematic approach throughout the entire company, making sure that communications, compensation, job responsibilities, and appraisals all fit together like a finely crafted cabinet. That means no rough edges, mismatched corners, or poorly hung doors. (Somehow, using a "well-crafted shoe" just didn't do it here.)

The details

Every action item in your plan, whether it is conducting an employee survey or chartering a team to design a new recognition package, follows a similar format. Each action item should

- ✔ Support your Desired State (see Chapter 13)
- ✔ Focus on one specific area
- ✔ Improve operations or eliminate obstacles
- ✔ Be clearly written
- ✔ Be measurable
- ✔ Have a person accountable for its completion
- ✔ Have predetermined start and completion dates

The CMT writes every action item in your implementation plan. The members also select who is accountable for the actions, charter subteams when appropriate, and determine when each item is successfully completed.

Just in case you're wondering what action items look like, here are two examples. Assume that you're merging two departments as a result of an acquisition. Of the many issues you're faced with, one of the most frustrating is ever erupting turf wars between the two newly merged groups. You need employees working together, not at each other's throats — fighting over who does what. Here are two actual action items that one CMT created for this very problem (but they called themselves the Steering Committee or SC):

- ✔ "The SC will define the top ten core processes for the department and develop draft block diagrams for each one by 1/1/97. *[The two companies were doing the same work differently, so the first step in getting people to work together required creating a common understanding of the workflow.]*
    - Implementation Accountability: The SC
    - Measurement Accountability: [Vice president, Quality]"

- ✔ "We will charter a team for each of the ten core processes by 2/1/97. Each team will reach common understanding of their documented process and identify the roles and responsibilities for each function by 7/1/97. Readouts to the SC will be completed by 8/1/97. *[Each person needed to clearly understand how his or her job fit into the greater whole thereby eliminating overlaps.]*

> • Implementation Accountability: Process team leaders
>
> • Measurement Accountability: [Vice president, Quality]"

Yes, it is possible to get lost in the nits and gnats of detail. You can create the perfect plan with level upon level of detail while talented people flee, competitors steal your customers, and costs escalate out of control. You need to find a balance between rushing in planless, where angels fear to tread, and getting lost in a jungle of dense detail. We wish we had a simple answer for you, but there isn't one. Only through experience and common sense does each CMT find its own level of comfortable, common-sense detail.

Focusing on the Technical Side

The technical side of your plan is the same organizing and planning stuff that you always do. It includes a step-by-step definition of the work that must be carried out, as well as timelines with start and completion dates for each step. We don't spend a lot of time in this section because the mechanical steps are mostly common sense and usually included by most managers.

Action items that define the technical steps include the following:

✔ Estimating cost — labor and financial

✔ Developing the implementation schedule

✔ Getting approval from the powers that be (if necessary)

✔ Contracting with outside suppliers (if necessary)

✔ Preparing information that employees need and can refer to (this information could be contained in organizational charts, procedure manuals, HR policies, or time reporting codes).

✔ Selecting and training subject-matter experts

✔ Testing change in small group trials

✔ Preparing employee orientation material

✔ Designing measurements to track effectiveness of change

✔ Tracking implementation of change

Mistakes or omissions made here often result from missing information. If in doubt, you can test this technical piece of your plan with a small group of knowledgeable employees. Usually, they surface missing data — critical information and valuable tools needed to get the job done.

We told you this was going to be a short section.

Reasons mergers fail — the human factors

A business article in the October 30, 2000, edition of *The Wall Street Journal* analyzed the reasons that "some of the highest profile deals of the 1990s have become major disappointments for acquirers and their shareholders." For the reporters, the two most obvious reasons, but the least interesting, were the difficulties integrating operations and overpaying. Less obvious, but probably more significant to the reporters, was inadequate planning — particularly in the areas of assimilating cultures, retaining talent, and other "soft" human areas. It seemed that for the less lucrative mergers, executives and their investment bankers focused on the financial issues almost to the exclusion of the human concerns. Successful mergers, however, resulted when planning also encompassed the more elusive human factors.

Focusing on the Human Side

The bottom line in getting your changes successfully implemented is reducing employees' reasons for resistance, eliminating excuses, and responding to uncertainties and fears. If you can do this, and some managers do, then step right into the winner's circle.

A new appraisal system or new outpatient center doesn't metamorphose from its old counterparts on its own. The transformation occurs because of employees' commitment, creativity, hard work, and motivation. Anything less from people, and you get a less successful product — or no product. That's why we focus so much attention on the human side of your plan.

Targeting the five reasons people resist

If you haven't read Chapter 5, then all this information about resistance hits you cold — if you need only a quick overview, then stay put. But if you're facing employees who sabotage your changes or openly rebel against new directions, then maybe you should take a detour to Chapter 5 and then come back here. You'll find the time well spent. Should you have already read Chapter 5, then this is a mini-review for you with an emphasis on implementation plans.

How does the CMT know what human action items to include in their plans? Their first guide is to focus on the following five causes of resistance. As you and the CMT create your action items, ask: Will these help people feel more in control? Are we keeping the number of change efforts within reason so that people aren't drowning? Will this action help the naysayers see something positive in the initiative? How are we proving that this time we'll succeed? And finally, is this plan protecting peoples' self-worth?

✔ **Feeling out of control.** Uncertainty intensifies peoples' stress levels and significantly reduces their productivity. If you want to increase productivity, then give employees greater feelings of control over a change. First, share the plan with them so that people actually see what's going to happen and who's doing what and when. Then make sure that you include items that reduce ambiguity and conflict. That may mean actions that clarify roles and responsibility, document confusing processes, or clearly define long-term goals and immediate objectives. The greater control employees feel, the less they oppose you.

✔ **Drowning in change.** People only have so much physical, intellectual, and emotional energy to give. The more changes you pile up on them, the more you drain their energy reserves — until they're empty. Obviously, you can reduce the number of changes you throw at employees. But you can also carefully plan each change and design each item in a way that keeps disorder and disharmony down to a bare minimum. Another option includes creating specific actions that focus on stress reduction, new skills development, or upward feedback opportunities. The less overwhelmed employees feel, the less resistance you face.

✔ **Thinking it's a terrible idea.** Even if you do everything right in the planning process, some employees may still consider your change a dumb thing to do. Before you go chopping off heads, find out why they feel so negatively. They may have valid information that you and the CMT are lacking. Or people might lack important data that is already addressed in your implementation plan. All you have to do is walk them through your action items. Then again, nothing may work, and this is when you need the resiliency characteristics that we discuss in Chapter 21.

✔ **Seeing too many past failures.** The more past changes that employees have watched bite the dust, the greater their reasons to distrust you and your present change. The only way that you can persuade them how trustworthy you are is by implementing this one successfully. First, begin by honestly analyzing what went wrong in the past and create action items that focus on those areas. Then, using your implementation plan, show employees how you're avoiding past mistakes, and in turn, past failures. You can also include a section in your initial kick-off meeting (see Chapter 15) that addresses the ways you aren't repeating the past.

✔ **Protecting their self-worth.** Most people vigorously fight against anything that denigrates their dignity and their positive image of themselves. It can be something as simple as having their job title changed or as complex as being appraised by their "subordinates." During the creation of your plan, the CMT should brainstorm ways they can safeguard employees' self-esteem. In addition, how you actually introduce your change is important — making sure that you start off describing what employees have done well before jumping into all the things that aren't going right (that's discussed in Chapter 12). Also, sharing your implementation plan shows people that you consider them important. How you share it also directly impacts employees' self-worth. Do you listen to their issues, respect their concerns, and answer truthfully? In a business world that historically overlooked peoples' self-worth, this new focus is in itself a major change.

Targeting excuses

If people are going to resist your change, they need to look in the mirror and justify their actions with a valid, rational or excuse. Chapter 4 discusses the eight most common excuses that employees employ. Rather than diving into each of the excuses, we focus on only three to give you a taste of how implementation plans reduce your vulnerability in this area. Should you be interested in exploring the world of employee excuses, then now's a good time to flip back to Chapter 4.

Your planning approach for dealing with excuses is very similar to the technique for minimizing the reasons that cause resistance. First, the CMT examines the excuses most likely to arise and then counters them with specific, customized action items. You can jump-start this process using our list of eight excuses in Chapter 4, but make sure that you also consider ones unique to your organization and change.

And now, on with excuses.

- ✔ **"I don't understand why we need to change."** What may seem obvious to you after days and months studying a problem inside and out, upside and down, side to side, and front to back, most likely doesn't appear obvious to someone focusing on looming project deadlines, teaching a class of 35 energetic children, calming unhappy customers, or helping distraught patients recover from major surgery. You must include action items in your plan that focus on marketing your change to employees. The most logical place to include these items is when you plan for your initial communication meeting. (You can read about that in Chapter 15.) Specifically, you want to make sure that before you go into describing in all the gory details of what employees must do, you build a very clear and concise case for changing — one that makes sense to them.

- ✔ **"Our policies and procedures don't support the change."** Rarely do the present HR and other policies work across the board when you're creating a new culture, moving to process teams, or designing a customer call center. Old appraisal systems, overtime guidelines, and compensation packages usually reward old behaviors, not the new ones that you're trying to encourage. An action item in your plan may be the identification of where policy disconnects exist or will occur. Following that, you may want to write action items that focus on creating policies or procedures consistent with your new change effort.

✔ **"Nobody knows who's supposed to do what."** Just because people have gotten new job titles doesn't mean that they'll automatically know what their roles and responsibilities are and what boundaries define their jobs. In our previous example of how to write action items, we focused on identifying and defining processes. The reason we're repeating it here is that most managers overlook this area, thereby setting themselves up for massive migraines and creating constant conflict for their employees. Because many changes involve people doing work differently, you usually remain vulnerable in this area — so don't get blindsided.

Choosing from a menu

You're in luck. A single action item often simultaneously addresses both the reasons employees resist and their excuses. Two for the price of one isn't doing too badly. Plus, it does reduce the number of items you need in your plan.

To help you decide what you should include in you implementation plan, we're giving you a menu of the "human side" action items. You probably won't choose all of them, and you probably have some of your own to add. But this list should get you started.

Make sure that you match the number and timing of the action items to your available resources. If resources are limited, spread the timing out so that you don't overload anyone. Don't try to move the whole mountain in a single week or month.

Your change effort determines the type and number of items that you include. Something as straightforward as a new expense voucher may require only two actions from the following list. But if you're moving from an autocratic, top-down culture to a free-agent, people-focused one, then you may need all the action items listed, and even more.

✔ **Clarifying processes.** Having seen this item in two previous examples, you've probably figured out that you use this when turf battles rage, quality begins slipping, and finger-pointing abounds — which happens frequently during major changes. You need action items that:

- Document work flow

- Identify responsibility for each work function

- Create a common understanding

✔ **Strengthening leadership development.** Management and leadership skills, like any other expertise, require constant upgrading — especially during times of upheaval. You also need managers walking the talk of continuous learning if you expect employees to follow. To ensure that managers have the leadership skills and behaviors you require, create action items that:

- Define outstanding leadership skills

- Evaluate your managers' present capabilities

- Update your present workshops

- Identify new training seminars to fill the gaps

✔ **Developing new employee behavior.** Use this item when productivity is being damaged by accelerating conflicts, increasing employee stress, and high turnover, or if you have escalating customer complaints. Obviously, people need to work differently. Here you create action items that:

- Examine your employees' attitudes and perceptions (see Chapter 6)

- Review your issues and concerns list (see Chapter 12)

- Identify where problems exist

- Define the desired behaviors you want (see Chapter 13)

- Design a plan to change employee behaviors from today's unsatisfactory ways to the descriptions in your Desired State.

✔ **Supporting employee development.** Obviously, if you're implementing TQM or a new computer system, you'll need employees trained in specific technical skills. But don't forget that you need a workforce that's current, not only in technical areas, but also in customer care, conflict management, and stress reduction — the human side of their jobs. To keep a "state of the art" workforce, you need action items that:

- Define the skills your organization requires for the 21st century

- Assess employees' current capabilities

- Evaluate your present training program

- Find additional training workshops that meet your requirements.

✔ **Creating a consistent culture.** Culture usually nourishes or undermines your changes — rarely is it neutral. If you feel that your present culture conflicts with, or can be perceived to conflict with, the change, don't wait; decide which aspects of your culture are in conflict and modify them. You do this by creating specific action items that target the inconsistencies. For example, in the past, managers may have primarily cared about expense budgets and quantity of product output. If your change involves customer satisfaction and retention, then you need to find ways to demonstrate that the customer is now of equal priority. (Should you want more information about the power of culture, look in Chapter 4.)

✔ **Updating policies and procedures.** Yup, you read this one as an antidote to employee excuses. Existing practices that are out of step with your change create logical justifications for resisting. Therefore, you may need several action items to modify the conflicting practices. Building on the preceding example from culture, if you want delighted customers you may need to modify your annual goals and objectives, create a different set of performance measurements, update the appraisal form, and modify the content of monthly reports.

✔ **Designing the initial communication package.** This is your kick-off meeting where you announce to the world how you're turning it upside down and why. No matter how simple your change, you should make this a mandatory item in your plan. From a small staff meeting to a worldwide dog and pony show, you need to carefully plan what you say and how you say it. Chapter 15 gives you details about planning for and creating your here's-another-change presentation.

✔ **Maintaining ongoing communication.** Don't stop with your great kick-off meeting — which is what many managers unfortunately do. People need you to keep them in the information loop — plus it significantly reduces resistance. Your plan for ongoing communication, (see Chapter 18) can contain

- Visiting work sites for meeting with people

- Holding video conference calls

- Having monthly meetings with direct reports

- Sharing score card status with all employees

- Establishing intranet chat rooms

- Conducting annual employee surveys

✔ **Providing for a scorecard.** How do you know when you've met your objectives or what has slipped? You need a tracking device. Therefore, in your plan assign responsibility for someone to create and maintain a scorecard that follows the progress of each action item. For scorecard reviews, once a month usually works best. If you want to see a sample scorecard from a real, live organization, see the sidebar "A sample scorecard."

✔ **Reviewing and revising your plan.** Your implementation plan is a living document that should change as your world changes. It's not written in stone. Therefore, at least once a year, examine all the action items, eliminating those that are completed, and inserting new items that address arising issues and concerns. At the end of your action plan, include one simple item (aren't you relieved?) stating that the CMT will review and revise their plan on such and such a date. Nothing could be simpler, but it's usually overlooked by many managers.

A sample scorecard

In order to become more competitive, a small multiinternational software company embarked on a radical culture change. They wanted to enhance teamwork, customer loyalty, and process management. The following are five action items from their scorecard of 23 commitments. Because a scorecard is a tracking tool, an action item need not be written in its entirety, but rather referred to in "shorthand." To respect confidentiality, we changed people's names.

Item #	Action Item	Accountable	Target Date	Actual Date
6	Recognition Plan [They had no formal way of recognizing people's successes.]	LeeAnne		
	• Team Formed		2 Sept.	29 Aug.
	• Recommendation Due		7 Oct.	7 Oct
7	Goal Setting/Appraisal [No link existed between goals and how people were appraised.]			
	• Team Formed		1 July	24 June
	• Recommendation Due		1 Aug.	11 Aug.
8	Communications Plan	George		
	• Team Formed		4 Sept.	3 Sept.
	• Recommendations Due		7 Oct.	7 Oct.
13	Baseline Survey. [The first in their annual employee survey.]	Claudia		
	• Initiated		4 Sept.	4 Sept.
	• Completed		15 Oct.	24 Oct.
	• Team Feedback		6 Nov.	1 Dec.
22	Disaster Protection & Recovery [They had no formal process for protecting their products.]	Marilyn		
	• Team Formed		18 June	18 June
	• Phase 1: Recommendation Due [These were the Initial manual procedures.]		1 July	1 July
	• Phase 2: To Begin [Study what to do on a permanent basis.]		7 Oct.	7 Oct.
	• Phase 2: Recommendation Due		2 Dec.	12 Jan.

Chapter 15

Now, What Do You Tell Your Employees?

> *"I'd settle for a simple 'this is what we're doing and why,' rather than the light and sound show. If they want to spend money like that, they can put it in my paycheck. I'll put it to better use."*
>
> Middle manager
> Telecommunications company

*F*irst impressions set the stage for everything that follows — and are often the most lasting ones. For a national leader, like a president, prime minister, or chancellor, the inaugural address and the first 100 days are critically important in setting the tone for the administration. For you, the kickoff meeting becomes an important occasion when you set a new direction for your employees. Now is your time to inspire employees and begin building their commitment to the change, as well as demonstrating your own firm commitment. This also becomes the time that you reaffirm your credentials as the leader, at the same time making it clear that success depends as much on them as it does on you.

There's an old rule in organizing a presentation: "Tell them what you're going to tell them. Tell them. Then tell them what you told them." Throughout the entire time that your meeting lasts, you and your managers, if you're not going it alone, need to repeat what the change is and the reason for making it. Of course, you wouldn't use the same words, but rather, package it differently and from different perspectives. Hopefully, you reach most employees so that, by the end of your presentation, very few walk out of the room unsure or misinformed.

In this chapter, you see what goes into your kickoff meeting and how to present all the information. Larger meetings require a more formal presentation, while informal talk (but still well planned and documented) works better with a smaller group. While we provide you with the basic foundation for your kickoff, your ultimate success depends on customizing the presentation to your change effort, your audience, your organization's culture, and your own personal style.

Preparing for Your Inaugural Address

Make sure that, when you walk into the auditorium or conference room, you come carefully prepared with a clear agenda. On the one hand, for the leaders of large organizations, the planning process begins with your direct reports. Together you and your team decide what employees need to know and who should handle what. While you want to personally establish your role as directing the change, your employees must know that all your managers stand firmly with you.

If, on the other hand, you're the first line supervisor, then you're responsible for clearly and accurately communicating all the information you received from your manager. Hopefully, he or she, and their managers, followed the suggestions in this book so that you have all the information you need when you meet with your team. If not, all's not lost. This chapter tells you how to customize your own smaller kickoff.

Your journey begins with creating your meeting map — the agenda. Because this pivotal document guides both you and your listeners, you must make sure that:

- The agenda covers not only what you think is important, but also what employees consider to be critical. While you're the boss, you also need them to buy into your new e-mail system or expense reporting process. Therefore, your presentation should focus on both telling and selling.

- The agenda should be distributed (electronically or manually) to all attendees before they walk into the room. Employees not only need to know what you're covering, but also need to have an opportunity to prepare questions they want answered. The advance agenda and chance to prepare helps people feel more like active participators than passive observers.

What should you include in your agenda? The following sections list the "major eight" items that every kickoff meeting should include, but, of course, you're not limited to them. In the following sidebar, you also see how one manager adapted the eight areas to accommodate his needs.

Kickoff meeting agenda

The director of a 52-person accounts payable department created the following agenda to discuss his department's reorganization. In his pre-meeting work, he collected his data by talking with employees individually. And then he met with his direct reports to finalize their new organizational structure. Here's his agenda.

1. Welcome
2. Purpose of this meeting
3. How I collected my information
4. First impressions

- What's going well?
- What are the issues?

5. Where do we want to go and why we must go there
6. Bumps in the road
7. How are we going to get there?

- Action items
- Accountability
- Needed time frames

8. Your questions

Why are we gathered here today?

By the time you walk into the room for your kickoff, most of the people waiting for you have already developed their own version of what the change is all about — and rarely does the rumor mill create positive images. You're most likely facing an audience with some anxiety and lots of misconceptions. That means, right after welcoming everyone, thanking them for their time, and reviewing the agenda, you clearly, and logically describe what you're changing and why — with a couple of concise sentences. In the rest of the meeting, you provide the details.

Research shows that adults absorb information best when they receive *advance organizers* — high-level, generalized summaries that come before the presentation of details. Advance organizers provide listeners with a framework for organizing new information, integrating new data with the old, and remembering what they've heard.

Make this opening piece personal and informal. Talk without charts, and preferably without referring to notes, as if you were sitting in a living room. Tell employees what caused you to consider the need to make a change. It may have been serious problems that they also see. It may be future dangers that you see on the horizon. Or perhaps it's great opportunities opening up if your organization can move quickly. At this point, only give highlights and assure people that they will hear more detail later on in the meeting. Sharing personal thoughts in an informal way helps you build a "human to human" bridge with your listeners.

A meeting of this enormous significance — it sets the whole stage for your change — should start off as strongly as possible. You need to grab their attention — not illicit a "ho hum" reaction. Therefore, especially with larger audiences, don't hesitate to use powerful, inspirational language. Employees are bound to be skeptical — after all, many of them have heard all this before — so you need to clearly show them your personal commitment.

Don't give your introduction short shrift. Devote plenty of time and thought to its creation. You want it to be memorable, credible, and sincere.

What have you and your team done?

In addition to informing people about change, a kickoff meeting can help reduce employees' uncertainty and suspicions and reinforce that you think their opinions are important.

Start off by introducing your leadership team (if you're in front of a large audience) and explain how, as a team, you've all worked together in designing the new staff development program. For a smaller department meeting, you should also emphasize how you and your direct reports worked together on the new organizational design. It's important that people understand that you didn't come up with some idea all by yourself.

You want people to know that you made your decisions with their input. Whether your information comes from focus groups, individual interviews, or employee surveys (see Chapter 6 for a discussion of these information-gathering tools), you consider their concerns and opinions important. This meeting is the place to point out their participation in the events leading up to this meeting. They have been instrumental not only in identifying problems but also in suggesting how to solve them.

If you're holding this meeting before obtaining any employee input, then make sure that you have an action item early in your implementation plan that provides opportunity for employee participation. This isn't "nice to do" stuff, but rather a vital component of your change effort. As Chapters 4 through 8 demonstrate, the more employee input you have, the less resistance you get undermining both you and your change.

What's going right?

As the old saying says: "Accentuate the positive." Begin your change effort on an upbeat note. You have employees who are doing many tasks right, or you wouldn't be in front of them — you'd be out on the street if they were poor performers.

By emphasizing the pluses instead of the minuses, you enable people to take pride in their work, which, in turn, instills confidence and gives your employees a strong sense of optimism for future success. By starting off with listing the problems, you whittle away at people's self-worth and reinforce negative feelings toward your new direction and you personally. Your goal is to have employees leave the meeting with a "can do" attitude, a feeling that they can overcome any obstacles and reach any goals.

Be sure your what's-going-right list is genuine and credible. Employees recognize smoke and mirrors very quickly. If you want specific information on how to create your what's-going-right list, just flip to Chapter 12.

What are the present issues and concerns?

Face it. You wouldn't be going through all the headaches and frustration of an organizational change if everything were chugging along hunky-dory. Perhaps new ideas aren't reaching the marketplace in time to outpace the competition, or customer requirements are still being overlooked, or employees seem less motivated and productive. Whatever it is, you've got problems that need fixing.

At the same time you collected the "what's going right" data, you most likely also got an earful of what's not going right. Or you've been inundated with customer complaints. However you've gotten your information, make sure that you share the hows and whats with your audience.

Remember that your issues-and-concerns list is establishing the foundation for the need to change. Chapter 12 offers you techniques for developing the "issues and concerns" piece of your presentation.

Why must people change?

In the preceding section, you set the groundwork for telling people specifically why they must work differently. You create a common background and understanding about the general problems, now you move on to the specific reasons that you and your employees must embark on this present change effort.

The need to change is the lynchpin of your meeting, so you must deliver your message as strongly as possible. Employees must realize that you're not making changes because it's the latest management fad, but that you have legitimate reasons for asking them to alter course. So, describe the need for change in vivid (but accurate) terms. While you may have been wrestling with these problems for a long time, many employees may react to this information with surprise. (But then again, they may also be wondering what took you so long.)

Some changes occur because of an immediate crisis with drastic consequences. In most cases, however, changes are made because management
has the foresight to see potential problems if they continue on the present
course or great opportunities if they alter the course. Obviously, you have an
easier time getting employees to buy into what you are saying when the
organization faces a four-alarm fire and everyone's paycheck is at risk.

If you don't have a genuine business problem to fix, then avoid making
changes that seem good but that don't impact the organization's success.
The last thing you need is for people to think you're turning their world
upside down for another "flavor of the month." Instead, making such a
change only reinforces employee resistance to this and all further changes.
Chapter 5 gives you more information about the causes of resistance.

As you talk about the need for changing, you must do so on two levels: the
organizational level and employee level. It's hard getting people to buy in
unless they have some clear idea of what changing or not changing actually
means to them — personally. For example, on an organization level you may
be talking about improving service to the customer. To the person on the
manufacturing line, you may be talking about changing the way he does his
or her task to improve quality and timeliness of the product. To the person in
the repair organization, you may be talking about moving from 8 a.m. to 5 p.m.
to 24 hour repair service response.

Where are we going?

In this section, you paint a detailed picture of where you're headed — a
picture that your employees can almost touch because it feels so real. While
some changes lend themselves to inspiring and inspirational language, such
as delighting the customer, a reorganization isn't one of them. Whatever your
change, describe it in the most positive and optimistic words you feel comfortable using. You must detail the benefits of your change, showing how the
organization and the people will benefit.

You most likely have skeptics in the audience. Therefore, you need to clearly
describe what your brave new world looks like in terms of products/services,
financials, and other departments. You must also include your vision of
values, culture, customer/supplier relationships, and employee interactions.
For each of these areas, explain what makes them important to you, the organization, and employees. The more detail you provide, the more real the new
direction appears to your listeners.

If you're faced with a major culture change, describing the future takes a vast
amount of preparation and creative word-painting. The smaller changes, such
as introducing flexible hours (flextime), still take careful preparation, but
require less time and effort to develop. If you want more information about
creating your picture of the future, Chapter 13 provides you with a template.

Where are the bumps in the road?

No change is ever problem free. Even things as simple as changing the vending machines, moving desks around, or creating a new time reporting process can make some people unhappy and can be susceptible to "Murphy's Law." There's no manager's crystal ball warning you where all the dangers are. With the help of your direct reports, employees, and your own experience, you can predict some frustrations and dangers — but never all of them.

Your goal, then, is making sure that you and your employees remain prepared for the snarl-ups that you *can* predict. This gives you more resources to survive the possible landmines. The less surprises you and your employees get hit with, the more mental, physical, and emotional energy you have for coping with unexpected disasters. Tell your people where to expect trouble.

There's also another reason that you want to discuss potential problems. You're showing your employees that you know what you're doing — that you're on top of issues. While you may not have total control over the latest benefits package or reorganization, you still have a firm hold on the change effort. Chapter 10 describes what happens when people lose trust in their managers' ability to lead. Don't let this happen to you by allowing your people to get blindsided.

What goes into your implementation plan?

Never hold your kickoff meeting without describing how you propose to get where you're going. You not only look unprepared but also communicate that you aren't serious about what you're asking employees to take seriously. If it's important to do, then it's important for you to have a plan for doing it.

Obviously, a complex change, such as merging two companies, would require a more involved plan than merging two departments. But each plan must contain specific action items, who's accountable for each item, and how the implementation of each action item will be tracked. For more information about implementation plans, refer to Chapter 14. The important thing is to show employees that your plan is practical, well designed, and responds to the critical issues facing them.

Your audience wants to know that you know what you're doing. So talk briefly about each specific action item. Emphasize that a committee will be established for each action item, which means that there is opportunity for employees to participate. For the smaller, less complex plans, you can hand out hard copies of the entire document and walk people through it.

Lastly, focus on your plan's *score card* — a document for tracking all action items. Identify the person who maintains it (if it's not you) and how you and your team will review it every month. Here you loudly tell employees how committed you really are — enough to track systematically the progress of your change. Of course, just because you tell them doesn't mean that they instantly believe you; that only comes when you do indeed review the score card each month and share the progress with them.

Getting the Most from Their Questions and Your Answers

The Q & A session is an opportunity to sell your change. Questions and answers (Q & A) give you a great chance to show people how committed you are and how much you respect their opinions. As much as some managers dislike and would like to avoid employees' Q & A, the questions indicate that people haven't tuned-out and turned-off. Individuals care enough to still probe and challenge you.

When it comes to answering questions, one of the first you must answer comes in the planning phase — do you encourage questions during your presentation or ask people to wait until the end? The answer depends upon the type of meeting you're holding. With a formal presentation to a large audience, asking employees to wait until the end works best. You don't want to get drowned in all their questions and never tell people what you've come to say.

If you're talking to a small group sitting around a table, then, of course, use your presentation as a vehicle for discussions. Should you occasionally get off the topic, or get too deeply embroiled in one detail, the damage won't be too great. But do remember, you must respect their time and the timeframes you gave them. So, while you are allowing open discussion, keep an eye on the clock — and keep moving along.

Q & A sessions can often be difficult because you're no longer in complete control of the meeting and employees usually toss you tough questions. Therefore, you want to:

- ✔ **Rephrase or summarize each question to make sure that you heard it correctly (and also ensures that everyone else heard it).** Doing so not only minimizes you possibly misinterpreting questions, but also gives you a minute or two for locating information in your mental data bank.

- ✔ **Tie each question back to your vision, goals, and relevant sections of your presentation.** Tying the question back to your presentation gives you a change to give an answer and reiterate your message while emphasizing the importance of the change.

- ✔ **Give as many employees as possible a chance to speak.** It's important for everyone to feel that you value his or her input.

✔ **Be prepared for many questions that raise excuses for resisting your change.** Keep your cool. How you answer, even the most off-the-wall ones, tells people how well you listen and how much you respect their opinions, and demonstrates that you don't shoot messengers.

As the Q & A comes to an end and as you answer the last question, restate your vision and reason for needing the change. Remember the speaker's motto: "Tell them what you're going to tell them. Tell them. Tell them what you told them." You want employees to walk out with the importance of your new direction as the last thing they hear.

Making Sure That People Leave with the Right Messages

The success of your kickoff meeting not only depends on the words you deliver, but the impressions you leave in the minds and hearts of your audience. You want employees to walk away supporting the move to centralization or your department's reorganization. Therefore, your presentation must deliver five key messages that create a solid foundation for the weeks and months ahead:

✔ **Message 1: You're committed.** By now, most employees have become jaded by quick fixes. It takes more than fancy slides and impassioned words to prove your commitment. You must also specifically tell people what you will do — how you're personally changing your day-to-day work. Plant the seed that this change isn't another "do as I say, not as I do" type of initiative.

✔ **Message 2: You've done a good job of planning.** The amount of detail in the implementation plan should leave no doubt in anyone's mind about how much time and thought went into your change. It shows that you know what you're doing and are in control. However, employees also need to know that the plan is flexible and open to adjustments as circumstances require.

✔ **Message 3: You respect and value your employees.** Managing change has two broad components — the technical and the human sides. In your presentation, don't spend all your time talking about numbers or the technical how-tos. Show that you understand what employees might be feeling as they face uncertainty and disruption. Emphasizing the human-focused action items in the implementation plan helps people see how important they are to you.

✔ **Message 4: You welcome their input.** How you respond to questions is a wonderful opportunity to encourage additional feedback. Your words, as well as your body language show them that you're comfortable with their questions — and criticisms. You want people to see that you don't have a fragile ego and want to keep the upward communications channel wide open.

✔ **Message 5: You'll keep people informed.** Make sure that employees walk away knowing that this kickoff meeting isn't a one-time communications event. They need tangible proof that you have a communication plan to keep them continuously informed. They must feel that you won't abandon them to the mushroom pile.

Chapter 16

Assessment: How's Your Management Doing with Planning for Change?

. . . .

In This Chapter

▶ Checking how you and your managers plan for change

▶ Interpreting your change-planning score

. . . .

In this chapter, you get a chance to evaluate how well you, your management team, and/or your own manager plan for changes. We've written this questionnaire so that you can answer it without reading all six chapters on planning for change (though, of course we hope that you do). After you have responded to the 14 statements, get out your handy calculator because you've got some simple addition and division to do. Or if you want to keep your arithmetic skill from getting too rusty, grab a pencil and paper.

After you've calculated (electronically or manually) your Planning Score, find the description that corresponds to your score. You can then judge how well your organization plans for change, as well as what you can probably expect from future changes. And by examining your response to each of the individual statements, you can get clues on how to improve your planning process.

Here are five ways for you to use this assessment chapter. You can

✔ Keep your evaluation to yourself — as a way to validate intuitions and gut feelings about how well changes get planned.

✔ Use it as a discussion topic with your own management or work team.

✔ Discuss your results with your manager (providing that he or she is open to discussions like this).

✔ Send your results to the people who manage the change you're presently struggling with, such as HR or a special task force. Or if you're part of the team that is planning and managing the change, use the results as a self-evaluation and guide for your planning process.

✔ Give the assessment to every one in your organization (if you're a manager), and ask that they fill it out honestly. Make sure that you protect their confidentiality.

No matter how you choose to use "Your Assessment" we hope that it provides you with useful information about the way your organization plans for change. If you find that your "Planning Score" falls into the "danger," "caution," or "optimistic" categories, read Chapters 10 through 15. They offer you tools for planning changes more effectively and improving the likelihood of success.

Recording Your View

When it comes to planning for changes, does your organization do it well, adequately, or just ignore it? Does your management develop complete implementation plans? Do they share those plans with employees? Circle the number that best represents how your organization handles the change planning process. Where **1 = never** and **6 = always.**

1.	Each major change has a team with responsibility for planning and over-all implementation.	1 2 3 4 5 6
2.	Employees have the opportunity to provide input into the planning process.	1 2 3 4 5 6
3.	Our implementation plans focus on both the and the human aspects of the change.	1 2 3 4 5 6
4.	Managers clearly and specifically explain the technical need for change to all employees.	1 2 3 4 5 6
5.	Management clearly and specifically describes how the change improves the organization.	1 2 3 4 5 6
6.	Managers share the actual implementation plan with employees.	1 2 3 4 5 6
7.	Throughout the change, employees receive status or progress reports.	1 2 3 4 5 6
8.	Implementation plans include action items to ensure two-way communication with all employees.	1 2 3 4 5 6
9.	Implementation plans include a review of our recognition process to make sure we reward those people who support the change.	1 2 3 4 5 6

10.	When there are changes in work processes or job responsibilities, the implementation plan has items that reduce confusion, misunderstandings, and conflict.	1 2 3 4 5 6
11.	Each action item in the plan has specific dates for starting and completing that item.	1 2 3 4 5 6
12.	Each action item has a person or team accountable for its successful completion.	1 2 3 4 5 6
13.	All the changes that are underway get integrated into one overall implementation plan.	1 2 3 4 5 6
14.	Because plans are living documents — and life constantly changes — we update them at least annually.	1 2 3 4 5 6
TOTAL		

Tallying and Interpreting Your Score

Total of responses is
(Score is total divided by 14)   _____

Score is   _____

Your score is 1–1.9

Danger: Your organization appears to place little emphasis on the up-front planning for its change efforts. Management seems to jump right into changes — and then hopes for the best. Subsequently, issues important to employees remain ignored, managers get blindsided by problems, and measurements are nonexistent, making it impossible to track progress. Because they see a change initiative that lacks organization, commitment, and strong leadership, people, in turn, lack enthusiasm and see no reason to waste their limited time and energy on probable failures.

Your score is 2.0–3.5

Concern: While managers go through a planning process, their actual implementation plans fall short of providing a guide for successful change. Unforeseen problems crop up; communication with employees remains spotty; leaders appear inconsistently committed; and insufficient measurements hamper the tracking of progress. In your organization, change initiatives often appear disorganized and out-of-control. Some planning, on the one hand, is always better than none. But on the other hand, inadequate planning lulls managers into a false sense of security allowing them and employees to get blindsided by a barrage of "unexpected" consequences.

Your score is 3.6–5.0

Optimism: Your managers appreciate the need for strong pre-change planning. However, their actual planning process and/or the plans themselves sometimes fall short of expectations. Managers may occasionally overlook employee input, not including important components in the plan, forget to share it with people, or not measure every action item. This inconsistency naturally makes employees feel insecure — will this change succeed or fail or just wobble along? In turn, many people hold back support — usually at the most vulnerable early stages — until they see signs of success. Yet, even with less than perfect planning, your organization has had enough successes to persuade many cautious employees to eventually take a chance and climb onboard.

Your score is 5.1–6.0

Celebration: Your managers carefully plan both the technical and human aspects of major change efforts. They focus on maintaining communication, avoiding glitches (as much as humanly possible), strengthening their own personal commitment, addressing employees' concerns, and measuring progress. In addition, implementation plans do not sit ignored on the shelf, but become guides for encouraging and supporting employee participation. Let your managers know how much your appreciate working in a change-smart organization.

Part IV
Leading the Charge

The 5th Wave   By Rich Tennant

"One of the first things you want to do before implementing change in your organization is to fog the employees to keep them calm during the process."

In this part . . .

Leadership is just as important as planning when it comes to implementing change. In this part, you find out what it takes to be a change leader, as well as the little things that add up to success, such as communication and recognition.

Chapter 17

The Many Faces of Leadership

"In my 20 years of working, I've never had a better boss than my first supervisor. He understood people and how to motivate them. He could be tough and caring at the same time. And he was never afraid to say he didn't know something. We would have followed him anywhere. I wish there had been some way that we could have bottled him."

Vice president
Fortune 100 company

*I*n the early 1940s, Prime Minister Winston Churchill rallied a starving and battered England to hold out through months of Nazi bombing. A few years after that, Mahatma Gandhi led India against the might of the British Empire to win his peoples' independence — without the use of violence. Almost 20 years later, Dr. Martin Luther King, Jr. inspired a massive civil rights movement to confront head-on centuries of discrimination against African-Americans. Then, in 1980, Candy Lightner and a small group of California women established Mothers Against Drunk Driving (MADD), which forced changes in federal and state laws that significantly helped reduce alcohol-related traffic accidents and deaths. In the close of this century, Nelson Mandela showed the world the power of leadership by becoming the first elected black president of the Republic of South Africa, following decades of apartheid and brutality.

What do these five people have in common? Their values, passions, and talents persuaded others to follow them — and to courageously take action in the face of daunting odds.

But not all leaders draw history's spotlight. Every day, millions of men and women motivate others to change a small corner of their world. Whether it's in the fight against AIDs, the campaign to make schools safe for children, or the struggle to keep an organization healthy and growing, people work tirelessly without publicity or fanfare. You find leaders at all levels of society — and organizations. Leaders are diverse as society itself, you can't pigeonhole leaders; each leader's style and skill remains uniquely his or her own.

Don't worry, you won't get an academic discourse on leadership. We'd get bored writing one. Instead, this chapter looks at the human qualities that cause people to trust and follow other human beings. Some managers make outstanding leaders, while others win the Boss from You-Know-Where contest (see Chapter 2). What do outstanding leaders, at all levels, do to motivate employees to abandon the safety of the known and risk the unknown? What do leaders do to keep employees dedicated and inspired even during disappointments, disruptions, and disasters? This chapter addresses those questions.

Completing the announcement of your change to the employees doesn't mean it's time to kickback for a little rest and relaxation. You still need to lead the charge. You still need to keep encouraging, persuading, and nudging employee along their bumpy journey. Here's where you enhance your various leadership skills.

Leaders Are Many Different People

No carpenter would use only a hammer to build a house, nor would a surgeon rely solely on a scalpel to remove a tumor. Neither should you rely on a single style for leading people through a merger or a company-wide integration of your information systems.

Motivating people to give up the familiar and to leap into the unknown requires ambidextrous leadership. It's about creating options, understanding situations and people, and being flexible. It isn't about one style of thinking or acting. Successful change leaders understand this. They consciously develop and use multiple methods for encouraging employees to embrace the future.

We present six different styles that successful managers often adapt when leading the charge. But rarely does each one exist in its purest form because managers evolve their own personal ways of operating.

Leaders Are Coaches

Simply put, coaches impart knowledge and skills to others — along with boosting self-confidence. They can help their teams to win six NBA championships, to work successfully with process management, or to build a loyal customer base. Regardless of the arena, the goal is the same — beating the competition. (If you're interested in more information about coaching, then turn to Chapter 12.)

How are a leader and an elephant alike?

One day, the king in a far away land heard about a strange beast. So he sent his five blind wise men to investigate. After a half-day's journey, they came upon the creature. The wise men began their investigation. The first, coming upon the tail, decided that "it" was most like a rope. The second wise man grasped a tusk and thought "it" was much more similar to a spear. With the third hugging a powerful leg, the beast became a tree. Encircled by the trunk, the fourth thought that it had to be a powerful snake. To the last wise man, grasping a waving ear, the elephant became a large fan.

Trying to describe a leader is similar to those men trying to describe the elephant. It's impossible to truly see leadership in its complex completeness. First one aspect comes into view and then another. How easy it is for individuals to fasten onto one characteristic thereby limiting their understanding of the whole. While people may laugh at those "wise men" for missing the whole elephant, many managers do the same thing with leading people. They find one style that works and then hold on to it for dear life.

Managers as coaches help people learn new, more effective ways of doing things. That doesn't sound very exciting on the surface, but it's extraordinarily challenging when you realize how different individuals are. Each person brings a unique set of factors to the change process: personality, learning, history, acceptance of risk, adaptability, and individual skills. In other words, an entire life experience. No two people are motivated the same way; what energizes one employee may turn another off. When you think about it, a successful manager with ten direct reports constantly modifies his or her own style to accommodate ten vastly different employee styles. Not so easy after all.

What do coaches do? Basically, coaches explain, support, and provide feedback so that athletes, actors, and singers improve their skill. When it comes to change, managers-coaches must help employees develop new skills, work with customers in new ways, and interact with each other differently. To accomplish these objectives, here are some of the coaching skills that managers must perfect:

- **Clarify.** Make complex ideas, new goals, and confusing situations clearer and more easily understandable. Your clarification includes explaining the reasons for particular decisions and breaking the change down into bite-size pieces so that employees can digest what's happening to them more easily.

- **Synthesize.** Take the different problems and the various people involved and show how everything and everybody all fit into one change package. The implementation plan described in Chapter 14 assists in this area.

A coach's coach

In his book *Sacred Hoops,* Phil Jackson wrote about his years coaching the Chicago Bulls basketball team. He described how he had to approach each player differently. Some needed forceful feedback, others a pat on the back, and still others time to be alone. Jackson understood (as much as anyone can) what made his players tick. He took the time to discover the individual keys that unlocked their hidden talents. Whether it was giving up the ball for the good of the team, approaching each tick of the clock with a focused mind, building self-confidence or obtaining some self-control, Jackson helped each player reach for his personal best.

But Jackson did more than create a dominating dream team. His players often said that he helped them, not only with the game of basketball, but with the game of life.

✔ **Question.** Probe to better understand what employees' find unclear, have problems with, or outwardly resist. But for this skill to succeed the manager must also have the next one, too.

✔ **Listen.** Make a conscious effort to hear both the employee's words and the emotions underlying the words. Only then can a manager know what support or information individuals need.

✔ **Know employees.** Recognize the strengths and areas of vulnerabilities of each employee. Understanding individuals helps managers to build upon strengths and provide focused development and support.

✔ **Know the team.** Understand how well people work together and what areas cause friction. By also knowing each individual, managers can then use employees combined strengths to compensate for individual weaknesses.

✔ **Build confidence.** Increase employees' belief that they can succeed in their change effort. This includes convincing them to trust not only themselves, but also the performance of other team members and the manager.

Yet, no matter how technically skillful and knowledgeable a manager may be, as a coach, ultimately his or her success depends upon the willingness of team members to accept coaching — and that manager's coaching specifically. It all comes down to the interpersonal relationship between manager and employee. Does the manager respect the employees as unique and valuable human beings, do employees feel respected, and in turn, do they respect the manager?

Leaders Are Models

Of all the responsibilities that managers get evaluated on and paid for, role modeling usually isn't high on the list. Think about it. Does your organization's appraisal form list role modeling as one of your job responsibilities? Was that a topic on your last feedback session with your manager? Probably not.

It's easier to measure concrete things like market share, revenue, production numbers, tax savings, outpatient visits, customer complaints, and room occupancy. But less easily defined, let alone measured, is role modeling. Role modeling is such a nebulous concept that it rarely gets more than an honorable mention in management and leadership books or seminars.

In situations where one person has the power to reward or punish another, the more powerful individual usually functions, by default, as a model. Parents, teachers, and athletic coaches naturally come to mind, but rarely managers. However, you should add them to that list. By the very nature of writing appraisals, controlling paychecks, bonuses, and stock options, you control people's lives — their ability to provide for family and future. When you have that kind of power over another person, is it any wonder that employees may unconsciously absorb your gestures, expressions, or attitudes?

Many people become uncomfortable thinking that others may follow (or imitate) what they say and do. This type of thinking puts a huge burden on managers. It reduces your freedom to act spontaneously. It means that you have to constantly monitor what you say and what you do so that you don't provide the wrong model. Many managers find it easier just to pretend that modeling isn't an issue and live their work lives as they naturally see fit — unburdened by restraint. As one vice president said, "I'm tired of being an example for every one else. I want to do my work and let them do theirs."

Just because you ignore your impact on others doesn't mean that your employees cease soaking up what they see and hear. Whether you like it or not, manager and role model are synonymous.

You've heard the saying, "Do as I say, not as I do." That type of advice is no more effective with employees that it is with children. If you want them to adopt new behaviors, work differently, or think "outside the box," then you must provide the model by doing those very same things yourself.

Employees scrutinize everything that the boss does. Basic work habits, attitude about the change, personal values, response to frustrations, and willingness to learn new tools, all come under a high-powered microscope. When you control someone's bank account, nothing is sacred. Everything you do is open to evaluation and judgment.

How did you learn your people management skills?

In a study, we asked, 205 managers (12 percent of the total management team) what experiences in their organization helped them develop people management skills. Over 80 percent of the managers responded, "By the way I was managed." Their people management skills didn't come from weeklong workshops, two-hour seminars, or the latest management books. People simply and naturally learned by observing their own managers. They absorbed how they were treated and then passed it on to their people.

You can dictate a change, but employees will watch your actions and imitate what they actually see you doing. As Ralph Waldo Emerson said, "What you are speaks so loudly I cannot hear what you say."

Leaders Are Investigators

When you're the boss, you're supposed to be the person with all the answers. It takes a strong dose of self-worth to admit first to yourself and then to others that you don't have every answer. But that's exactly what change winners do. Regardless of title and office size, your strength and value as a manager comes from constantly learning new ideas, gathering new data, and finding new ways of doing things. You can't lead a change effort if you're stuck in the past and operating with incomplete information. No one follows leaders who are out of date, out of fashion, and out of their depth.

One of the requirements of becoming an investigator is accepting that the more you know about a topic, the more you realize how much you don't know.

As an investigator, you focus on two tasks. First, you gather the technical facts about what's happening with your change. You want to know such things as whether you are on schedule and what new resources are needed to accomplish your goal. Second, you determine how the change is presently affecting your people. What's working for them and what's standing in the way of getting their jobs done? Only by constantly collecting and analyzing data can you help employees merge two departments or increase output 25 percent.

Through your collection and mastery of information, you make a huge personal impact on your organization. You enhance your leadership credibility in the eyes of your people (and the powers above you). And you're seen as a valuable resource that employees — in your department and elsewhere — can turn to when problems arise.

You decide whether your organization is closed-minded or open-minded — each is equally contagious. You're the model. You set the atmosphere. If you want people who don't hide behind smoke screens and who admit when they don't know something or need more information, then you, too, must acknowledge that you don't know all the answers. Sometimes, both the manager and the employee find themselves in an information-gathering partnership — looking for answers that neither of them have.

We're not talking about knowledge for its own sake (though there's nothing wrong with wanting to know more about the reproductive habits of ringworms), but rather gathering information for a purpose. It's about digging beneath easy surface answers and suspending judgment until all the facts are in. Of course, simply collecting facts isn't enough. Next comes knowing how to use them to fix problems, support employees, and jump-start a stalled reengineering effort. Effective managers have the ability to not only absorb vast quantities of information but also to synthesize it, see new patterns, and create solutions.

Does this mean that you never make fast decisions? Of course not. Urgent situations abound — forcing you to make decisions on limited information. It's all about balance — knowing when you have the luxury of wearing the investigator's hat and when you don't.

It has been said that the only difference between a rut and a grave is the depth. Stagnation and eventual decay are inevitable when growth stops. Look at the plants, flowers, and trees outside your home or office. Either they're growing or dying, there is nothing in between.

Leaders Are Actors

By actors, we don't mean insincere, phony people who glad-hand their way across a room. We do mean that there are times in every manager's life when he or she would rather be sailing, golfing, or doing anything other than being in front of angry people who want immediate answers and the world returned to its original, familiar patterns. Standing in front of your employees is the time to temporarily put aside your own personal needs and give your all to your audience.

You have a job to do. Even if you're exhausted from an all-night party (or walking a colicky baby), hurting from a tennis injury, or struggling through a divorce, your people expect a professional performance. True, you're only human. You have times of crisis and loss when you just can't put on a happy face. That's when honesty works best; tell people as much of the truth as you can. They'll understand. But hopefully those times are few. Most often, the little things cause managers to respond emotionally, rudely, or callously. And those are the occasions when you become the actor, preventing later regrets and damaged relationships.

Here are examples of when you might want to slip into the actor's role:

- Someone asks a "dumb" question in a meeting. Instead of saying that it's the dumbest thing you've ever heard, you answer as if it were the most important question asked. By treating that person with respect and dignity you're clearly showing your audience that they, too, can trust you.

- Someone asks you a "dumb" question in private. You protect that person's self-worth even though there isn't an audience to applaud. It's the right way to treat human beings.

- You're visiting employees at their work location. Even though a million thoughts are swirling around in your mind, you give each person your full attention and treat everyone as if they are the most important people in your world, and their problems are your problems.

- A team that you empowered to create a recognition plan reports back to you with its first draft. You would have never designed it the way they did. However, as you discuss the finer points, you keep your tone of voice, body language, and facial expressions neutral, as well as looking for items to praise. You need motivated and productive people who get the job done, not demoralized employees who no longer care.

- You've repeated the same message to 12 groups around the country — and you have 6 more to go. You can see the slides in your sleep and wake up hearing the talk echoing in your head. But when you get in front of that room, those people are hearing you for the first time and deserve the same enthusiasm and energy that you gave on "opening night."

Your world is a stage

Over 400 years ago, William Shakespeare wrote these words in his play, *As You Like It:*

> All the world's a stage,
> And all the men and women merely players.
> They have their exits and their entrances,
> And one man in his time plays many parts.

"Assume" at your own risk

The General Electric Company has earned an enviable reputation as a highly efficient, well-managed organization. One of GE's most important tools is a quality program called Six Sigma (which was developed by Motorola). A key premise of Six Sigma is that nothing should be assumed. Employees don't operate on a hunch, but rather check everything out by gathering information.

For example, the *New York Times* reported in Fall 2000 that GE decided to set up a Web-based system in Home Depot that allowed customers to have appliances delivered to their homes. Managers at GE believed that customers would put a very high value on a schedule that guaranteed delivery in 24 hours. After conducting focus groups, however, the company was surprised to discover that quick delivery was not high on customers' priority lists. Instead, the most critical thing to them was that the delivery people were pleasant and professional. As a result, GE now makes sure that installers know how to treat every customer with the utmost respect and courtesy.

Managers, like actors, have a vision that they want to communicate. If you want your employee "audience" to think and feel positive about the new patient care program or benefits package, then you need to thoroughly understand your role and change-effort script, as well as your audience and what they like and dislike, and how to capture your audience's attention. That doesn't mean you exist in a world of only memorized lines and choreographed movements. Even the most experienced actors forget their lines, find props missing, improvise when another actor misses a cue, or even restart in the middle of a scene if a power failure temporarily interrupts the performance.

As an actor, you're prepared for anything and everything — making sure that the show always goes on.

Leaders Are Builders

You're building a future. And you're building a support system for that future. Whether it's creating a lean-mean-competitive machine or simply a new way of responding to unhappy customers, you're building employee commitment to the unknown. This isn't the easiest thing to do, but then you already knew that or you wouldn't be reading this book.

When building commitment, you focus on two main groups of people: the employees in your own organization and those individuals you interface with — mainly your internal customers and suppliers. For both groups, you have basically the same goal: building cooperation. That means opening avenues of communication, creating respect and understanding, and breaking down suspicion and defenses. You want your own organization working as a single team focused on common goals. You want your external partners providing assistance and encouragement. You need both groups working along beside you. As much as you might like to, it's impossible to create a successful change all by yourself.

Building a team

Few people would openly poo-poo teamwork. But not everyone wants to tie his or her star to someone else's wagon. In fact, most Western countries reward individual contributions rather than team performance. Just look at your own appraisals and compensation — how much focus was on team-work? Probably not a lot; but probably more than role modeling.

Nevertheless, your strength and your organization's success come from all of your people working together. That means that you have to find a balance between supporting independent performance and encouraging team synergy.

If you want to build a team that supports you and your new direction, don't leave it to chance. It won't happen. You have to carefully plan for and diligently work at creating "a single team focused on common goals." You do this by:

- ✓ **Developing a vision.** If you want everyone pulling in the same direction, employees must clearly see where you're heading. They must find your vision meaningful and all supporting goals logical. Plus, you'd better be totally committed to that vision yourself, or nobody else will be.

- ✓ **Clarifying processes and roles.** You want employees working together not squabbling over who does what. Well-documented processes keep everyone following the same plans and knowing who does what. You also simplify everyone's life so that each has the energy left to focus on implementing your change.

- ✓ **Providing team recognition.** Most likely, you work in a culture that rewards individuals, but you probably also have some flexibility in how you recognize employees. So, find ways that you can measure and reward team efforts. You'd be surprised how many of opportunities magically appear once you start looking for them. For more information about recognition, check out Chapter 19.

- ✓ **Safeguarding communication.** Never let the channels of communication get clogged. That means always keeping your employees updated, remaining open to their upward-feedback, and making sure that they can continually share information with each other. You can read more about the many opportunities for improving communication in Chapter 18.

By no means is this a complete how-to list on team building. Volumes have already been written on the topic. But it gives you an idea of what we mean.

A bundle of strength

Napoleon Hill told the following story in his book the *Law of Success*.

There was a man who had seven children who were always quarreling. One day he called them together to demonstrate just what their lack of cooperation meant. He had a bundle of seven sticks, which he had tied together. He asked each child to take the bundle and break it. Each tried, but couldn't. Then he cut the strings and handed one of the sticks to each child, asking each of them to break it.

After the children had easily broken the stick that they were given, he said: "When you work together you resemble the bundle of sticks, and no one can defeat you. But when you quarrel among yourselves, anyone can defeat you one at a time."

Building an external network

If you and your organization existed in a vacuum, then you'd only have to focus on building a cohesive team of employees. But you don't, it doesn't, and you can't. Because no manager is an island, changes that you make impact others, and they impact you in return. Unless you're building alliances with your professional neighbors, then you might wake up one fine morning to discover that the foundations for your change program have collapsed due to lack of support.

To get buy-in, it's not enough for you to simply present a good idea and expect everyone to see it with the same wisdom that you do. Competing managers and interest groups fiercely protect their turfs and clamor for their must-do projects. You've got your work cut out for you. So, you need to prepare for time-consuming alliance building, a lot of hand-holding, and occasionally, hard negotiating. Consciously building and maintaining loyal partners involves:

- Building mutual trust and respect
- Encouraging individuals to openly share their issues and concerns with you
- Solving your partners' problems — not just your own
- Showing that you're working for the good of the company, not just your own glory
- Getting people to listen and objectively consider your proposal
- Persuading people to publicly support your change

The human face of Jack Welch

Back in mid-1998, *Business Week* described Jack Welch as a leader who "has delivered extraordinary growth, increasing the market value of GE from just $12 billion in 1981 to about $280 billion today." Not even Microsoft's Bill Gates or Intel's Andrew S. Grove or Wal-Mart founder Sam Walton had "created more shareholder value than Jack Welch."

Warner Books also thought that Mr. Welch held a special place in the leader's hall of fame because they shelled out $7.1 million for his autobiography.

Yet, could it be that within the bigger-than-life executive who led GE to such greatness also lurks a mere mortal? Just six months before his announced retirement, Welch spectacularly snatched Honeywell from the grasp of his long-time competitor, George David of United Technologies. With one of the biggest deals in GE's history, both the company's board and Welch decided that he should stay on to help with the transition until the end of 2001. Sounds logical enough.

GE has been held up as the end-all, be-all of succession planning. Welch, himself has publicly announced on numerous occasions that any number of top GE executives could step right into his office. So, why not let them? He correctly knew that his expertise would be valuable during the merger. However, he could have retired and still shared his expertise in an advisory role. Perhaps he was also influenced by how tough it is to give up power, prestige, and a job that he held for nearly 20 years. Because leading GE is Mr. Jack Welch's life. Because when you've reached the top where else do you go? Or because he's human, just like the rest of us.

The preceding is a brief summary list. The devil is in the detail. To accomplish each of the bullets, you'll spend hours and even days of your time. But it's well worth it. If you don't take that time, you'll spend even more time battling other organizations and repairing damage that they have inflicted. In the long run, building a supportive network is much easier.

Leaders Are Human Beings

Think about all the managers you've worked for or with. Were any two of them alike? Sure, they may have had a few similar characteristics, but fundamentally all those people were as different as . . . well, leaves on a tree. Why? Because getting anointed with a title, doesn't modify the basic person. It only superimposes an artificial identity on who that person is as an individual.

Underneath the fancy titles, you find ordinary human beings with the run-of-the-mill hopes and dreams — people who awake in the wee hours of the mornings with anxieties and fears, people who crave glory and recognition and who are disappointed that their careers didn't quite rise as high as their hopes. Regardless of their positions, all managers face life's fickleness and the same slippery slope of success. Not one of them is protected from getting colds, cancer, or wrinkles.

On cold wintry nights when the wind howls, you too may catch a fleeting glimpse of your own humanness. Nothing fancy. Just a basic human being who wants a speck more than what you've already got — a little more respect, money, office space, time on the project, visibility, or staff. You might find a person who's afraid of failing. Or you could get reacquainted with your desires to triumph over others and garner public acclaim. Regardless of who you meet, you'll see some things that you like and some things that you wish would go away.

If managers could only have a dollop of patience for their own struggle with picking up new skills, then they might also be more supportive as their people wrestle with new ways of doing business. If managers could accept that they too resist the unknown, then maybe they would develop more understanding and tolerance for employee resistance. Maybe if managers could find a certain amount of peace with their own natural human imperfections, then they might be a smidgen more open-minded to the diverse need of their organizations.

While you may wear different leadership "faces," one remains the core to who you are — your humanness.

Chapter 18

Making Communication Work for You

> *"We had a great quality kickoff meeting and that's the last thing we heard from management. It's as if they forgot about us. Or maybe they thought that quality appears by osmosis. Whatever the reason, we haven't seen hide nor hair of anybody in all these months."*
>
> First-line manager
> Private company

*I*n the early 1990s, researchers analyzing long-term, happily married couples made a curious discovery. Except for only one constant factor, successful marriages had little in common with each other. Each married couple created their own unique style and ways of interacting. What all couples did have in common, however, was an ongoing, open, and respectful sharing of thoughts and feelings. Yes, communication seemed to provide the sole link between the successful marriages.

Really, these results are not too surprising when you think about it. In all relationships — be they personal or professional, in marriages or businesses — communication provides the lifeblood that carries the "oxygen" to nourish and revitalize. Without communication, relationships wither and die, like the body without oxygen.

Most employees know what poor communication feels like — they spend their workdays like "mushrooms," kept in the dark. Some lucky souls, however, work in organizations where managers place communication high one their to-do list. These organizations are also the winners in the arena of change. In this chapter, you read about ways that change-winners keep communication flowing and their organizations growing.

Looking at Communication

Many managers use communication mainly as a tool for transmitting pertinent information about the job. What some don't realize is that communication is more than the mere transmission of information. It's a way to

- ✔ Build trust
- ✔ Reduce uncertainty
- ✔ Reduce fears
- ✔ Strengthen confidence in leadership
- ✔ Solve problems
- ✔ Build relationships
- ✔ Reduce misunderstandings and conflict
- ✔ Reduce rumors
- ✔ Increase motivation
- ✔ Reduce resistance
- ✔ Show employees that you respect them

With all the benefits of communication, it behooves managers to make communication a priority — with careful planning and constant attention. Communication won't survive if it's abandoned on the nice-to-do pile of people stuff.

Here's a little scenario for you. Think about orchestras. Conductors do all the necessary planning, selection of the music, and rehearsing with the musicians for the upcoming performance. But on the night of the concert, the conductors fail to show up — they are just too busy planning for the next set of important performances. Sounds ridiculous? You're right. It would never happen. But it happens every day in organizations around the world. Managers work hard designing and planning their new budgeting system or distribution process, but fail to show up for the "performance." They're off working on the newest great leap forward, leaving employees to figure out how to make the current change happen on their own.

While employees, unlike musicians, don't need someone directing their actual "playing," they do need someone regularly communicating to them as they struggle with a changing culture or a new marketing plan. People need to know what's happening, what rumors aren't valid, what problems are getting fixed, and that management is still interested. Without that stream of nourishing information flowing freely, employee support quickly dries up.

Creating Powerful Messages

Some may never hear you. But over time your powerful messages will reach the majority of your employees.

Your kickoff meeting, which we discuss in Chapter 15, gives employees that initial explanation of where you are today, why they need to change, where you want to go, and your plan for the journey. But please don't stop there. In truth, your work is just beginning. Your speeches, e-mails, videos, and conference calls provide the oxygen that your organization requires to keep chugging along.

But quantity, unfortunately, doesn't equate to quality. Many messages, whether written or oral, aren't effective. They seem unfocused, rambling, unnecessarily long, and frequently irrelevant to the needs and concerns of the audience.

Regardless of whether you're communicating to one person or 100,000, whether you're giving an informal ten-minute briefing or an hour-long formal presentation, your message must be clear and meaningful. Usually this means that you need to

✓ Customize the message to your audience.

✓ Develop a central point that's easily understood.

✓ Show how employees are and will continue benefiting.

✓ Deliver your message with passion.

And do it over and over again.

The rest of this section focuses on eight areas to help you to prepare and present your messages.

Know that the same words mean different things to different people

As a child, perhaps you played telephone with your friends. You sat in a circle and whispered a message to the person next to you. Then that person repeated it to the next person, and so on until the message went around the circle with the last person stating it out loud. How different the message had become from what you originally communicated.

The children heard words that were different from what was said to them, had difficulty understanding what they heard, or missed something all together.

The same thing happens in adult-managed organizations. Communication easily gets garbled and misunderstood. Individual words have different meanings when heard by employees with different backgrounds. (If you're interested in exploring why the same words mean different things to different people, turn to Chapter 3.) And some messages just never make it into an employee's mental data bank.

When the communication process breaks down, blaming your audience is easy. "What's the matter with those people?" managers have said to us. "Why couldn't they understand a simple message?" The message may have seemed simple to the managers who created it. But it may not be quickly and easily meaningful to the audience who is hearing it for the first time. In fact, employees may actually hear the exact opposite of what was intended.

Protect yourself and your people from the "telephone game." Test yourself by having an objective, honest, and gutsy person review what you're communicating.

The responsibility for effective communication rests with the sender, not the receiver. It's up to you to make the communication process work.

Establish your key messages

As the manager of your reorganization or customer call center, you must also be its chief salesperson. This means crafting and communicating a consistent central message. We should really say messages, because there are two levels: the emotional, "right brain" rallying cry that people personally relate to and the more objective "left brain" facts that meet employees' intellectual requirements.

For the first level, you want simple, persuasive words or phrases that you can repeat over and over again every chance you get. They're designed to focus your people's efforts on your new direction, just as a magnifying glass focuses the light and heat of the sun on an object. Over time you ignite a fire of commitment within employees. Just make sure that you keep it simple and succinct.

The second level of key messages provides the intellectual substance to your emotional rallying cry. Here, you continually review the information that you created for your initial kickoff meeting. You know — the reasons for the change, where you want to go, and your plans for getting there. (All this information is in Chapters 12 through 15.) When people find themselves in a topsy-turvy world, it's helpful for them to remember why they're disrupting their lives in the first place and that there is a light at the end of the tunnel (not an oncoming train). Going forward, as you carry out each step of your implementation plan, you should also communicate the status — the progress made, where you've slammed into roadblocks, and how you're going to get back on track.

Regardless of the content of your key messages, deliver them continuously and consistently.

Know your audience

When you work hard to create an oral or written message to your employees, it's easy to focus on what you want to say and forget how people may interpret it.

As important as your ideas are, your thoughts don't exist in a vacuum. Your audience is the customer and you are the supplier. Selling change is like selling any product. You have to understand the customer, recognize what the customer wants and get them to buy.

A four-word mantra

A large manufacturing firm in the Midwest had languished for several years with declining sales until a new president achieved a turnaround. He developed a simple, four-word mantra that encapsulated not only his vision for the company but also the strategy that he had in mind for achieving it. "Quicker, Sharper, Brighter, Longer."

The company had to get its new products to the customer quicker. Managers had to be sharper in preparing for customers' future needs. Employees had to be brighter, which meant better and more broadly trained so that they could switch jobs easily. And everyone had to work longer, putting in more hours to not only accomplish the day to day work, but also overtake the competition.

"Quicker, Sharper, Brighter, Longer." This was the president's message — and he kept repeating it over and over at large employee gatherings, small meetings and in one-on-one conversations. In a short time, those words became a reality and the company moved into profitability.

Generally, people tend to see others as they see themselves — and develop a message that they would want to hear. But this isn't the way successful communication works. It relies on your ability to put yourself inside the heads of your audience.

Communication and community have the same root. They imply a common bond that unites people. Effective communication involves creating a common bond by finding what connects you with your listener or reader. It means seeing the world from their point of view. To do this, ask yourself some questions about your audience. These questions fall into three categories.

- **Employees' attitudes toward management.** Do people feel positive or negative about the new direction? Do they trust management to look after their interest, or do employees have reasons to mistrust leaders' motives? Do employees have confidence in managers' judgment to make good decisions, or is that getting shaky? Does a good working relationship exist between managers and employees, or is there friction? (These are tough questions to answer honestly if you're "management.")

- **Employees' attitudes toward the change.** Is there a history of flavor-of-the-month efforts, so that they expect this one also to fade? Do employees see this change as important to the organization and them, and if not, why? What problems have people already identified that will make success difficult? Are employees supportive, indifferent, or antagonistic?

- **Employees' personal concerns.** Does the change modify or disrupt the way people do their jobs. Will team and networking relationships be damaged? Do employees have to learn new skills? Will people lose power and control over their work? Does the change require extra work and additional hours above and beyond what employees already give? Do they even have a job?

How you answer these questions helps you decide and shape what you include in your communication. It also helps you determine how much selling you must do to get your audience's support.

Craft your message to specific groups

The second element to knowing your audience is understanding their professional world. When you talk or write to employees, put it in terms of their vocabulary and their workplace — marketing and manufacturing often seem to be from different planets (but we won't hazard a guess from which ones).

For a good example of what happens when managers fail to customize a change, you can look at TQM. Once the business community pigeonholed TQM as "a manufacturing thing," employees and managers had difficulty seeing how they could use it in other areas such as payroll, sales, or R & D .

(research and development). Unfortunately, most of TQM's examples and training material focused on manufacturing, even when the audiences were accountants, marketing specialists, research engineers, or human resource specialists. True, a few companies like Motorola took TQM, renamed it Six Sigma, and customized it to all aspects of their business; but banking, health-care, education, and insurance, just to name a few, had (and many still do) difficulty refashioning a manufacturing paradigm into an industry-specific tool.

Managers also fall into the same trap when they communicate with employees. Often, they use the same examples and stories for all departments, whether the audience comes from purchasing, housekeeping, or benefits. Yes, something that crosses all departments, such as a culture change, requires a basic platform; but employees also need to know what it means to them in their unique corner of the world.

If you want to sell your new appraisal process or e-mail system to multiple departments, maintain the same basic message, but vary it's packaging to fit your audience. You also get a side benefit from doing all this extra work. The same presentation delivered again and again becomes monotonous for you very quickly, which can make you boring to your audience. By bringing each communication alive with new examples, you keep yourself energized, bring credibility to your words, and hold listener interest.

By customizing your communication to where people live 8 to 12 hours a day, you're also showing that you care enough, not to present a canned, off-the-shelf communication, but to prepare something specifically for them.

Build an internal sales team

Being bombarded with an unceasing torrent of information, employees have constructed bomb shelters to protect themselves from data destruction. One great speech and a few bring-them-up-to-date e-mails won't get past their sophisticated defense systems. So, you must reach-out to people with a chorus of voices. Eventually, messages slip past protective shields and get heard.

Anyway, you can't carry the whole communications burden alone. If you're a first-line supervisor, use the informal leaders in your organization to help you talk-up and encourage support among their peers. If you have a management team reporting to you, then they should become your sales force.

In the organization of the 21st century, don't expect your managers to parrot the party line. And they certainly won't sell something they don't believe in. That means, you better do a good job of building consensus and getting their buy-in before you send them on the road. Only then do your managers deliver similar messages (in their own words, of course) and, hopefully, with the same commitment that you feel.

What do you get when you enlist your managers as part of your "sales force?"

✔ A change that employees know how to integrate into their day-to-day work.

✔ People who missed your presentation or didn't "hear" your message get a second and third chance.

✔ Employees who weren't comfortable asking "the big boss" questions, have a chance to ask their supervisor (who they know on a personal basis).

✔ Different ways to present the same thing so that, over time, more and more people understand it.

✔ Employees knowing that the person who writes their appraisals believes in the new direction. (Let's face it, if the manager doesn't support your change, it's not too likely that his or her organization will do so, either.)

Meet regularly with your direct reports to discuss the change messages and to make sure that everyone is on the same page when they deliver oral or written communications. Your direct reports should do the same thing with their own teams.

Open all channels

Successful marketing campaigns use a variety of channels to present their messages. These include television and radio, billboards, print media, and the Internet. Although the channels may differ, you should conduct your marketing campaigns similarly because the principles remain the same — you want employees to buy your change effort.

In traditional advertising campaigns, the media for communicating is predominately one way — out to a potential buyer. In your change campaigns, you need methods that work three different ways: one from you to the employees, one from the employees to you, and one between the two of you face-to-face. All three ways provide valuable avenues and meet specific communication needs.

Whatever channel you use, always customize your communications to meet the size, "personality," and needs of your organization. That also means that different managers rely on one of the following three channels in different proportions.

✔ **One way, from you to them.** This includes channels, such as videotapes, e-mails, messages (or even video clips) posted on an intranet site, personal letters, newsletters, and posters, that allow you to reach a lot of employees fast. But there is a downside. You may be writing or saying what you think individuals need to hear, but you can never be sure how they interpret it. In addition, people often find these channels cold and impersonal.

✔ **One way, from them to you.** You can create a number of ways for employees to give you input and ask questions. These channels include e-mail, a message board on your company's intranet site, voice mail, letters, suggestion boxes, focus groups, and employee surveys (Chapter 6 discusses many of these). All options offer employees varying amounts of anonymity, and therefore, can provide you with different degrees of candor. You definitely hear about what's not working with your merger or new product line. You even get a surprise or two. Additionally, get prepared to receive input that has nothing to do with your immediate change, some of it valuable and some going back to decades-old personal grievances.

Whatever way you chose to obtain feedback from employees, make sure that you also create a process for responding. People interpret a lack of response on your part, as a lack of interest. So, never ask for information unless, at the same time, you have ways to show employees that you heard them.

✔ **Two-way, between you and your employees.** When possible, face-to-face communication provides the best results. This lets people respond immediately to your message, and it allows you to show them what a good listener your are. Both you and your employees get the added value of hearing vocal tones, watching facial expressions, and seeing body language (and these are a major part of communication). While technological advances make meetings possible between people in Fez, Morocco, Auckland, New Zealand, San Juan, Puerto Rico, Hong Kong, or Scottsdale, Arizona, nothing beats being in the same room with each other.

Even though two-way communication gets your message across the most effectively, it's also the most stressful on the speaker. You're vulnerable to angry comments and hostile questions. Plus, you're responding in real time with no opportunity to carefully craft soothing statements. So make sure that before you step out in front of an audience you've done your homework: you truly believe in what you're doing, have analyzed the major issues, and understand the concerns and mood of the people in front of you.

Listen, listen, listen

Successful sales people will tell you: If you want individuals to listen to you, first show them what a good listener you are.

Once upon a time when the boss spoke, subordinates stopped what they were doing to listen. But that automatic, attentive audience has followed the direction of carbon paper — it doesn't exist much anymore. Now, managers must convince employees that it's in their best interest to listen.

Not an easy job to do. Research shows, that on average, people listen to only 25 percent of what they're told. That means you may not be listening to your employees as completely as you could, and they probably aren't listening to you as well, either.

What prevents managers from being better listeners?

✔ **Distractions.** An employee is talking to you, but you're worrying about a project that's behind schedule. Or perhaps the speaker says something that triggers a thought on a different topic, and off you go analyzing it. Or the individual takes such a long time to get to the point that you grow impatient. Whatever the reasons, your mind is not 100 percent engaged. (But, we bet that when the CEO is doing the talking, you keep distractions way down. So, good listening is possible.)

Most speakers talk at 160 words per minute, but you absorb information at least three times more rapidly. This means the more patience you develop, the easier it is for you to stay focused on what people are saying. (You can read more about mental focus and patience in Chapter 21.)

✔ **Interruptions.** People were taught that it's impolite to interrupt others, but they still do it. There are two main reasons that managers interrupt their employees: They work in an instant e-communications world and expect to receive answers immediately (just like their manager and customers do); they may think they know where the speaker is heading, so they jump in with comments or even conclusions. Either way, the speaker is insulted and the manager misses valuable information.

✔ **Selective listening.** Most people have the tendency to hear only what they want to hear and screen out the rest. So, managers often listen only to those things that confirm their own attitudes and beliefs. Or they tune out until they hear the part that answers their questions or focuses on their problem. Whatever the cause, managers lose vital information and may walk away with faulty "facts."

Information is power. The more you get and the more accurate it is, the more prepared you are to meet what customers, competitors, and change initiatives throw at you. For more on information gathering, you can turn to Chapter 6.

Listening becomes especially important when miscommunication and conflict occur. During times of tension, rarely does one person see the whole picture or have all the answers. If fixing the problem is more important than being "right," then you should start with careful listening.

Presenting Powerful Messages

While print communication is a great way to reach lots of people, it often lacks the immediacy of talking with people face to face. Whether it's one person in a cubical or 100 in an auditorium, the most successful way to sell your message and achieve buy-in is to talk with employees. Therefore, if you're in a large organization, get ready to add public speaking skills to your managing-change tool kit.

By creating a powerful presence, effective public speakers strike a resonant chord in people. In addition to being competent, credible, and listener-focused, accomplished presenters bring passion and proficiency to their message. Getting people to give up the known and follow you into the unknown requires that you reach into their hearts, not just their heads.

If you don't have much experience in public speaking, think about a training course. Your company may already offer public speaking workshops. If not, see if your HR department will get you an outside communications firm. A simple two-day program can achieve wonders for your speaking skills.

Say it like you mean it

Tell it to them with enthusiasm, emotion . . . passion. If you lack passion when talking about reengineering or relocating your headquarters, don't expect your employees to jump up and cheer. They'll be just as unenthusiastic as you are.

Emotion doesn't replace intelligence. It enriches the facts with a fire. You've done your homework. You've built a logical and factual case for reengineering the product development process from idea to cash register ring. Now wrap it up with passion. Help employees feel the same urgency that you do. Help them envision how much more effective and efficient the new process will be and how they can do their jobs better. Help them to see how they can leave the competition in the dust. Show them how much you believe in it.

Present your message with skill

Obviously, factual information and passion by themselves can't carry you forward nor hook your audience. But when you unite your data and enthusiasm with skillful presentation techniques, then you have a presentation that's hard to beat. Expert use of gestures, voice, and eyes combined make you a strong and forceful presenter.

To help you package your presentation about the new customer call center, here are some public speaking props for you. They enhance, reinforce, and strengthen your message, but they don't replace the power of your knowledge and passion.

✔ **Gestures.** Perhaps some well-meaning person told you to "stop waving your arms around when you talk." Forget it! Gestures add emphasis to your words. They bring your entire body into action, showing people that "all of you" is involved. Use gestures to reinforce and enhance what you're saying.

✔ **Vocal techniques.** How many speakers have you heard drone on in a dry, boring monotone? It's enough to put anyone to sleep (including the speaker). When used effectively, however, your voice becomes a powerful instrument. By raising the volume of your voice, you add emphasis to specific words and phrases. Lowering the volume draws people forward to listen more intensely. A pause just before you deliver an important thought builds anticipation in your audience and draws attention to what you say. Your voice offers a variety of options for you — so try out all of them.

✔ **Eye contact.** Don't hide behind the podium or stare at your notes as you deliver a presentation. Look at your audience. As you deliver each thought, make eye contact with an individual listener and speak directly to him or her. Even in an audience of 200 people you can select people in various locations so that you're talking to the entire room, not to one section, the back wall, or the ceiling. Looking at employees as you talk personalizes your presentation and gives it more power. It also helps the listeners feel more connected to you and what you're selling.

Well-programmed presentation techniques that lack a core of feeling and sincerity appear phony. You're turned off by people who deliver stilted, artificial talks, and so are your employees. Make sure that you develop a style that's natural to you and still incorporates valid presentation theory.

Finish it with finesse

Most managers put the majority of their effort into crafting their speech and leave the questions-and-answer sessions (Q & A) to luck. It almost appears as if they find Q & As a necessary evil — something to get through quickly so they can get on with the next presentation or conference call. In fact, Q & As often form the heart of your presentation.

What make Q & As so valuable? When done well, you

✔ Show employees that you respect them.

✔ Get valuable insight into people's thinking and feelings.

✔ Obtain warnings about problems before they become disasters.

✔ Head off rumors at the pass.

✔ Discredit rumors that have already taken hold.

✔ Help employees feel valuable and a part of the process (or at least less isolated and alienated).

Q & As are the toughest part of your presentation. It's here that listeners take the measure of the manager. They observe, by your words and your body language, how comfortable you are interacting with them. If you seem uncomfortable, they may conclude that you're hiding something or that you lack leadership skills. Employees also detect from your voice and your gestures whether you're committed to what you're telling them, or simply going through the motions.

In this concluding phase of your presentation, you can't hide behind prepared notes. You can't depend upon perfectly crafted sentences. You must rely totally upon your own expertise and knowledge.

Handling Q & A sessions takes practice just like everything else.

✔ **Anticipate questions and prepare your answers.** You won't predict all of the questions, but some preparation is better than hitting every question cold.

✔ **Listen carefully to employees' questions.** If you want to maintain their respect, don't interrupt individuals or assume that you know the question and stop listening before they've finished.

✔ **Handle even the most aggressive questions with composure.** Some people may try to provoke you. Others may look to see how well you respond under pressure.

✔ **Tell listeners when you don't know the answer or when information isn't publicly available.** If you need to research any questions, then get back to the people who asked them as soon as possible. Otherwise you lose credibility.

The best speech in the world can't compensate for a presentation that ends with a lukewarm, let alone disastrous, Q & A session.

If you have managers reporting to you and expect them to participate in the communication process, make sure that all of them are trained in handling Q & A sessions, as well as other elements of effective public speaking.

Planning Your Communication Strategy

No manufacturer of toothpaste would think of selling its new, all-in-one-tube cavity-fighter, teeth-brightener, and breath-freshener with only one quick announcement. The proud manufacturer tells perspective buyers over and over again how the new toothpaste will save dental bills and make every user the most popular person around the water cooler. But the manufacturer doesn't stop there. Marketing campaigns also focus on different parts of the population, such as children, singles, coffee stained 50-somethings, or porcelain smiles.

But rarely do managers put the same value on creating their "marketing" plan for a new reorganization. What causes the difference between the external marketing and internal marketing perspectives? Usually employees aren't seen as customers buying a product — in this case, what management is selling. Then again, managers don't think of themselves as needing to sell their ideas to "subordinates." Finally, communication occurs naturally all the time, so managers can't see why they should waste precious time planning for something in which they continuously engage — talking with their people.

Don't get trapped in this kind of faulty thinking. You need to plan your marketing strategy for a new customer care program just as carefully as you do any other product or service. You're enlisting employee support and personal commitment.

How does the communication plan fit into the overall implementation plan that we discuss in Chapter 14? It's part of the domino effect. When you implement a major change effort, it consists of a series of minichanges (or not so mini, depending on what they are) that you must complete in order to succeed. These include, but aren't limited to, changing how you appraise and reward people, revising policies for overtime, or clarifying roles and responsibilities.

Of all the various miniplans that you must do, one of the most important is communication.

Your communication plan focuses on you, your managers, and your employees. All action items in your plan should speak directly to one of these three.

What's your purpose?

Your communication plan spells out the commitments, opportunities, and channels for managers and employees to communicate with each other on an ongoing basis. It builds from the action items in your overall implementation plan, which ensures that all aspects of your change effort fit together.

You use your communication plan to

- ✔ Create a to-do list that defines what is necessary to make sure that good communication happens.
- ✔ Role model the communications style and work atmosphere you want for your organization.
- ✔ Show your employees that you're serious about the change underway and tell them what to expect in the way of communication from their managers.
- ✔ Establish channels for manager-employee exchange and ensure that you obtain ongoing input.

What are you going to do?

Your communication plan describes the personal action or commitments of the manager. These items must be tailored specifically to you and the circumstances of your organization. The action Items must feel right to you. What is logical and makes sense in one organization and with one management style may be ridiculous in another.

Your personal communication commitments might include such items as:

- ✔ I will visit each of the five geographic locations at least once every quarter. I will spend at least two hours of the trip visiting with employees.
- ✔ I will conduct one-hour conference calls with all locations at least once each month. These calls will cover current issues facing the business/organization and respond to questions. Employees may submit topics and questions prior to each scheduled call.
- ✔ I will contribute a column in every monthly newsletter on issues critical to employees.
- ✔ I will hold an "all management meeting" at least twice a year to discuss both technical and people issues.

Don't build a list of so many to-do's that you can't deliver all of them. Missed personal commitments destroy your credibility as a leader and tell employees that you aren't serious about your change.

What are your managers going to do?

Employees have difficulty supporting your change, unless they also see their immediate supervisors and the managers above them supporting it. So, include action items for all the other management levels in your organization. Here again, be careful to keep the list for your managers to a reasonable number. Then make sure that you hold them accountable for successfully completing each item.

Typical communication actions on your manager's list might include:

- ✔ District Managers will hold all employee meetings in each of their locations at least once a year.

- ✔ Managers (all levels) will hold at least one small group discussion each month to solicit input from their team, listen to their issues, and respond to their questions.

- ✔ At monthly or weekly staff meetings, each manager will begin by updating employees about how the change is progressing.

- ✔ Managers will receive a monthly "Key Message" discussion package that they will use with their own organization.

- ✔ Managers with employees in multiple locations will visit all locations at least once a quarter.

What are the employees going to do?

You also want to ensure that employees have easy, nonthreatening channels for communicating with you — even opportunities for anonymous upward feedback. Establishing and maintaining these channels not only provides valuable information, but encourages teamwork, builds morale, improves productivity, helps your employees feel that you value their opinion, and many other good things that you already know about.

A list of possible communication actions include:

- ✔ We will continue the monthly newsletter with the addition of a "Letters to the Manager" feature.

- ✔ We will trial an electronic "Question and Answer" process for employees using our e-mail system.

- ✔ We will provide employees with an e-suggestion box that supplements the existing paper process.

- ✔ We will conduct our annual employee survey each October.

Don't establish great sounding objectives if you aren't prepared to invest the time and money necessary to make them work effectively. Also, if employees commit personal energy preparing input for you and then get no response or a brush-off, they'll quickly conclude that you really don't care about what they think. And they'll stop wasting their time. And people will spread the message that communicating with management is a waste of time. However, when done well, communication is one of the best management tools you have.

Chapter 19

Celebrate Successes

● ●

In This Chapter

▶ Using recognition as a tool for supporting your change

▶ Creating rewards that reflect your culture and employees' desires

▶ Developing your recognition plan

● ●

"It really hurts when you've done a good job and nobody cares enough to say thank you. Yeah, I'd like to see a fatter paycheck, who wouldn't, but what really angers me is that no one has ever acknowledged all the money I've saved this company."

Vice President,
Fortune 500 company

*N*ow that old-fashioned lifetime employment and loyalty have gone the way of typewriter ribbons, what keeps bright, talented, and creative people from looking for greener pastures? Making sure that you have the greenest pastures around. And that doesn't mean just more money, it also means making sure that your people enjoy their work, feel challenged, have opportunities for professional growth, and feel personally rewarded.

Human beings (regardless of job title) need to know that their efforts make a difference. Yes, people require their own personal sense of accomplishment — fulfillment that accompanies a job well done. But also, employees need to feel valued by the people they work for and with. One senior vice president admitted that it had taken her far too long to understand this simple, common sense fact of life. She had demanded so much of her employees that, as soon as they achieved one goal, she raised the bar and set another objective for them. Finally, she realized that they needed time to catch their breaths and the opportunity to celebrate their successes. As she said, "I may be a slow learner in some areas, but once I learn a lesson I don't forget it."

Most people desire recognition; indeed, it motivates them to continue working hard and achieve superhuman feats. What kind of recognition? There's no single, simple answer. And that's what this chapter is all about — helping you create a successful, customized recognition program for your change effort, a program designed to your organization's needs so that it has the most powerful impact.

Understanding Recognition

From a human point of view, saying "thank you" when people give their best is the right way to treat others — with courtesy and respect. Saying "thank you" makes them feel good about themselves and their work.

From a more simplistic point of view, when you recognize people for their accomplishments you motivate them to work a little harder (sometimes much harder) and to keep plugging away at their job.

Managers who successfully lead changes know what their less-than-successful peers miss — that recognizing employees is one of the most powerful motivating tools that they have. When used correctly and wisely, recognition

- ✔ Reinforces the desired, new behaviors in your change
- ✔ Demonstrates leaders continuing support of the change
- ✔ Enhances people's self-worth
- ✔ Builds loyalty and commitment (when both are on a national decline)
- ✔ Creates a work culture that nourishes successful people

Celebrating success isn't only for managing changes, however. It's just plain, good people management. So, even if you aren't beginning or in the middle of a change effort this very minute, you can still use the information in this chapter.

Creating Many Small Successes

With free agents swelling the workforce ranks and employees marketing their own personal images, you don't have the luxury to wait until a project is completed before you acknowledge hard work. People involved with big change efforts, such as culture changes, mergers, or new distribution processes, used to celebrate successes at completion time. They would get anything from T-shirts to elaborate dinners with spouses or significant others. However, big projects take months and usually years to complete. What recognition usually happened between the kickoff meeting and the celebration dinner? Often, very little.

HUMAN INTEREST

Small things mean a lot

Roscoe, a second-level manager on the "fast track," took over his new assignment in Detroit — an office of 28 people. After about three months on the job, his vice president (four levels above him) paid a visit to Roscoe's organization. The VP assumed Roscoe would organize the meeting the same way that the previous managers had: initially spending time alone with the VP to review performance, discuss the good things that were happening, share plans to improve operations, and then take a tour of the office to meet people.

Instead, Roscoe highlighted his employees, not himself. He immediately introduced the VP to each individual. Roscoe told the VP how long each person had been with the company, something about them personally, and described their job and responsibilities. Most important, Roscoe related a specific accomplishment or skill unique to each employee. He found something that he could publicly and honestly recognize about every person. Then he stepped back to let the employee and VP visit for a few minutes. For many people, it was the first time they had actually talked with their VP.

Roscoe understood the power of recognition. There was no question in those folks' minds — their manager understood and appreciated what they did.

Big change projects continue abounding, but the number of people willing to defer their rewards keeps shrinking. If you want to retain well-trained employees who work hard and remain committed to the success of the organization, then you need an economic way of continuously showing appreciation for all their small achievements along the change journey, not just a fancy finale.

There's no doubt that money talks loudly, but it's not the only voice of reward. Just because people appreciate bigger paychecks, doesn't mean that they reject other forms of recognition. In fact, employees seem the most motivated by a combination of money and personal tribute. Creative and caring managers amazingly find innumerable ways to appreciate employees between the bonus checks. Often times, the little things end up making the difference, such as

- Saying thank you in notes, e-mails, voice-mails, and in person
- Having a special recognition lunch for everyone when interim dates are met
- Giving time off for working overtime
- Bringing in pizza for late night crunches
- Letting people go for requested training (even if it's tough on you)

✔ Taking everybody out for an impromptu breakfast before the day spirals out of control

✔ Letting the people who actually do the day-to-day work make the status reports and presentations

If you sit high up in the company and have the financial resources, you can always do something dramatic. One manager unexpectedly arranged a fair to reward her group that had achieved outstanding results. The fair included concession stands, food tables, various games of skill, and a rock band. We know CEOs that have taken out full-page ads in local and national newspapers thanking all employees for contributing to the success of the organization. Most people loved the gestures — as a one-time deal — but not as a substitute for the small day-to-day personal appreciation.

Few things damage your credibility more than showering employees with insincere recognition. If you don't feel it, then don't say it. You'd be surprised how quickly people see through insincerity — just as fast as you do.

Avoiding Great Ideas that Sour

Vacation trips, special bonuses, restaurant dinners, and theater tickets are the traditional elements of recognition programs. And, to this day, organizations continue using them to reward top performers. These high-level, big hitters stay meaningful for a long time if you use them sparingly for major accomplishments, and (this is really important) everyone agrees that the selection process is fair.

But what about the day-to-day small acts of heroism? How do you keep people motivated to slug through chaos and uncertainty caused by changing their work world? The smaller tokens of appreciation never go out of style. However, a person can only use so many gym bags or pocket calculators or refrigerator magnets. That means that you need to keep your recognition program fresh and relevant. This section explains how to keep rewards from turning sour and people, bitter.

Don't make one shoe fit all

The bottom line is not what *you* find rewarding, but what your people do. Your employees embody unique experiences, wants, and values — different from you and from each other. What one person or group might find rewarding could just as easily anger another employee or team. For example, one manager may take individual people out to lunch when they do something special. Another group may feel that the focus on the individual is embarrassing and the antithesis of teamwork; when they celebrate successes, they always do so together and never single out any one person.

If you're a manager of a large organization with different departments or teams, then you need to remain aware of unique differences between your groups. While the individual departments or teams share the umbrella culture of the "parent" organization, each also has its own special environment, personality, makeup of people, and informal culture. Therefore, you need an overall recognition plan (that we discuss in the next main section) and individual recognition programs specific to each of your groups.

Is this starting to sound complicated to you? You're right, it is. One of the most difficult aspects of motivating people, whether it be during a time of change or not, is finding the right rewards. The last thing you want is to spend time and money on a recognition program that demotivates people. But you've got help on the way — your employees. They're the best resource you have.

Don't create a recognition plan in isolation

We've seen the best recognition programs backfire — creating cynicism and bitterness. Employees thought either the rewards were insulting or the recipient undeserving — or both. All because managers sat behind locked doors in isolation creating what they thought was a wonderful reward program. In fact, you're better off doing nothing than having a recognition program blow up. Once that happens, people reject future efforts hands down.

The best way to protect change efforts and your organization is to engage the people who are to receive the recognition. Nobody knows the people in your organization better than they know themselves. So, let them help you design your organization's recognition program — one that works best for them. This doesn't mean that employees have unlimited freedom to plan South Pacific cruises or weekly distribution of lottery tickets. You give them guidelines, budgets, and cautions. You also have the final approval.

A menu of rewards

An office of 100 clerks in Phoenix, Arizona, presented the management team with a challenge: find rewards that pleased everyone. What a single parent of three found rewarding was not the same as what an unmarried 30-something person found rewarding. No matter what managers, tried somebody loudly voiced his or her displeasure. Instead of motivating people, managers found their efforts were only breeding dissension. Finally, one of the supervisors came up with the idea of creating a menu of rewards from which employees could choose. After canvassing employees, items on the menu included gift certificates to local stores, restaurant certificates, time off, cash, and choices out of a catalog for personal and home-related gifts. An amazing change in morale occurred by allowing employees to choose what they wanted — now they looked forward to their rewards.

The fishbowl — a story of success

We'll let this leader tell the story in his own words.

"As part of our effort to become more competitive, my management team and I redesigned our region's desired culture. We wanted 6,000 people to become more customer (internal and external) focused. To reward employees for living by the new behaviors, we created a region-wide recognition plan, but also asked middle managers and their people to develop their own personalized recognition program.

"One manager had an organization of 200 clerical employees. He formed a committee that came up with a simple approach. They put a fishbowl, literally a fishbowl, in the back of the room. As employees saw a coworker using the new behaviors, people simply wrote that individual's name on a slip of paper and dropped it in the fishbowl.

"Prior to his monthly all-employee meetings, the manager tallied the number of votes for each person in the fishbowl. Then at that meeting, in front of all 200 employees, he recognized the person who received the greatest number of votes.

"The manager asked me to attend one of his monthly meetings. At the end of the meeting, he handed me the envelope containing this month's winner. I opened it and read a lady's name. It turned out to be a woman in her early 50s who had worked for the company for over 30 years. When I announced her name total bedlam broke loose with people whooping, hollering, clapping, cheering, jumping up and down, and standing on chairs to salute her. It was the greatest outpouring of support across a team that I have every seen. The lady sat there with tears pouring down her cheeks.

"As the leader of the region, I would never have built a recognition program like the one that clerical team created. No way would I have thought of using a fishbowl in the back of the room. Using their frame-of-reference, they designed a very powerful recognition program that financially cost the price of a fishbowl and a few slips of paper. What tremendous payoff to the region and company, and what a powerful tool for changing behavior. I still stand in awe of their creation."

Here's a process to help you and your employees create a successful recognition program:

1. Form a small committee of employees from different work teams. Have them create a questionnaire to survey all the people in your organization. (Or if you've got a small organization, they can come up with their own ideas.) Incidentally, no single rule exists for how people should be picked for committees. Asking for volunteers should get people who want to participate. At other times, you may select the committee members because specific experience or expertise is needed, or you may just need to avoid people who are not team players.

2. Let the committee analyze the results of the survey and recommend a recognition program based on their analysis. This includes the actual rewards, how people are selected, when the rewards are given out, and tracking measurements to see how it's working.

3. Review with them their recommendations making sure that they stay within the parameters that you gave them. Remember that this recognition is for your people, not you. So trust them even if you're not thrilled with what the committee designed.

4. Share the plan with everyone in your organization. Ask for their feedback. You might find that some fine-tuning is necessary.

5. Implement the recognition, and within at least six months, review to see how the plan is working and what needs changing.

Developing Your Recognition Plan

If you're a first-level manager of a single workgroup, then you probably won't immediately use all the information in this section. However, if you plan on moving up the ladder or want to see what your boss or boss's boss should be doing, then read on. For those of you who manage a large organization with multiple departments, your multilevel recognition plan is a valuable tool — both during times of change and for everyday motivation of people.

Like individuals, departments, and organizational changes, each recognition plan has a unique personality but also similar elements. Plans that work share the following characteristics. They

✔ **Reflect your organization's values.** What you reward should reinforce the values in your group. If teamwork is important then focus rewards on team accomplishments, rather than individual contributions. That doesn't mean you can't reward some one who does an extraordinary job, but the bulk of your recognition should focus on teams. Should delighting customers be a strong value in your organization, then the rewards should focus on employees who develop loyal and happy customers.

✔ **Describe clearly the criteria for receiving rewards.** Make sure that you clearly state in your plan how employees are selected for their special recognition. People must agree that you have fair and legitimate selection criteria. This way you avoid turning a positive experience into bitterness and anger. By making sure that the selection process remains uncorrupted by politics or favoritism, you preserve the integrity of your recognition efforts.

✔ **Remain flexible.** In other words, besides awarding special recognition plaques, include fun pat-on-the-back things to do. One vice president of a research and development group included in his plan a pancake breakfast for each of his four sites. As a way to say "thank you," he and his direct reports donned white aprons and chef's hats to make and serve pancakes before the workday began. To say the least, employees loved it. If you're not interested in something so fancy and involved, then you can commit to, twice a year, spending a half-day with each of your departments (and having lunch brought in).

✔ **Allow for multiple ways to select recipients.** Sometimes peers have a much better idea of who contributed beyond the call of duty. Other times, it's the customers who experienced outstanding service. Or, the vice president who convened a task force to solve a major crisis. In other words, design a plan that allows nominations to bubble up from all levels and directions of your organization.

✔ **Are updated annually.** You must keep your recognition plan fresh and meaningful to employees. People change, jobs change, goals change, and changes change — so too should the way you reward employees. Therefore, include in your plan a specific date on which you and your direct reports — or better yet, the recognition committee — can annually review and revise the recognition plan. To assist the people entrusted with updating your recognition plan, provide a way for employee evaluations of the plan. What worked one-year may not work two years later. Your people will gladly tell you what to keep and what to dump and what needs to be added.

Do not create your recognition plan in isolation. This is a task where your employees know more than you do about their preferences and needs. Check the preceding section if you want more detail.

HUMAN INTEREST

A recognition plan

Following a reorganization of a company from the traditional functional structure to four self-contained Business Units (BU), an employee recognition committee for one of the newly organized BUs developed the following recognition plan. (The committee asked that we respect their confidentiality, so we have eliminated all references to organization names. Also, for the purpose of this book, we omitted considerable detail.) As you read the recognition plan, it may appear cold and impersonal. We assure you, that when managers and employees actually recommended and rewarded outstanding employees, the events were truly ones of celebration, and at times, became emotional. Management continually received positive feedback from the people. Employees were pleased that the BU's leadership not only thought recognition important, but also made their commitment in writing.

Here is a modified version of their recognition plan:

I Shared Vision. We want to establish a non-bureaucratic way to recognize individuals and teams for their contributions to our business.

II Categories and Methods of Recognition. Three recognition categories (or tiers) and suggested methods of recognition are listed in the following table.

III Nomination and Selection Process.

✔ **Tier 1:** Nomination of an individual or team may be made by any one within the BU. These may be informal (for example, verbal) or formal (for example, memo or letter) submitted to the appropriate supervisor, who is also responsible for selection and administration.

✔ **Tier 2:** Nomination of individuals or teams are made by any individual using the Departmental Recognition Committee (DRC) form and submitted to the appropriate supervisor. The supervisor will forward the forms to the DRC who is responsible for selection and administration. If the supervisor is part of the nomination, the form may be sent directly to the DRC.

✔ **Tier 3:** Nomination of individuals or teams is made by any individual for the BU President's award. These nominations are first submitted to the DRC who will review and forward qualifying nominations to the BU President's Recognition Committee (BURC). The BURC is responsible for selection and administration.

Categories and Methods of Recognition

Tier	Recognition Category	Characteristics of Qualifying Activities	Methods for Recognizing Individuals or Team Members
1	Supervisor Group	They demonstrated behavior producing results or other improvements that had a positive impact on their team.	Personal thank you from the supervisor. Personal note of recognition and appreciation from supervisor. Public thank you at team meeting. Token gift under $25.

(continued)

(continued)

Tier	Recognition Category	Characteristics of Qualifying Activities	Methods for Recognizing Individuals or Team Members
2	Department	They demonstrated behavior producing results or other improvements that had a positive impact on the department.	Personal verbal thank you from the department head (DH).
			Personal note of recognition and appreciation from the DH.
			Personalized certificate signed by DH.
			Breakfast or lunch with DH.
			Article in Department publication.
			Token gift under $25.
3	BU President	They demonstrated behavior producing results or other improvements that had a positive impact on the BU.	Personal verbal thank you from President.
			Personal letter of recognition and appreciation from President.
			Personalized certificate signed by President.
			Breakfast or lunch with President.
			Article in Company publication.
			President's award/gift certificate.

Chapter 20

Assessment: How's Your Management Doing with Leading the Charge?

*N*ow's your chance to evaluate how well you, your management team, and/or your own manager actually lead change. We've written this questionnaire so that you can answer it without reading all three chapters on leading change (though, of course we hope that you do). After you have responded to the following 12 statements, get out your handy calculator because you've got some simple addition and division to do. Or, if you want to keep your arithmetic skill from getting too rusty, grab a pencil and paper.

Once you've calculated (electronically or manually) your Leading-Change Score, find the description that corresponds to your score. You can then judge your effectiveness at leading employees through change, as well as what you can probably expect with future changes. If you're not happy with your score, examine your response to each of the individual statements. These responses can give you clues for improving your change-leadership skills.

Here are five ways for you to use this assessment chapter. You can

✔ Keep your evaluation to yourself — as a way to validate intuitions and gut feelings about how well your organization leads changes.

✔ Use the evaluation as a discussion topic with your own management or work team.

✔ Discuss your results with your manager (providing that he or she is open to discussions like this one).

> ✔ Send your results to the people who manage the change you're presently struggling with, such as HR or a special task force. Or, if you're part of the team that is leading the charge, use the results as a self-evaluation and guide for improvement.
>
> ✔ Give the assessment to everyone in your organization (if you're a manager) and ask that they fill it out honestly. Make sure that you protect their confidentiality.

No matter how you choose to use your assessment, we hope that it provides you with useful information about the way your organization actually leads change initiatives. If you find that your Change-Leadership Score falls into the Danger, Caution, or even Optimistic categories, read Chapters 17 to 19. They offer you tools for leading change more effectively and improving the likelihood of success.

Recording Your View

When it comes to leading change, does your organization do it well, adequately, or merely give it lip service? Does your management provide clear and ongoing guidance? Do managers demonstrate their support by their own actions? Circle the number that best represents how your managers lead the charge — where **1=never** and **6=always.**

1.	Managers build support for changes by their own enthusiasm and personal commitment.	1 2 3 4 5 6
2.	Managers care enough about people to spend personal time coaching.	1 2 3 4 5 6
3.	Managers actually make the same tough changes that they ask of employees.	1 2 3 4 5 6
4.	In our organization, working well with others is as important as getting our individual jobs accomplished.	1 2 3 4 5 6
5.	Managers consider communication so important that they create a specific communications plan during times of major change.	1 2 3 4 5 6
6.	Management uses multiple channels of communication — for example, meetings, e-mails, newsletters, and videos — to keep employees informed.	1 2 3 4 5 6

7.	Employees hear a consistent and unified message from all levels of management.	1 2 3 4 5 6
8.	We have multiple opportunities to discuss our issues and concerns with management — for example, Q & As at meetings, focus groups, and informal gatherings.	1 2 3 4 5 6
9.	Management creates recognition plans that reinforce the "new" skills and behaviors required by the change effort.	1 2 3 4 5 6
10.	Employees at all levels receive public and private recognition for their change implementation work.	1 2 3 4 5 6
11.	Our organization celebrates small successes, as well as the bigger, high-visibility projects.	1 2 3 4 5 6
12.	Employees have input as to who, what, and how people get rewarded.	1 2 3 4 5 6
TOTAL		_____

Tallying and Interpreting Your Score

Total of responses is	_____
(Score is total divided by 12)	
Score is	_____

Your score is 1 — 1.9

Danger — Management doesn't appear to recognize how valuable the human components of leading change really are. Planning for and maintaining open two-way communication, coaching, teamwork, and recognition aren't high priorities for them. Therefore, implementing change means high levels of uncertainty, frustration, and wasted effort for you. Because managers aren't willing to personally make the changes they're asking of the organization, neither will employees. Sadly, many of your changes fail.

Your score is 2.0 — 3.5

Concern — Management's approach and commitment to change seems erratic. Occasionally, you receive excellent communication, while other times you feel shutout. Teamwork is talked about, but inconsistently supported. When recognition occurs, it appears haphazard and not part of a consistent plan. Finally, those changes that are personally important to managers get their attention; others, even if they are important to your organization, sit abandoned. As a result, management appears to be undependable change leaders.

Your score is 3.6 — 5.0

Optimism — More and more, management values the "human side" of change. Managers know that their actions and behaviors impact success. They intellectually understand the power of role modeling, coaching, communication, teamwork, and recognition. But, in spite of good intentions, management doesn't consistently follow through with its plans and commitments. This lack of follow-through often causes confusion and discouragement. Yet, even with these occasional lapses, employee loyalty and dedication help the majority of changes succeed.

Your score is 5.1 — 6.0

Celebration — Congratulations, your organization's managers are change winners. They recognize that the "human side" of change is critical to its success. Whatever they ask of employees, they also demand of themselves. Coaching, communication, teamwork, and recognition all get equal billing with the technical demands of the change effort. Take advantage of your good fortune. Watch what your managers do and borrow it to develop your own style of managing change. Make sure that you become a change winner (and say thank you to your management).

Part V

Taking Care of Yourself — No One Else Will

The 5th Wave   By Rich Tennant

"Sometimes I feel behind the times. I asked my 11-year-old to build a web site for my business, and he said he would, but only after he finishes the one he's building for his ant farm."

In this part . . .

Sometimes things are beyond your control. But when it comes to taking care of yourself, you're the one in charge. In this part, you discover ways to maintain your mental and physical health during tumultuous times.

Chapter 21

Five Keys to Mental Mastery

> *"Today, [people] of all stripes are using mental conditioning not just as a means to a better golf swing but also to make them better corporate competitors, more creative artists, and, some argue, better human beings."*
>
> Jay Tolson
> *U.S. News and World Report*
> July 3, 2000

*Y*ou're reading a book about managing change — and that also includes how you manage it in your own life. You can't always (or even sometimes) make people and events conform to your needs and wishes. But you can control how you respond when life doesn't go your way. Psychologists studying people who successfully cope with change have found a variety of mental skills that set change winners apart from change losers.

While none of these experts on human behavior compiled the same list of characteristics, the mental attributes that they identified are similar. Dr. Martin Seligman, a psychologist and professor at the University of Pennsylvania, concentrates on optimism with its positive self-talk. Then you've got Dr. Suzanne Kobas, who as a professor at the City University of New York, developed her three psychological characteristics of stress hardiness: control, commitment, and challenge. Dr. Daryl Connor, psychologist and President and CEO of ODR, Inc., has five characteristics of resiliency: positive, focused, flexible, organized, and proactive. And the most familiar of all the experts is Dr. Stephen Covey with his seven habits of highly effective people: personal vision, personal leadership, personal management, interpersonal leadership, empathic communication, creative cooperation, and balanced self-renewal.

The five keys discussed in this chapter help you to become less vulnerable to your external world by keeping your internal world strong and healthy. You're less dependent on what other people say and do. You don't need others to change in order for you to have less stress and a happier life. Mental mastery gives you control when everyone around you is losing theirs.

Reviewing New Research

If so many great lists are floating around out there, why do we need to create a new one just for this book? Why not take one that already exists and be done with it? That's because experts, like Covey or Connor, didn't have the benefit of the newest mind-body research coming out of the medical centers. Over the last decade, the field of *psychoneuroimmunology* (psycho-neuro-immunology), or PNI, has gained significant respectability (and momentum) in the scientific community. The research at medical schools such as Harvard University, University of California at Los Angeles (UCLA), Rochester University, Stanford University, Ohio State University, and the University of Massachusetts (to name a few) have all shown the interconnection between emotions, the brain, and the immune system. (You may have even read about PNI research in your local newspaper or a national magazine.) Therefore, any "list" of what constitutes successful personal change management should now build upon the latest PNI research. (For examples of some of that research, please refer to the accompanying sidebar and Chapter 22.)

We've based the five keys to mental mastery on the work of those who have come before us, the most recent PNI research, and the program conducted by the Stress Reduction Clinic at the University of Massachusetts Medical Center. The five keys to mental mastery — successfully managing changes in your life — are

- ✔ Flexibility
- ✔ Mindfulness
- ✔ Positive thinking
- ✔ Patience
- ✔ Compassion

One powerful, but basic rule that links together all five keys is that you have control over what you put into your mind and how you act. You aren't a puppet. Nobody is telling you what to think and feel. Sometimes you may not like the choices life dishes out, but you can always choose how you respond to any given person or situation. You, and only you, are responsible for the thoughts you hold, which in turn shape the life you live and impact your health.

Mind over body

The following are just a small sampling of the tens-of-thousands of studies in psychoneuroimmunology (PNI) research.

Psychologist Sheldon Cohn at Carnegie-Mellon University and scientists at a specialized cold research unit in Sheffield, England conducted a rigorous study that proved that stress weakens the immune system. They evaluated almost 400 healthy subjects for how much stress they were experiencing in their lives and then systematically exposed each individual to a cold virus. Cohn found that people with the higher stress levels were the most likely to "catch" a cold. For those subjects with minimal stress, only 27 percent caught colds. However, of those with high stress levels, 47 percent became sick.

In the *American Psychologist* journal (42, 1987), Howard Friedman and S. Boothby-Krewley reported their findings from combining 101 smaller health studies into a single larger one. Applying a special statistical analysis to several thousand people, they confirmed that negative emotion adversely impacts peoples' health. Individuals with long-term problems such as anxiety, depression, stress, and hostility had double the risk of illnesses that included asthma, headaches, arthritis, high blood pressure, and heart disease.

Dr. Redford Williams of Duke University Medical School and his collaborators found that the higher the feelings of hostility (as measured on a psychological test) among their subjects, the greater the chance of death from heart disease. In fact, male doctors, who as medical students were in the high-hostility group, had a death rate 25 years later six and a half times higher than those doctors who were in the low-hostility group during medical school.

Cardiac researchers at Yale School of Medicine found results similar to the study at Duke University Medical School. Studying over 1,000 men with a history of one previous heart attack, researchers noted that those men who scored high on tests of anger and aggression suffered more second heart attacks and were three times more likely to die of heart attacks than those men who had lower scores.

Peggy Huddleston, Project Director at the Center for Psychology and Social Change, an affiliate of the Department of Psychiatry at The Cambridge Hospital, Harvard Medical School, put the mind-body research to practical use with presurgery guided imagery to reduce pain and speed healing of post-operative patients. The following three women all followed Huddleston's program described in her book, *Prepare for Surgery, Heal Faster.* June K. needed only Tylenol to control her post-operative pain following a mastectomy and reconstruction surgery. After hip replacement surgery, Patricia F. left the hospital a week early because she used Huddleston's approach. Maureen K.'s doctor warned her about excruciating pain following her plastic surgery, but instead, as she told *The Boston Globe* (10/29/1996), "I didn't have any pain at all." These women, and thousands of other surgery patients, have learned how mental mastery helps to protect and heal their bodies. (Should you or a friend have surgery on the horizon, then you may want to visit their Web site www.healfaster.com.)

More mind over body

To directly experience how quickly your mind impacts your body, try these two simple experiments.

Think of a big juicy lemon. Do you see that lemon in your mind? Now take a knife and cut that lemon into quarters. Holding one quarter in your hand, take a big juicy bite out of it. What's happening to your mouth, and even your body? You probably feel your mouth puckering slightly and a little extra saliva forming. Your body may even be pulling back, in rejection of the sour taste.

For those of you who like eating lemons, here's another visualization. Think of a chalk board — you know, those big old fashion blackboards that you find in school classrooms. Now imagine scraping your fingernails down that board. What do you feel? A few shivers? Did you want to pull back your hand?

What you put into your mind has a direct and immediate effect on your body. The same thing happens when you practice the five keys of mental mastery. By using your mind, you can cause stress to relax its deadly grip, and disease-fighting antibodies come to the rescue. But when you dwell with bitterness, judgmentalness, and anger, your body remains a prisoner to stress and becomes flooded with immune-destructive chemicals.

Every moment during the day, you choose where to focus your attention.

Fortifying Your Flexibility

Trees that can't bend and move with the wind often lie broken after a great storm. So, too, with people who face life's storms. Less flexible individuals stubbornly struggle against rough weather. They're like those inexperienced sailors who fight against the wind rather than using it to reach their destination. The more flexible human beings adjust to and creatively accommodate themselves to life's disturbances.

Flexible individuals:

- Don't get derailed too long by unforeseen circumstances.
- Know that situations contain both positive and negative elements.
- Don't expect events to unfold or people to act in a predictable manner.
- Accept the fluidness and impermanence of life.
- Are comfortable with the diversity of others' opinions and operating styles.
- Are not tied to one way of doing something.
- Can see problems from multiple perspectives.

An aspect of being flexible is acknowledging that flexibility doesn't work in every situation. Most individuals have a basic core of values that remain fairly constant — you don't want to be flexible about them. There are company policies that you must follow; government regulations don't permit flexible interpretation, unless, of course, you want to spend the money defending yourself in court or time in jail. When taken to the extreme, being so "flexible" that you can't make decisions causes you to appear "weak" or "wishy-washy."

But for the majority of experiences that you encounter, your personal and professional success often depends upon responding to life's fickleness with flexible thinking and actions.

Offshoots of flexibility

Concrete advantages that you get from being flexible include having greater adaptability and creativity. Both skills greatly enhance a manager's ability to cope with a changing workforce, unpredictable business environment, and demanding customers.

- ✔ **Adaptability.** When you find yourself confronting unexpected situations, you create advantages by quickly adapting to the new circumstances. That usually means swiftly changing course, easily juggling multiple demands, rapidly shifting priorities, and integrating diverse frames-of-reference. Those managers that lack well-developed adaptability skills end up like the dinosaurs — relics of the past.

- ✔ **Creativity.** This second offshoot of flexibility requires original and imaginative thinking. It's seeing unique and unexpected ways to solve problems and get work accomplished. Creative people look at life from new perspectives. They combine nontraditional elements and take new approaches to standard and traditional ways of doing a job. They find patterns and relationships that other, less creative people miss.

Tools to try

Flexible managers don't waste time and energy agonizing over things that don't happen as planned. They don't destroy their immune system by angrily wishing that people or situations were different. They have a mental attitude that helps them successful accommodate life's fluidness.

The following are four tools that can help you expand your own flexibility skills.

✔ **Minimizing avoidable suffering.** Life gives us enough pain and suffering in the forms of illness, accidents, and other uncontrollable events. But human beings seem to compound their unhappiness by creating additional, avoidable suffering — by wanting to control the uncontrollable or fighting battles that they can't win. An example of avoidable suffering is the manager continuing to chastise himself for a bad presentation that he made six months ago. St. Francis said, "May I have the strength to change the things I can, the patience to accept the things I cannot and the wisdom to know the difference."

Practice flexibility — recognize what you can't and can control. Then let go of what you can't change and use your creativity on what's left.

✔ **Accepting duality.** People often get surprised when positive experiences have negative consequences and when negative experiences have positive outcomes. Yet inherent in most events and people are the seeds of both the good and the bad. By initially focusing on only one attribute (the positive or negative), individuals get locked into a one-sided perspective and never see the whole. Managers can end up discouraged or bitter when they find that their perfect employee isn't so perfect. Or they can fail to act on a valuable recommendation because it came from an employee they didn't like.

Practice flexibility — accept that most things in life come as double-edged swords. That means gracefully working with the "imperfections" inherent in our world.

✔ **Seeing it another way.** When you're caught up in anger, an experience that you detest, or a frustrating communication, stop for 30 seconds and ask yourself, "Can someone else see this situation differently?" If your answer is "yes," then you don't have to be locked into one way of reacting. You actually have options for responding differently — options, that aren't destructive of your health and welfare. As the French playwright, Molière wrote in the mid-17th century, "Things only have the value that we give them." You decide how you want to respond to a situation by how you chose to interpret it.

Practice flexibility — know that you can interpret the same event in multiple ways. You become a more effective person and manager when you avoid getting chained to a single way of seeing situations.

Maintaining Your Mindfulness

Living mindfully is the focus of the Stress Reduction Clinic at the University of Massachusetts Medical Center. Over the past 22 years, more than 11,000 people have walked through the doors of this center and found a way to successfully reduce stress and heal their minds and bodies. Often referred by their doctors, people have come with a wide range of medical problems such as headaches, high blood pressure, heart disease, cancer, and AIDS. They were young, old, and everywhere in between. And they all lived tied up in knots of fear, anxiety, and anger. After attending the program one day a week for eight weeks, over 95 percent of the people left with reduced levels of psychological and physical stress — with healing minds and bodies.

If you want to read more about the mindfulness work at the University of Massachusetts Medical Center's Stress Reduction Clinic, we recommend *Full Catastrophe Living: Using the Wisdom of Your Body and Mind to Face Stress, Pain, and Illness* by Jon Kabat-Zinn.

Basically, *mindfulness* means paying attention to what is happening as it's actually occurring. It's living each moment, instead of mechanically stumbling through life on automatic pilot, unaware of what you are doing or experiencing. With mindfulness, you no longer waste enormous amounts of energy unconsciously reacting like Pavlov's dog to every little offense that life tosses your way. (See Chapter 8 for more information about Pavlov and his dogs.) You bring a conscious awareness to each situation and how you respond to it.

Being simple doesn't mean it's easy

Whether it's slicing a tomato with a sharp knife and finding your finger in the way or walking down three backyard steps and missing the last one, most accidents occur because people weren't paying attention to what they were doing. They weren't mindful.

If mindfulness is simply the act of paying attention to what is happening in the moment, then why do people need to go to high-powered medical centers to learn something so basic? That's because, even when you want to concentrate on a given task, your mind has a "mind" of it's own. A mind gets easily distracted, wanting to wander off into the past or get lost in the future. In fact, staying present is tough and takes a lot of practice.

Two ways to break rocks

Richard Fortey, a senior paleontologist at the Natural History Museum in London, understands how each mind interprets experience differently. In his book *Trilobite!,* he described his early professional years spending long fascinating summer days pounding rocks in the Arctic cold of Norway. Musing on how rarely people see things the same way, he observed that hardened criminals also pounded rocks, but as a punishment, until governments banned it because it was being inhuman. But Fortey loved the experience.

For example, you can be enjoying a few peaceful moments during a Sunday afternoon — walking the dog, reading the newspaper, or making lasagna — and all of a sudden you're hijacked back to the past. You start replaying a frustrating meeting at work, feeling angry all over again that someone hadn't yet returned your second phone call, or enraged that an employee missed a vital deadline making you look incompetent. In the blink of the eye, your body's flooded with adrenaline, making you feel stressed out — all because your mind leaped spontaneously from resting in a peaceful Sunday moment to agonizing over something that happened in the past. If you want to exert more control over your mind, see the section ahead called "Giving these a try." You can also find additional information in Chapter 22.

When driving your car, have you ever made a wrong turn or missed your exit because your mind wasn't on where you were heading, but on all the things you had to cross off your to-do list? Hopefully, you've never experienced the shock of running through a stop sign (and hitting someone else) because you weren't paying attention to your driving.

To watch your unruly mind in action, try this simple exercise. Close you eyes and spend three minutes concentrating on your breathing. Just feel yourself inhale and exhale — nothing fancy. If you're like most people, your concentration might last for three or four breaths. Then all of a sudden your mind starts telling you, "This is dumb; you should be going through all your e-mails," and you jump to thinking about the presentation you're giving next week at 11:30, and that starts you fretting over whether people will listen because they'll be thinking about lunch, which makes you wonder what you're going to have for lunch an hour from now, and then on to how hungry you feel because you had to rush out of the house earlier this morning missing breakfast, which in turn moves your thoughts to the garbage you forgot to take out, and you're on to feeling tight and tense because you're life is running out of control. All this occurs when you were just trying to spend three minutes focusing on an activity that you've done during your entire life.

Should you decide to develop your mindfulness concentration, gracefully accept the fact that your mind won't always stay in the present. Watch your thoughts and actions, withholding judgment of good or bad. When you start to criticize what you do, how you do it, or what you're not doing, you're only heaping greater stress upon your already pushed-to-the-wall body. As you watch your life unfold, do so with an open, nonjudgmental mind.

Getting the most from your time

When you aren't fully living in the present, you've lost that moment forever. Even if you live for 70, or even 100 years, missed moments still add up to a missed life.

Mindfulness goes mainstream

Two celebrities, one a star golfer and the other a talk show host, have incorporated mindfulness into their lives. While their ways of living in the present differ, they both understand the power of focusing on the moment.

First, there's Tiger Woods. He applies mindfulness to his golf games. His physical and mental mastery of golf has been called "being in the zone," "flowing with the game," "mental control," "transcendent calm," and "stay-in-the-present focus." Whatever the name you give his mindfulness, the outcome is the same — he routinely sinks 8- and 10-foot putts for par or better. According to Jay Tolson in *U.S. News*

and World Report (July 3, 2000), Wood's "internal calm and power" added to his gift for golf and hard work and helped him post "the biggest margin of victory in the history of golf's four 'major' annual tournaments."

Then you've got Oprah Winfrey. The talk show host and magazine publisher sees mindfulness as a personal way of life. In her new magazine "*O*" (July–August, 2000), Oprah described how she celebrates each day rather than waiting for a tomorrow that is not promised. She lives her life "consciously, aware that each moment you breathe is a gift."

Yes, you do have memories, but research shows that people remember only bits and pieces (and even things that may not have actually occurred). True, you also have a future, but who knows what that holds for you. Just ask Christopher Reeves who leaped tall buildings as Superman. His future didn't turn out as he expected. So, "living" in a time and place that may not occur doesn't make any more sense than living in the past. That leaves only one thing you can count on that is totally yours: the present moment.

Looking beyond mindfulness

Does being mindful mean that you don't learn from the past or plan for the future? Of course not. You still need to make sure that you don't repeat mistakes. You also need goals for which to strive and dreams in which to believe. You need to anticipate problems so that you can stay healthy and retain satisfied customers.

Mindfulness is not meant to place blinders on you, but rather to help you dump unnecessary and unwarranted stresses. It's also to help you avoid accidents and stop spinning your wheels so that you can find a moment of peace in a frantic world.

Life only unfolds in moments. Every moment you miss means that you've shortchanged yourself.

Giving these a try

Regardless of where you are on the business ladder, you made it there because you can focus your thoughts and energy to get a job done right. Now it's just a matter of applying those same skills to more and more aspects of your life. Here are three techniques to help you practice mindfulness. If you find that you want to bring your "mind" under more control (rather than you being controlled by it), then Chapter 22 gives you additional tools.

✔ **Brushing your teeth.** This simple activity takes only a few minutes. The next time you brush your teeth, keep your mind focused on the actual act of brushing. Feel the toothbrush in your hand, the movement of your arm, the bristles against your gums, the foaming of the toothpaste in your mouth. But also watch as your mind zooms off frequently to past incidents or future events. Observe how difficult it is to keep focused on one short, simple act.

Practice mindfulness — when your mind flits off while you're brushing your teeth, return it to the present moment. And don't worry if at first you have to do it over and over again.

✔ **Stuck in rush traffic.** Even telecommuters have to get into their cars now and then. The next time you're rushing somewhere only to be stuck in traffic, take a few minutes to focus on the sensation within your body. As you get agitated, where do you feel your muscles clenching? As the adrenaline begins pumping through your body, is your heart pounding or is a tingling sensation creeping across your skin, or both? Watch how your frustration hijacks your body — but watch nonjudgmentally. As you begin the simple act of observing what's happening, you may begin noticing that you're less swamped with anger and agitation. They don't magically disappear, but you do become less of a prisoner to your flight-or-fight chemicals.

Practice mindfulness — when traffic gets you tied into knots, focus on the sensations you feel rather than the appointment you're late for. You can't control the traffic, but you can control your responses to it.

Perceiving the Positive

Almost every motivational speaker and self-help book brightly announces the importance of positive thinking. Even Scott Adams used positive affirmations 15 times a day as a way to help him stay motivated while struggling to syndicate his *Dilbert* comics. Yes, there is something positive about positive thinking. But as you can see reading this section, it's not unrealistic optimism. Rather, it is looking for the realistic, positive aspects or opportunities of an apparently negative event. It's making a conscious choice — choosing to focus on what you can do, not what you can't.

What do these four people have in common?

- ✔ Eileen Collins. In 1999, she became the first woman to command a space shuttle mission. At the time she entered the Air Force, Collins was one of the first women to go through pilot training. However, a federal law forced her to fly only transport planes because women were denied fighter pilot training. However, she didn't let discrimination or a dead-end career stop her from excelling. Collins' outstanding performance led her to astronaut training and a major leadership role in space exploration.

- ✔ Benjamin S. Carson, M.D. A professor of neurosurgery and director of pediatric neurosurgery at the Johns Hopkins Hospital, he's an international expert in his field. Carson is also one of the few African-American neurosurgeons in the world. But his career wasn't handed to him. As a child, he didn't always excel in school. And during his first year in medical school, Carson's advisor told him that he wasn't medical school material, recommending that he drop out. Carson didn't listen. Instead, he listened to his inner voice, pursuing and excelling in a career that some considered an impossibility.

- ✔ Sarian Bouma. The CEO of Capitol Hill Building Maintenance, Inc., in Washington, D.C. won the office-cleaning contract for the nation's New Executive Office Building. Twenty-four years earlier, deserted by her husband, she didn't even have enough food stamps to buy milk for her baby son. While living in a homeless shelter, Bouma decided to turn her life around. She took job-training courses and eventually became a bank teller. As a second career, she decided to start her own business. On her small-business loan application, she wrote that she someday wanted to have the office of the president as a customer. Four years later, her company cleans the offices of the president's staff.

These three people faced obstacles that would have crushed most other individuals. But with their ability to focus on the positive, while keeping feelings of helplessness and hopelessness at bay, they turned probable defeat into success. Meeting life with determination and optimism, they conquered their fears, depressions, and disappointments. Their positive thinking wasn't some unrealistic view of life, but rather a deep-seated belief in themselves and an ability to focus on the possibilities instead of the impossibilities.

Search for the positive or remain stuck in the negative — the choice is yours

What exactly do positive thinkers do? First, they admit that nothing is perfect, that everything has the seeds of heartache and failure. Then they immediately draw on their flexible thinking skills to acknowledge that everything also contains the seeds of joy and success. (See the section "Fortifying Your

Flexibility.") Next comes a choice: On which of the two sides of the coin do they focus? The winners consciously zero in on the positive — what they can do, what they have control over, and what lessons they can learn.

By contrast, negative thinkers remain trapped on the side of heartache and failure. They lament what they can't control rather than looking for what they can. They focus on loss rather than potential gains. They see events and life as static — remaining forever bad — rather than as a cycle where good appears, like spring following winter. They live as victims.

Life throws everybody disappointments and suffering (true, some people receive more than others), but how each person responds is what counts. You always get a choice — maybe not the options you would have scripted for yourself, but a choice nevertheless. Do you emphasize all that's not right or look for ways to create a masterpiece out of a flawed situation?

Art historians believe that Michelangelo, the 16th-century sculptor, painter, and architect, created his magnificent statue of David from a block of stone that another artist abandoned because of a flaw. Michelangelo saw the possibility of greatness where others saw only failure.

For more information about how to think more positively, try the book *Learned Optimism: How to Change Your Mind and Your Life* by Martin E.P. Seligman.

Be realistic

We're not suggesting that you walk through life thinking that everything is sweetness and light. You definitely experience situations when you don't want to optimistically leap before you look. You must constantly keep your guard up to avoid mistakes and search out defects. One Titanic was one too many.

Here are some of the times when you don't want an optimistic view:

- An airplane pilot taking off in a freezing winter storm assumes that everything is fine and skips de-icing the plane.
- You have chest pains and numbness down your arm, but dismiss it as only heartburn.
- The car's gas gauge is nudging empty, but you're not really going too far.
- A jogger thinks it's safe running in a city park late at night.

Nor is acting artificially upbeat and merry going to help you. In fact, unhappiness and pain can be warning signs that tell you to make a change, to protect yourself. A number of psychologists also feel that the unrelenting pressure to always act cheery forces people to deny and bottle up their emotions, causing even greater damage, as well as giving them a big dose of guilt for not being chipper all the time. Finally, artificial optimism causes individuals to set unrealistic goals, which in turn sets them up for failure and defeat.

You might say that life is 10,000 joys and 10,000 sorrows. When you're trapped in one of the sorrows, mindfulness and flexibility come in handy. Acknowledge what you're feeling, even when it's disappointment, anger, humiliation, depression, or searing pain. They're all valid human emotions, even though you may hate experiencing them. With mindfulness, you can treat each emotion respectfully and nonjudgmentally. When the turmoil inside of you subsides a little (and it always does), use your flexibility to see what lessons you've learned and what new doors have opened. Even though you may not be able to hold on to the happy times permanently, one of the benefits of life's impermanence is that the bad times don't stay around forever.

Gravitate to gratitude

An aspect of positive thinking is the feeling of gratefulness for the wonders that do fill your life. Most people reading this book have something about which to be grateful. The very fact that you have sight, know how to read, can hold the book with both hands, and have the financial flexibility to buy it are remarkable, given how the majority of human beings' struggle to survive.

Here's a quick mental exercise for you. Take a minute to think about one thing that you're grateful for. Do you have it? Now, how does your body feel as you contemplate it? Probably a little more relaxed. Next think about something that angers you. Do you have it in your thoughts? Now how do you feel? Probably tenser with subtle feelings of unhappiness. Go back to the positive thoughts — about something that you're grateful for — and let your body relax again.

In every instance during your day, you control what you focus on, just as you did now. You were the person who shifted your thinking from the feeling of gratitude to anger back to gratitude. In any given moment, gratefulness or bitterness remain options for you. No one forces you to select one over the other — you make that choice yourself.

Give these a try

You're reading this book because you believe that you can discover something positive. The following suggestions are ways of strengthening those positive feelings that you already possess. None of the four positive-enhancement tools are written in stone. Feel free to modify them to fit your style and life situation.

How you explain things might save your life

About three decades ago, researchers began examining how people describe events that happen to them. Those who use pessimistic explanations, such as considering situations as all-bad or feeling that bad times would last forever, had poorer physical health and were more prone to depression than people who held a more optimistic view. In general, optimistic people looked for and found the positive side in tough situations and believed that good times were just around the corner (which corner they weren't always sure, however).

Now a Mayo Clinic study (*Mayo Clinic Proceedings,* February 2000) revealed a significant correlation between optimism and living longer. Between 1962 and 1965, 723 general medical patients took the Optimism-Pessimism (PSM) scale of the Minnesota Multiphasic Personality Inventory (MMPI). Thirty years later, analysis of subjects' medical records revealed that a statistically larger proportion of people who scored high on pessimistic thinking had died than had the optimistic thinkers. In fact, as pessimism scores increased, so, too, did mortality rates.

✔ **After you get into bed for the night, think of five things that you're grateful for.** Okay, that sounds corny, but you'd be surprised how quickly your body begins releasing tension and relaxing and how you begin to see that the day wasn't a total disaster. Not to mention that you fall asleep a lot easier. Should more than five things pop into your head, go ahead and think about them. No one's limiting your gratefulness to a set number.

Practice positive thinking — at the end of each day, choose to be thankful for what you have rather than despairing over what's lacking. Even on bad days, you can find something for which to be grateful.

✔ **Remind yourself that most everyone has some positive qualities.** Yes, even your boss from you-know-where isn't all bad (even when he or she seems that way on some days.) Just as nobody is 100 percent wonderful, rarely is anybody 100 percent bad. You choose where to focus. If you want to increase your anger and continue destroying your health, then hold on to the negative attributes of a person. If you want to reduce stress and protects your health, then take time to discover what's positive about that individual.

Practice positive thinking — shift your thoughts to what is good about a person. Nobody is worth destroying your health over. (Besides, look at all the power over your life that you're giving them.)

✔ **Be kind to yourself.** When you make mistakes, ease up a little. Most often people harshly criticize themselves by saying such things as "you idiot" or "how stupid can you be" (out loud or in their thoughts). You have other options, such as saying, "Oops, you weren't paying attention here" or "That was a good learning experience." How you interpret your mistakes either supports or undermines your self-worth.

Practice positive thinking — when you fall short of perfection, give yourself a break. You've got enough people out there waiting to criticize you for acting human; you don't need to do the same thing.

Persisting with Patience

Patience and passivity aren't synonymous. All you have to do is observe a cat watchfully waiting for a mouse or a mountain lion intensely anticipating the right moment to attack an unsuspecting moose. Neither of those animals is moving a muscle or twitching a whisker, but each is still 110 percent engaged. Both were actively awaiting the perfect time to pounce. That's patience!

Some human beings substitute projects and promotions for mice and moose. Those who have developed patience determinedly trained their minds to:

✔ **Tolerate ambiguity and uncertainty.** They don't make unsound snap judgments due to lack of adequate data. Patient individuals work with unclear or inadequate information, knowing that with continued effort they'll find the right solution.

✔ **Wait until the time is right.** They don't plant corn in the winter or push an idea that others aren't ready to hear. Patient individuals do, however, prepare the "fields," pausing only for that window of opportunity to open — and then move quickly.

✔ **Persevere through failures.** They don't expect solutions to come smoothly. Patient individuals tolerate disappointments and delays and learn from their mistakes, while never losing sight of their goal.

✔ **Reduce stress.** They don't struggle against situations or people that they can't control. Patient individuals conserve physical, mental, and emotional energy for those battles that are winnable and those projects that are achievable.

✔ **Defer gratification.** They don't indulge in immediate personal or professional satisfaction at the expense of long-term gain. Patient individuals keep a focused perspective on the future, knowing that the results justify the self-denial.

✔ **Have self-control in the heat of conflict.** They don't destroy relationships with emotional explosions and irrational fury. Patient individuals maintain self-discipline when others lose theirs.

Know when to hold and when to go

Patience doesn't work in all situations all the time. When a person violates company policies isn't the time for patience. When your company's expenses are climbing, you don't wait for some miracle to save you. When you have severe pain in the lower right side of your abdomen (most likely your appendix), don't grit your teeth and bear it.

But most of life isn't emergencies that demand immediate action. Instead, success often comes from making an ally out of time and becoming friends with frustration. As Thomas Edison once said, "Many of life's failures are men who did not realize how close they were to success when they gave up."

Reap the benefits of resolve and restraint

Patience, like intelligence, is a *construct*. It's a concept that is made up of related behaviors. It's something that you know when you see it.

For example, there's no such thing as a specific behavior called *intelligence*. There are a set of skills that make a person *intelligent*. In fact, the definition of intelligence varies depending upon the behaviors used to describe it and the tests used to measure it. Some abilities that comprise the construct of intelligence include verbal understanding, word fluency, numbers, short-term memory, long-term memory, abstract reasoning, spatial relationships, and perceptual speed. Actually, one psychologist came up with 120 different abilities that comprise intelligence.

Psychologists haven't given the construct *patience* the same scrutiny; though philosophers have written eloquently on the subject. For a workable definition of *patience,* the dictionary still remains your best source. *The New International Webster's Concise Dictionary* defines patience as: the "exercise of sustained perseverance" and the "quality of enduring without complaint." We call the first characteristic "resolve" and the second one "restraint."

Resolve

You've probably heard the saying "great oaks from little acorns grow." That's certainly resolve, growing from a tiny acorn into an 80-foot tree, with branches spanning 100 feet. We should all have such resolve.

For the actor Harrison Ford, resolve held a personal meaning: "I realized early on that success was tied to not giving up. Most people in this business gave up and went on to other things. If you simply didn't give up, you would outlast the people who came in on the bus with you." Of course, patience alone won't do it; you also need talent, hard work, support from others, and luck.

Here are some of the things that you get when you have the resolve to keep on truckin'. You:

- ✔ Don't have to settle for second best because you want "it" now.

- ✔ Feel the freedom to be creative and take risks because you're not desperate for an answer.

- ✔ Have the freedom to break big problems into smaller, manageable ones because you aren't frantically trying to solve the whole thing at once.

- ✔ Find failures a learning experience because you know the journey is as important as the destination.

- ✔ Agree with Dolly Parton who said, "If you want the rainbow, you gotta put up with the rain."

Restraint

For some individuals, restraint smacks of self-deprivation. For this book, *restraint* means mastery over one's emotions, particularly in times of stress and conflict. It means not letting others control your thoughts, actions, and feelings. With restraint, you're in command.

Every time you let another person make you angry, you're giving that individual power over you. Like Pavlov's dog, that person "rings a bell," and you automatically respond with a conditioned response.

When you lack restraint in an emotionally charged situation, you come out the loser. You:

- ✔ **Look unprofessional and out of control.** Think about the last time that you saw people "lose control" and get angry. What did they look and sound like? Probably, their faces became red and distorted, their voices got thin and higher pitched, and their bodies shook with their hands flaying around in the air. Not a pretty sight. But that's how everyone looks when they "lose it."

- ✔ **Can't accomplish your objectives.** Anger shuts down the analytical part of your brain. You think less clearly and rationally. The very time that you need your "wits" about you, they've been hijacked by your out-of-control emotions.

- ✔ **Say and do things that make the situation worse.** When you get angry, you unintentionally or intentionally hurt, humiliate, and/or anger another. Instead of solving a problem, hostilities escalate, and conflicts accumulate. You've also created an enemy who's out to get you — sabotaging your efforts and refusing to help when you need support.

Thomas A. Edison — his patience helped to change your world

Thomas Edison patented more than 1,000 inventions, including an improved version of the stock market ticker tape, the electric light bulb, the phonograph, and the motion picture camera. His resolve gave rise to the electric utilities industry, the music recording industry, and the film industry. The years between 1879 to 1900 became know as the Age of Edison.

None of his major inventions came easily. Success demanded that he persist through thousands of failures.

✔ The telephone that Alexander Graham Bell created in the mid-1870s could operate only over a 2- to 3-mile distance (3 to 5 km). Edison put his creative and patient mind to work. After hundreds of experiments, he finally created a phone that carried clear speech over longer distances. In March 1876, Edison's telephone system connected New York City and Philadelphia, a distance of 107 miles (172 km).

✔ A year later, in 1877, Edison was working on the *phonograph* — a metal cylinder covered with tinfoil. He ran into one problem:

The cylinder couldn't reproduce the "s" phoneme of "sugar." After steadfastly working 18 hours a day for two years, Edison finally solved his problem, creating a phonograph that could reproduce all sounds and words.

✔ In the 1920s, the United States was highly dependent upon imported rubber for tires, manufacturing (conveyor belts, rollers, machinery mounting, and so on), medical tubing, storage tanks, and power transmission belting, to name just a few. In the event of another world war or natural emergency, the country wouldn't have been able to obtain an adequate supply of rubber. So, at the age of 80, Edison directed his ingenuity and patience to finding a rubber plant that could grow in U. S. soil. Over a four-year period, he tested 17,000 different plants, narrowing his count to 1,200 and then to 40 plants before he settled on one, the goldenrod. Then with careful crossbreeding, he finally produced a taller plant with a greater rubber content.

Restraint doesn't mean denying or repressing your feelings of anger. It does mean remaining totally aware of what you're experiencing in that moment, while consciously determining what you want to do and say. It means having the first two characteristics of emotional intelligence — knowing your emotions and managing them. (For more about emotional intelligence, look in Chapter 8.) You may still choose to act on your feelings, but when you do so, it is you who are in control. You won't be driven by mindless reactivity or unrestrained fury.

Give these a try

The president of a private company said to us, "Can't you give me patience now?" He isn't alone in his demand that life and people give him what he wants, when he wants it. Unfortunately, impatient people charge into "battle" poorly prepared and against unfavorable conditions. They set themselves up for failure and frustration. The following exercises won't magically give you more resolve or restraint, but when practiced, they do increase your store of patience. And when it comes to succeeding, every little bit of emotional fortitude helps.

- **When things aren't moving fast enough, ask yourself "Does my survival depend upon getting this now?"** If your well-being and that of your family's or organization's is threatened, then press on with all due haste. But rarely are you faced with life-threatening or job-endangering situations. In fact, seeing most things as a crisis causes you to keep toxic chemicals flooding your body, destroy your immune system, and stress your heart. By constantly living in a state of impatience, you're slowly killing yourself. Few things are worth that price.

    Practice patience — separate the normal projects and the to-dos of everyday living from those rare "life-and-death" circumstances. You need to conserve your emotional and physical energy for the times you're hit with one of life's whoppers.

- **Learn to see successes in small accomplishments.** It easy to want the whole enchilada and feel angry if you don't get it. Often, it's just a matter of letting time work its magic. So, while you and time trudge on together, treat yourself to a few celebrations along the way. When you take your eyes off the "gold medal" for a minute or two, you'd be surprised at the number things you've achieved.

    Practice patience — take pleasure in your small successes. Each day, you have many moments worth celebrating. And, who knows what the future holds.

    In writing this book, we practiced the preceding exercise over and over again. If we had thought of the "whole" book as our one and only goal, we'd have given up early on. But by setting our sights on a chapter, a section, or even one paragraph, then success became more attainable. This view of success helped us maintain our resolve during the thousands of steps and missteps in the book-writing process. And slowly, over time, "just this one paragraph" became a section, then a chapter, and finally the book you're holding.

- **Find out the warning signs of anger before they hijack you.** As you begin feeling your body preparing for war, ask yourself, "Do I want to give this person control over my mind, body, and emotions?" And then remind yourself that every time you get angry, you end up the loser @ even if you "won" that battle. True, anger is occasionally the appropriate response, but more often you may not have all the answers or see all the issues or be the only "victim."

Practice patience — respond to conflict with control of yourself and the situation. Some of the brightest people (intellectually) have been done in by not being able to control their anger. Their emotional intelligence wasn't developed quite as well as their mental intelligence.

Cultivating Your Compassion

Compassion? What's that doing in a business book? You're right; compassion isn't a concept that you normally find in typical business publications. Neither is it a behavior that managers usually practice in typical business environments. A vice president in a telecommunications company once told us, "I know all about compassion, and it's got no place in our dog-eat-dog world."

But the times, they are a-changing, and so are the people who fill an organization's cubicles. Today's employees demand a higher quality of work life than what previous generations expected and received. They want to work in an environment that treats them as valuable human beings, as well as valuable employees.

Helping yourself with compassion — a paradigm shift

To understand what compassion is, it may help to first see what it isn't. It isn't coddling people. It's not pitying the less fortunate from a position of superiority. It's not a mushy, bleeding-heart, touchy-feely soft skill that makes you a weak, pushover manager.

You can view compassion as something that you do for or give to others. It runs the gamut from just listening and being supportive to actually helping with a problem. Compassion has historically been viewed as the "the right thing to do for *other* people."

And now for the shift in paradigms.

Another way of viewing compassion focuses not just on the person receiving it, but also the person doing the giving. Yes, that's right, individuals who treat others with compassion also gain — even on the job. We know that our perspective of compassion modifies the "traditional" paradigm that most people hold. However, some great minds through the centuries have explained that, while compassion makes the world a better place, the giver also gets great rewards.

In its most simple form, *compassion* is the ability to step out of "my" needs, "my" concerns, and "my" pain and freely feel another's needs, concerns, and pain. It's acknowledging that underneath all surface differences, you and everyone else are all together in the same boat — an imperfect vessel called life. You recognize that all people want to wake up in the morning feeling good about themselves, experiencing joy, facing minimum disappointments, and living free of pain and suffering. Individuals with compassion look beyond titles, cultural differences, and job functions to see the "we" as in "we are all human beings."

So, how does compassion help you in a dog-eat-dog world? When you operate from a value system that says all human beings deserve respect and dignity, and then treat them that way, you:

- **Have more peers and employees willingly support you.** Genuine self-interest recognizes the self-interest of others. By showing people that you sincerely respect them as individuals (that doesn't mean you agree with what they do), you're giving them something that they value. In turn, employees begin perceiving you in more positive ways and will more likely give you their support.

- **Improve your health.** Scientists have found that feelings of compassion increase the amount of infection-fighting antibodies floating around in your body and reduce stress-related illnesses. Sociologists have discovered that disaster victims who helped others recovered faster from the trauma and protected themselves from future related psychological problems. Finally, medical researchers observed that people who spoke mostly about themselves — used lots of "I," "me," and "my" in their interviews — were more likely to develop coronary heart disease than individuals whose focus was less self-centered. Scientists aren't sure how the feelings of compassion actually interact with your body, but they know that having empathy for others does help you heal and protect yourself.

- **Preserve a positive personal life.** You don't work 24 hours a day. When you leave the office, you most likely want your life outside of work to provide support and a safe harbor. But who you are on the job — values and behaviors — don't get left behind when you walk out the door. If you humiliate and demean coworkers, that's what you bring home. If you treat employees with respect and dignity (even if you don't always like them), then that's what follows you into your living room.

- **Feel good about yourself.** If positive thinking can improve your immune system and help you live longer (see the Mayo Clinic research in the section on positive thinking), then feeling positive about yourself should also boost your health and well-being. When you treat others with compassion, you know that you've done something worthwhile, that another person is better off because of you. Or, if instead of a "good deed," you just treated a coworker with respect during a disagreement, you know that your actions haven't caused another harm. Either way, your self-worth receives a little extra lift. And there's nothing wrong with feeling good about yourself.

Restraint knows no boundary

Traveling across time and borders, you see that human beings have always struggled with and aimed for self-mastery.

✔ "If you are patient in one moment of anger, you will escape a hundred days of sorrow." An ancient Chinese proverb

✔ "No man is free who is not master of himself." Epictetus, a Greek philosopher in the beginning of the first millennium

✔ "He that would govern others, first should be the master of himself." Philip Massinger, an English playwright in the 17th century

✔ "Speak when you are angry — and you'll make the best speech you'll ever regret." Laurence J. Peter, a mid-20th century Canadian writer.

Observing compassion at work

Some managers find it hard to imagine how compassion can operate in a business environment. Yes, they'll agree that there are special situations when compassion is appropriate, such as an employee whose child has cancer or a peer whose parent suffers from Alzheimer's. But except for those rare occasions, the majority of time compassion doesn't seem consistent with the bottom line.

For other managers, however, most situations require successfully balancing compassion with doing-what's-right for the business. Here are two examples of how they integrated compassion and hardheaded business thinking.

✔ **Downsizing.** Whether it's due to technological advancements, terminating a product line, or cutting expenses, there are times you need to reduce headcount. Once the decision has been made, the next question becomes how to let people know that they're out of work. When Ron needed to let five people go in his engineering department, he knew that nothing he said would reduce the pain of losing their jobs. At the same time, he didn't want to add to their pain. Ron worked hard to handle this distasteful effort with care. For example, he met with each of the five individually and privately. He carefully and honestly explained the reason for the headcount reduction. He took time to listen to their frustrations, questions, and comments. As Ron said to us, "I tried to treat them the way I would have wanted to be treated if the situation was reversed."

✔ **Reducing a bonus.** Even when bonuses seem a given, the amount still depends upon job performance. Terry had one middle manager who steamrolled over everybody. Even though Terry had talked to the manager about his leadership style, he still didn't show improvement. So, when bonus time came, Terry informed the manager that the bonus reflected only his technical skills; there was no money for leadership performance. Terry went on to say how much he valued the manager's knowledge and knew that his leadership ability could also be outstanding. Terry offered him an opportunity to attend a special two-week leadership development program so that the next year he'd receive a full bonus. For Terry, "This wasn't an easy thing to do because he's one of my top technical managers, but I also need quality leaders. I hope I found a way to communicate honestly and still keep a good employee."

Compassion doesn't mean denying reality or avoiding tough choices. It does mean, however, that when you implement decisions at work, you do so with respect for the individual. Furthermore, as a manager you work in a "glass" office. What you say to an employee and how you say it often finds its way throughout the organization — reinforcing your reputation as a "people" person who's good to work for or a callused clod that employees shun.

Giving these a try

Is there any time that you should treat people without compassion? It's rare. Is it possible to always operate with compassion? That is rare, too. Sometimes your own frustrations and angers get in the way. But that doesn't mean you should stop striving to treat coworkers (and others) with empathy and dignity — thereby increasing your allies and decreasing your enemies. The following are three exercises that you might give a try for applying compassion on the job (or even in the home if you're so motivated).

✔ **Find something that you have in common with a person who rubs you the wrong way.** Having strong negative feelings about another employee makes it difficult to build a productive work relationship and may even cause you to say or do things that you later regret. However, when you identify a common interest that the two of you share, such as you both like golf or are loyal to the company, it helps dilute negative perceptions. And the less negativity you feel, the more options you have for successfully dealing with a tough situation. Rarely do you work with someone who is devoid of any human feelings or interests.

Practice compassion — look beneath the work personality to find the human being. Any way that you can minimize your aversion toward a coworker will make you more effective in dealing with that person and doing your job.

✔ **Before you give another person bad news, ask yourself, "How would I want to hear this information?"** You're applying a variation of the Golden Rule (see Chapter 5). On the one hand, there really isn't a "perfect" way to tell people that their performance doesn't meet standards or that they're out of a job. On the other hand, certain styles and techniques can soften the humiliation and pain. And usually those are similar to what you would want if you were in the same situation.

Practice compassion — take a moment to put yourself in another person's "shoes." Being a manager who makes tough decisions doesn't preclude you from also being a manager with compassion.

✔ **When a person does something that frustrates or angers you, stop before you respond and ask yourself, "If I were in his or her place could I have, just possibly, acted in a similar way?"** Maybe your answer is a resounding "No." But most likely, you may be able to identify with a tiny piece of that individual's actions. Your objective is not to justify behavior that you disagree with, but to help yourself respond more productively in difficult situations, as well as maintain a productive relationship. Usually, intelligent people have some logical reason for doing what they do — as dumb as it may look to you. Plus, they don't usually think of themselves or their actions as "stupid."

Practice compassion — put yourself in another person's situation in order to find the logic behind the behavior. Taking a second look before you leap may save you and others a lot of grief.

Two centuries and two cultures, one concept

Compassion begins with acknowledging that all human beings share common life experiences. And in the end, regardless of wealth or title, one bell still tolls for all. Therefore, rather than emphasizing how individuals differ, compassionate people focus on what all people hold in common.

In 1623, John Donne, the English writer and clergyman, touched the heart of compassion when he wrote: "No man is an island entire of itself; every man is a piece of the continent, a part of the main. If a clod be washed away by the sea, Europe is the less, as well as if a promontory were, as well as if a manor of thy friend's or of thine own were. Any man's death diminishes me, because I am involved in mankind. And therefore never send to know for whom the bell tolls: it tolls for thee."

In 1998, His Holiness The Dalai Lama described in *The Art Of Happiness* a similar shared humanity when he said, "Whenever I meet people, I always approach them from the standpoint of the most basic things we have in common. We each have a physical structure, a mind, emotions. We are all born in the same way, and we all die. All of us want happiness and do not want to suffer. Looking at others from this standpoint rather than emphasizing secondary differences such as the fact that I am Tibetan, or a different color, religion, or cultural background, allows me to have a feeling that I'm meeting someone just the same as me. . . ."

Chapter 22

Powerlifting for the Mind and Body

"You've read all about road rage and air rage, but now I'm beginning to see desk rage around here. People are really stressed out, and they're not coping very well with it. No fights yet, but we've had a few tossed phones, aggressive and nasty e-mails, some yelling matches at meetings, and one kicked over cubicle [wall]. But the company won't acknowledge that we've got a problem. I'm just holding my breath hoping nobody gets hurt.

Director of Human Resources
Private Company

A softening economy, merger mania, grueling commutes, fewer people to do more work, less time to do more work, catacomb-like cubicles — and the list goes on. Mix in all the changes individuals grapple with in their personal lives, and it's no wonder that frustration, short tempers, and anger are busting out all over — as well as heart disease and hypertension (high blood pressure). If you're interested in the multiple ways that stress can destroy your health, Chapter 21 is a good place for you to turn.

Some companies, like General Motors, offer employee stress-reduction support such as meditation and tai chi, but they're the exception. Most organizations don't recognize the growing problem of employee stress and pent-up "desk rage," don't have the financial wherewithal to deal with it, or don't understand how to help, so they do nothing.

But you don't have to suffer with mounting stress.

And that's what this chapter is all about — options for helping you eliminate stress rather than stockpiling even more of it. If you're going to survive c onfrontational peers, to accept a high-visibility project, to struggle with centralization, or to keep one-step ahead of demanding customers, then you need a well-tuned mind and body. We offer you four ways to keep your cool and maintain your health during all those crazy, unpredictable, exhausting times that never seem to end.

Mind-Body Connections

It's nearly impossible for you to have a strong body without getting your mind involved. And it's just as difficult for you to maintain a strong mind without getting your body into the act.

Somehow, people in the West came to the conclusion that the mind and body operated independently, even though they were housed together. You know: The mind had the intelligence and did the "thinking," while the body chugged along doing its thing, such as pumping blood, digesting food, healing injuries, and fighting invaders. By the 1980s, however, molecular biologists and neuroscientists had proven unequivocally that a vast and intricate communication network exists between the brain and the physical body. Inside of you are neuropeptides and other "messenger molecules" zipping information from your body to your brain, from your brain to your body, between organs within your body, and all of them communicating with your immune system.

The barriers separating mind and body are crumbling. *Intelligence* exists in all of your cells, not just the gray ones between your ears — which means that your heart and intestines aren't passive, but actually passing information on to the brain. And your thoughts and emotions don't exist in isolation, but influence your immune system by the messages they send. Just how all this works, scientists don't know yet. But they're working on it, and each day brings more and more evidence that all parts of you operate as a single, dynamic whole.

Before we move on to the four mind-body techniques, however, it might help for you to get some idea about how all the research applies to real people in real-life situations. To translate the new molecular studies from the laboratory into life-enhancing medicine, a new discipline called *psychoneuroimmunology* (psycho-neuro-immunology) developed. (For more information about psychoneuroimmunology or PNI as it's known, jump to Chapter 21.) Slowly, but steadily PNI scientists are convincing the medical community to shift its focus from an either/or "mind" or "body" approach to the concept of mind-body as a single entity. The following four examples give you an overview of how PNI research converts to the everyday world. Plus, you can find additional PNI research in the following section on meditation.

✔ Dr. Dean Ornish, the Director of the Preventive Medicine Research Institute at the School of Medicine, University of California, San Francisco, demonstrated conclusively that you can reverse severe heart disease without using drugs or surgery. Using his program, patients with reduced blood flow to the heart meditated, practiced yoga, met in small support groups, walked for exercise, and ate a very low fat vegetarian diet. Over one year, 82 percent of his patients reduced their artery blockages and increased blood flow to their hearts. When Dr. Ornish originally started his study in the early 1980s, the medical community responded with skepticism and even outright hostility. Twenty years later, major insurance companies are now providing reimbursement to similar programs throughout the country. Dr. Ornish has shown that you can heal a damaged heart without expensive and intrusive surgery.

✔ In 1989, Dr. David Spiegel, the Director of the Psychosocial Treatment Laboratory at Stanford University School of Medicine, conducted a landmark study of breast cancer. Women with metastasized breast cancer were randomly assigned to two research groups. Both groups received conventional medical care, such as surgery, chemotherapy, radiation, and medication. However, one set of women met in small support groups for 90 minutes once a week for a year. The groups were led by two therapists, one whose own breast cancer was in remission. The other (control) group received no special emotional support except from family and friends. Dr. Spiegel expected his study to show little difference between the two groups. To his amazement, however, he found that the women in the weekly support groups lived, on the average, twice as long as did the women who didn't have the formal support system. In fact, all those women in the control group had died, while most of the women in the support group were still living. Furthermore, the women in the support group who did die lived significantly longer than the nonsupport group women. It appears that the ability to honestly express fears and emotions in a supportive and loving environment adds a healing ingredient that traditional medical treatment lacks.

✔ Two researchers gave birth to the term *energy cardiology* in 1993. Dr. Gary Schwartz at the University of Arizona and Dr. Linda Russek of Harvard University began investigating how cells and organs, especially the heart, naturally store information once thought to exist only in the brain. Data for their investigations have come from an unusual area, heart transplant patients. Here is one woman's (brief) story about the intelligence of the heart:

In the spring of 1988, Claire Sylvia received the first heart-lung transplant in New England at Yale-New Haven Hospital. As Sylvia described in her book, A Change Of Heart (1997), after three days of living with her new organs, she began craving beer — something she never liked. As time went on, she found herself adding green pepper to all of her meals — a vegetable that she previously would remove from her food. And on the day she began driving again, her car "practically steered itself to the nearest Kentucky Fried Chicken." She hated fast food, but here she was craving chicken nuggets.

All her life, Sylvia suffered from low blood sugar, but now it vanished. Similar changes occurred in all aspects of her life. It wasn't until years later, after meeting her donor's family, that Sylvia learned how "Tim" [as she called her donor] loved beer, green peppers, and fast food and how so many other changes she was undergoing matched his personality, behavior and lifestyle. Sylvia isn't an exception; many heart transplant patients tell similar stories about unusual changes in their lives, but not all of them have had the opportunity to talk with their donors' families.

✔ The *Tufts University Health & Nutrition Letter* (October 2000) reported a study conducted by researchers in Sweden and Thailand. In the mid-1990s, these investigators discovered that people's emotional response to food affects how well their body absorbs nutrients. Researchers fed women from both cultures the same Thai dish of rice and vegetables spiced with chili paste, fish sauce, and coconut cream. The Thai women liked their meal and absorbed significantly more iron than did their Swedish counterparts who found the food too spicy. When that same meal was "all blended together in a high-speed mixer to form an unappetizing paste," Thai women's absorption of iron fell by 70 percent. The same significant reduction in iron absorption occurred when the Swedish women had to eat hamburger, string beans, and mashed potatoes (a meal that they usually liked) puréed into unappealing goop. Researchers believe that your emotional reaction to food directly affects your body's ability to produce digestive enzymes necessary for food absorption, as well as actually digesting that food properly.

The preceding examples of PNI research illustrate the close connection between your mind and body. Bodies naturally breakdown under the stresses of living. When you sever the mind-body connection, damages occur sooner, are more severe, and heal slower and less completely. The four techniques we present in this chapter help you to strengthen your mind-body bond — which in turn helps you to remain healthier and heal faster.

When it comes to managing change, the first place to begin is with yourself.

Meditation

Should we, or shouldn't we? That is the question. Given the discomfort of some people with the term *meditation,* should we risk writing about it? Obviously, we decided to. That's because meditation is rapidly gaining respectability in the health and scientific communities. It's no longer relegated to navel-gazing, blitzed-out hippies. It doesn't require that you join a cult or wander the Himalayas following gurus. Now, fiscally conservative insurance companies support meditation practice for fighting heart disease; hundreds of traditional medical centers use meditation as the core of their successful stress reduction programs; and the cautious National Institute of Health (NIH) is funding major research into meditation's unique ability to lower hypertension (high blood pressure) without drugs.

The questions are no longer Does meditation heal? or Does it improve the quality of your life? but rather How does it work? Scientists are trying to understand how 20 minutes of focused attention a day helps to reverse the damages of stress on your body, slow the aging process, heal a diseased heart, reduce chronic pain, sharpen your concentration, and increase mental alertness.

All this good stuff may sound like some flimflam, cure-all snake oil. But it isn't to the 11,000 people who have successfully completed the stress reduction program at the University of Massachusetts Medical Center or to Phil Jackson, the coach of the LA Lakers basketball team and past coach of the Chicago Bulls. For these people and hundreds of thousands like them, meditation improves their quality of life at home and their performance on the job (even when it's a basketball court). For a brief overview of the research on meditation, take a look at the sidebar "The science behind meditation."

Understanding meditation

Meditation crosses all religious and cultural boundaries. Whatever your beliefs and background, you can tailor meditation to fit your personal lifestyle. Simply stated, meditation increases your mental discipline, giving you more control in an out-of-control world.

You might call meditation a mental balancing act because you're actually developing two separate qualities simultaneously:

- **Concentration.** You sharpen your mind's focus. In meditation, your mind settles down to one sensation or object — learning to ignore all the other jabbering thoughts bouncing through your head. Concentration provides the power that allows mindfulness to develop.

- **Mindfulness.** You take your mind off automatic pilot, becoming aware of what's actually happening moment by moment. In the here-and-now world of meditation, you dwell less often in a haze-filled past or a non-existent future. Mindfulness grows as you settle down in the present moment and become comfortable with all experiences as they appear and disappear. (You can find more information about mindfulness in Chapter 21.)

With concentration, you focus your attention on one item, while mindfulness helps you notice when your concentration has slipped. The faster you notice when you've lost concentration, the quicker you return to your object of attention. Over time, concentration intensifies and mindfulness strengthens — which means chaotic thinking subsides.

The science behind meditation

During the past three decades, behavioral and medical researchers have investigated the influence of meditation on the human body. The following five studies give you a brief look at the diverse areas in which scientists have examined meditation's effects.

In 1978, R. Keith Wallace, a University of California at Los Angeles physiologist, studied the effects of meditation on aging. He used three biological markers for aging — blood pressure, the ability to see close up, and hearing — all of which are negatively affected by the aging process. He demonstrated that for long-term meditators, those biological capacities usually aged slower, and in many people, the aging process was reversed. In fact, meditators had a biological age five to 12 years younger than their actual chronological age.

In 1980, Charles Alexander, a Harvard psychologist, studied 60 residents in three separate nursing homes. All participants were over 80 years old. Some of the people were taught meditation, others received a nonmeditative relaxation technique, and the third group only performed creative word games. When the three groups were tested for follow up, the meditators scored the highest on low blood pressure and improved learning ability. They also reported feeling happier and younger than they did prior to meditating. However, the most remarkable results appeared three years later. When Alexander returned to the nursing homes, 24 of the participants in the relaxation and word-games groups had died — but all the meditators were still living.

In the late 1980s, Dr. Jay Glaser studied the effect of meditation on *DHEA* (dehydroepiandrosterone), a steroid secreted by the adrenal cortex. Now being considered as a "youth" hormone, DHEA reaches its maximum volume at about age 25 and declines until it reaches almost nothing by the end of life. In older people, higher levels of DHEA are associated with longer and healthier lives. Glaser compared the DHEA levels of 328 experienced meditators with those of 1,462 non-meditators. Dividing his subjects according to age and gender, Glaser evaluated their DHEA (specifically their dehydroepiandrosterone sulfate or DHEAS) levels. He found

- All women meditators had higher DHEAS levels then nonmeditating women.

- For eight out of the 11 men's groups, meditators had higher DHEAS levels. Specifically, in the over-45 groups, meditating men had 23 percent more DHEAS then their nonmeditating peers.

Also, in the late 1980s, the medical researchers at the University of Massachusetts Medical School looked at the effects of meditation on *psoriasis* (scaly skin patches caused by increased rate of skin cell growth). Dr. Jeffrey Bernhard in the division of dermatology, Dr. Jean Kristeller in behavioral medicine, and Dr. Jon Kabat-Zinn at the stress reduction clinic studied 23 patients with psoriasis. All subjects received the standard ultraviolet light treatments in the phototherapy clinic. Randomly assigned, one group of people meditated during their treatment sessions, while the others stood in the round light booth without meditating. Treatments occurred three times a week over 12 weeks. The researches found

- Scaly skin patches on the people meditating healed faster than patches on the nonmeditators.

- Ten out of the 13 meditators had totally clear skin by the end of the 12 weeks, while only two of the nonmeditators had skin that healed in that same time period.

In 1999, M. Specca, L. Carlson, D. Goodey, and M. Angen at the Tom Baker Cancer Center in Alberta, Canada, assessed the effects of meditation on 90 cancer patients' moods and stress levels. Outpatients (mean age 51 years with a variety of cancer diagnoses and stages of illness) were randomly assigned to either a meditation group or the control group that received no meditation training. All people completed the "Profile of Mood States" and the "Symptoms of Stress Inventory" before and after the intervention — with equivalent mean scores for both groups. At the end of the seven-week study, the meditators had significantly lower scores for depression, anxiety, anger, and confusion than the control subjects. The meditators also had significantly fewer overall symptoms of stress, such as cardiopulmonary and gastrointestinal symptoms, irritability, depression, and mental disorganization.

In his book *Sacred Hoops,* Phil Jackson described how meditation helped him become a "more focused" basketball player and coach by developing "an intimate knowledge of my mental processes" on the court. For example, Jackson writes, as a coach, "I often get agitated by bad calls, but years of meditation practice have taught me how to find that still point within so that I can argue passionately with the refs without being overwhelmed by anger." (Unfortunately, many great coaches have self destructed because they never found their own "still point within.")

It might help you to understand better what meditation is, by seeing what it isn't. Mediation isn't trying to blank out your mind so that you become a zombie; engaging in hypnosis; becoming an emotionless vegetable; performing a relaxation exercise; or escaping reality.

Meditation is focusing your mind and examining your thoughts. By increasing mental discipline, you gain greater power and control over your life. (Something that most people can use more of.)

Should you want more information, *Meditation For Dummies* (Hungry Minds, Inc.) by Stephan Bodian gives you an excellent review of the topic. We recommend this book not because it's another *...For Dummies* reference, but because Bodian presents accurate, clear, and detailed information about all aspects of meditation.

Setting the stage

Meditation is one of the few things in life that's healthy for your mind and body, but doesn't drain your bank account, require fancy equipment, or demand extensive travel. You can do it in your own home, sitting on your favorite chair, and wearing whatever you want (but we also show you how to meditate in less then ideal conditions, too). All you need is five things:

✔ **A quiet place.** It's hard to concentrate with kids battling, music blasting, and the TV blaring. So, whenever you decide to meditate, make sure that it's a quiet time. Many people find that early in the morning, before the house comes alive, works best. But that may be tough for you night owls, so it's okay to wait until every one has snuggled in for the night. What's important is that you find a time and place that's right for you and one that also gives you peace and privacy.

✔ **A comfortable and stable position.** You don't have to twist yourself into nasty-looking pretzel-like shapes. In fact, a comfortable chair is fine, so is a cushion on the floor, or even sitting on your bed (if that's the only private place you've got). An erect, nonforced posture makes breathing easier for you; in turn, breathing relaxes your body. If you use a chair, however, you might need a pillow under your feet so that the chair doesn't dig into the underside of your thighs. (For those readers with bad backs, it's also okay for you to lie on the floor.)

What's important is that you sit with ease, while maintaining a strong, straight (not rigid) back. Once you're comfortable and securely seated, then keep that position during your entire meditation. You should maintain complete physical stillness. If physical pain should arise, sit for awhile focusing on your discomfort, like a scientist looking at an experiment. If the intensity of the pain increases, then slowly, with awareness, shift your position. Meditation isn't supposed to be a test of your pain tolerance.

✔ **An object on which to focus.** Most people's "minds" really aren't very disciplined. Your thoughts have had a lifetime of doing what they wanted, when they wanted — chattering away, fretting, fantasizing, and bouncing between past and future worlds. By focusing your mind on one thing — your breath, a word/mantra, an image, a "centering prayer," or a picture — you calm and reduce unwanted distractions. Not only does your mind slow down, so does your body.

Take your breath, for example. (We use it as our "object" throughout this section.) Don't think about what your breathing is or should be doing. Just feel it coming in and going out. Nothing fancy. And every time your mind flits off, such as to your overdue expense report or next Saturday night's party, simply bring your focus back to your breath. If your mind wanders a thousand times, then you gently bring it back a thousand times.

✔ **A mindful alertness.** Thoughts, sounds, body sensations, and emotions may drift into your awareness — but you don't concentrate on them. You acknowledge the bird chirping, the itch in your ear, or your restless-ness, and then you let them drift off. Meditation doesn't block out experiences, but rather it helps you become more conscious of what's actually occurring around and in you — moment by moment. And what you'll find is that nothing really hangs around for long. Like the clouds in the sky, sounds, physical sensations and emotions form, dissolve, and then reform into something else.

✔ **A nonjudgmental attitude.** There aren't any "rights" or "wrongs" in what you experience while meditating. They are just experiences that are neither "good" nor "bad." Your mind flies off to a marketing presentation — that's okay, bring it back to your breath, doing so without criticism. Thoughts pop into your head that you feel aren't socially acceptable — that's okay, too. Just come back to your breath and don't judge yourself. You feel frustrated because you can't concentrate for longer than two breaths — notice (neutrally) your self-criticism and then return to your breath. Let the time that you're meditating be moments of unconditional acceptance — so rare in today's hypercritical world.

Making meditation user friendly

How does the average person, overwhelmed by work and personal commitments, find the time to meditate — to reduce tension and anxiety, slow the aging process, and heal a stress-damaged body? Here is the way that some people creatively integrated meditation into their lives. They do the following:

✔ Sit for ten minutes in the car before getting out and going into the office.

✔ Close their office door, forward the phone to voice mail, and spend five to ten minutes quietly focusing on their breath or special word.

✔ Use the quiet time in the car to meditate while waiting for their children during soccer practice, ballet lessons, or band practice.

✔ Walk to the coffee machine conscious of each step and breath.

✔ Grab 20 minutes to meditate on airplanes.

✔ Concentrate on their breath while standing in a line at banks, stores, or airports.

The next time you're in a long airport ticket line, watch disgruntled people shifting from foot to foot, looking at their watches, sighing loudly, and getting even more agitated — and remind yourself that they're damaging their immune systems.

With creativity, you'd be surprised the places and time you can find for meditating.

Giving it a try

Here is a simple process for meditating. Should you find that you want more instruction, then turn to the back of *Meditation For Dummies.* Bodian gives you suggestions for further reading and a variety of meditation centers, for all major religions and the nonreligious.

Give meditation a try. You have nothing to lose and a lot to gain.

1. **Find a quiet place and a comfortable sitting position.**

   If you've got a bad back, go ahead and lie on the floor.

2. **Decide on the length of your session.**

   For you first-timers, you may want to try ten minutes. Have a watch or clock that you can see, but please don't set an alarm.

3. **Rest your hands lightly on your thighs, in your lap, or any place that feels comfortable for you.**

   But wherever you decide, keep them there for the entire sitting.

4. **Close your eyes.**

   This is usually the best way for first-timers to begin.

5. **Feel your body settle into your meditation position and feel the chair or cushion against you.**

   Get a sense of the room around you.

6. **Begin focusing on your breath.**

   Let it move at its own rate — just feeling your inhalation and exhalation, allowing the process of breathing to find its own natural rhythm. When Beth does this, she says the word "exhale" on the out breath, and then just feels her in breath. Some people label both the inhalation and exhalation. Others just sit with the sensations. With practice, you'll find what works best.

7. **Focus on where you most clearly feel your breath.**

   That may be as the air enters and leaves your nostrils, as your abdomen moves in and out, or somewhere in between. The right place is what's natural for you.

8. **Notice that when you complete an inhalation, and before you begin the exhalation, there's a slight pause.**

   Also notice the pause between the end of your exhalation and the start of your next inhalation. Don't do anything with those pauses; just a quiet awareness is fine.

9. **Watch how your mind flits from your breath.**

   All of a sudden, you find yourself thinking about an unfinished report, worrying about what to fix for dinner, remembering a person you haven't talk to for 15 years, feeling bored, dreaming about the perfect date, getting antsy, worrying about bills you haven't paid, or wanting to sleep. As soon as you become aware of your thoughts, acknowledge what you were thinking, let them go, and then settle back with your breath.

Why all the fuss about the breath

In some traditions, the breath means more than the simple exchange of carbon dioxide for oxygen. For example, the Greek word *anima*, the Latin word *spirtus*, the Hebrew word *ruach*, and the Sanskrit (ancient Indian language) *brahman* all mean the same thing — breath and spirit or soul.

Breathing, in its exchange of gasses with the environment, unites all living things. In fact, all vertebrates breathe in basically the same way. You might call breathing a universal process. Furthermore, by its constant cycle of inhalation and exhalation, it mirrors life's cycles of birth and death. Breath mirrors life itself. In fact, it's what jump-started your life when you were born and never leaves you until you take your last breath.

Dr. Lucille S. Rubin, a New York-based trainer of CEOs, actors, anchors, and politicians, teaches that a powerful and compelling voice comes from deep inside a body firmly grounded in its breath. It also comes from what people know as diaphragmatic breathing.

From a more scientific perspective, James S. Gordon, clinical professor of psychiatry at the Georgetown University School of Medicine, considers slow, deep breathing one of the best antistress medicines there is. Deep abdominal breathing reduces heart rate, decreases blood pressure, allows muscles to relax, and helps to calm the mind. Dr. Andrew Weil, director of the Program in Integrative Medicine and clinical professor of medicine at the University of Arizona, reports that correct breathing also improves digestion, decreases anxiety, and enhances sleep.

10. **Accept nonjudgmentally each time your mind wanders from your breath.**

    It happens over and over and over again. And that's okay. You're just noticing what your mind has always been doing, but you never had a chance to "watch" it before now. Also, don't worry that you have less "self-control" than any one else — everyone has thoughts that jabber and jump around, even experienced meditators. Part of meditation is coming face to face with a rowdy, unruly mind. The fact that you're now aware of the issue means that you've started fixing it.

11. **Acknowledge sounds that you hear.**

    Whether they are dogs barking, the next-door neighbor's telephone ringing, or a motorcycle roaring by, acknowledge them. Then let all sounds come and go, always returning to your breath. If a sound persists, however, it's okay to shift your focus from your breath to that sound. It now becomes the object of your attention. When that sound is no longer intrusive, return to your breath.

12. **Acknowledge physical sensations that you feel.**

    Letting an itch continue to itch without scratching it or a tightness in your shoulders feel tight without shifting to get rid of it. Watch what your mind does when you feel something that you don't like. Do you fight it, pull away from it, feel scared, or get angry that you are in discomfort? Remember, regardless of what sensations you're experiencing, you're safely sitting in your quiet place. When the sensations fade, (and they usually do), return to your breath.

13. **Stay seated for a few minutes when your meditation time is over.**

    Let your mind and body slowly readjust to the chaotic world around you. But notice how much calmer you may feel, less caught up in all the soap-opera-like dramas. Remember, you always have your breath to give you some breathing room when work or personal situations become too "tight" or intense for you.

Meditation mirrors the unpredictability of life. In some sittings, you find great peace and concentration, while at other times you feel agitated and distracted. It's also like people, pets, and snowflakes — no two meditation sessions are ever alike. So, in every meditation, (to add another analogy), sit like the serene mountain that faces both sunny days and raging storms — always with firmness and equanimity.

Meditating their way

Tony Schwartz, a journalist and ghostwriter of Donald Trump's book *The Art of The Deal,* found himself trapped for almost two hours in a pitch-black, commuter train under New York City. While hundreds of other passengers became angry and stressed out, Schwartz meditated. Describing himself as the kind of "impatient person who considers waiting in traffic jams a personal affront," he turned to meditation to help him avoid a would-be traumatic experience. In his book, *What Really Matters,* Schwartz tells how he closed his eyes, repeated the word "one" silently "while breathing slowly and rhythmically." He became so absorbed in the meditative process that he lost track of time. At the end of 90 minutes, when power was restored, he felt "as relaxed as I could ever remember feeling." Not so with his trapped companions.

One woman, with three children, who worked and went to college, couldn't find a time or a place to sit quietly. Creatively, she turned washing dishes into her meditation. The children knew that dishwashing had become their mother's quiet time so they stayed out of the kitchen (not a bad deal for them). When she rinsed the dishes and loaded the dishwasher, she focused on her breath, listened to the sounds of dishes being washed, and felt the dishes in her hands and the warm flowing water. An experience that she once considered an unpleasant chore became a time for mindfulness, peace, and healing.

Exercise: Cardiovascular and Strength Training

Most people don't think of the run-on-the-treadmill, break-a-sweat exercise as mind-body fitness. That's because when they perform traditional exercise, people disengage their minds and let their bodies do all the work. However, pounding on a stepper or pumping iron is not the time to shut down your mind — not if you want to get the highest return on your investment and minimize injuries. Sports scientists have documented that exercisers who mentally focus on the muscles they're working actually engage more muscle fiber in the exercise, which means that they receive a more productive workout for the time spent.

Professional athletes now realize that personal power and professional success come from paying attention to the mind, as well as the body. Thirty years ago, Jim Loehr became a pioneer in sports psychology. Now he heads one of the leading sports motivational and training centers, LGE Performance Systems, in Orlando, Florida. Not only do athletes from around the world come to train at LGE, so do business executives. In fact, LGE trainers consider the mental, emotional, and physical demands on the Corporate Athlete frequently greater than those faced by professional athletes. So, LGE developed a special mind-body sports program specifically for stressed out, under-exercised executives.

Because only a few lucky souls attend LGE, we've put together our own brief overview of exercise for the rest of you. And you may also want to check out *Workouts For Dummies* (Hungry Minds, Inc.) by Tamilee Webb. By now you're pretty familiar with the benefits you obtain from exercising, so we won't destroy a lot of trees discussing the decades of research filling medical journals. Quickly, here's a summary of the great and wonderful things you get with moderate exercise (next we talk about what you get with more-than-moderate exercise). You:

- Maintain a healthy, fit body that handles stress more effectively
- Prevent muscle and bone loss (for both men and women)
- Have an easier time maintaining the "ideal" weight
- Protect joints and ligaments so that they don't get injured easily
- Improve cardiovascular fitness
- Improve the efficiency of your digestive system
- Sleep better
- Increase energy
- Reduce stress

Damaged cells = a damaged body

In the mid-1950s, Dr. Denham Harman, a scientist at the University of Nebraska, introduced the idea that *free radicals* might be a major cause of aging. When you convert food to energy or exercise intensely, your body produces atoms with an extra electron. These highly reactive, electrically charged atoms are called *free radicals*. In the attempt to neutralize their electric charge, they steal electrons from healthy cells, thereby damaging and even destroying those cells. Over time, as free radicals increase, so do the number of damaged and destroyed cells — which in turn reduces your ability to bounce back from injuries and fight diseases.

Some scientists believe that aging results from your body's inability to repair the damage that free radicals inflict on healthy cells millions of times a year. Additionally, free radicals are thought to contribute to life-shortening diseases such as strokes and heart attacks.

Like most things in life, however, free radicals aren't 100 percent bad. They do help your immune system's white blood cells bond to and kill invading bacteria and viruses. You just don't want an over abundance of free radicals in your system.

Now, here's what you get when you disengage your mind, stop listening to your body, and keep pushing yourself to exhaustion. You:

- ✔ Feel sluggish and tired all the time
- ✔ Increase the number of aches and pains
- ✔ Traumatize joints
- ✔ Have less time for muscles to heal and repair
- ✔ Diminish or lose hard-earned fitness gains
- ✔ Become more susceptible to injuries
- ✔ Impair the immune system
- ✔ Add stress upon the very stress that you're trying to release

When you sit for hours bleary eyed in front of a computer, scrunched in an airplane cabin breathing recycled air, or locked in a conference room fighting for head count, your body isn't doing what it was genetically designed to do. If you can't spend your days paddling a kayak, hunting wild game, or walking behind a plow, then you'd better find other ways to get the blood "flowing" and the muscles flexing. Humans weren't engineered to live sedentary lives — not if they want long and healthy ones.

Your two options for getting fitter, healthier and stress resilient are exercises that speed up heart rate, called *cardiovascular training,* and exercises that build muscles, known as *strength training* (or weight lifting). Because each helps your body in different ways, cardiovascular and strength training complement each other. They aren't mutually exclusive. Here's a brief look at what you get from each activity and why you need both of them.

Cardiovascular workout for your heart

Your heart is probably one of the most important muscles you own. When it stops working, you stop living. A great way to keep it strong is to give your heart a workout — like any other muscle. When you run, swim, dance, inline skate, walk, or take a spin class, you improve your cardiovascular system in four ways:

- ✔ Increase the volume of blood your heart pumps with each beat (especially important if you're more than 40 years old, because your maximum heart rate begins to decline).

- ✔ Make blood vessels healthier, which in turn improves circulation.

- ✔ Increase heart-protective HCL cholesterol levels.

- ✔ Use oxygen more effectively because you have more enzymes metabolizing your oxygen.

A healthy heart means more energy, reduced risk of heart disease, reduced risk of diabetes, and improved reasoning powers because you're getting more oxygen to the brain. Of course, don't forget that you also burn calories, while targeting the abdominal fat deposits that seem to suddenly appear from nowhere (along with the years and gray hair).

Strength training for your muscles and bones

It's time to trash all the false information about lifting weights. For most people, pushing weights doesn't build massive muscles. To bulk up with muscles, you've got to have a rare genetic predisposition, like Arnold Schwarzenegger (which very few people have). Or you're taking performance-enhancing drugs known as steroids, which is not recommended unless you are under a doctor's care. Otherwise, weight training won't give you ponderous pectorals (your chest muscles) or beefy biceps (your upper arm muscles). You just get stronger muscles that rev up your metabolism and build stronger bones that stay healthy longer.

Mad for muscles

As recently as two decades ago, weight lifting was relegated to muscle-bound bodybuilding fanatics. That's changing. Scientists from major medical centers now know that healthy bodies and minds depend upon maintaining strong muscles. The following is a quick overview of the data that researchers keep pumping out about strength training for a better you.

In 1985, Daniel Rudman, M.D., a scientist from the Department of Medicine of the Medical College of Wisconsin, described in the *Journal of the American Geriatrics Society* how body composition changes with age. When you're a healthy youth, your body weight is about 10 percent bone, 30 percent muscle, and 20 percent fat (the other 40 percent being composed of other organs and water). At age 30, inactive adults begin losing muscles at the rate of one-half pound per year, or five pounds per decade. By the time you reach 75, a typical body composition is now about 8 percent bone (occasionally even less for women), 15 percent muscle, and 40 percent fat. What happens is that as your muscles decrease with age, the calories that you once used for their maintenance now get stored as fat.

According to Dr. Miriam Nelson and researchers at the USDA Human Nutrition Research Center on Aging at Tufts University in Boston, weight training not only stops that downward aging spiral, but reverses it. The more muscles you have, the more metabolically active your body is, which means you burn more calories, which also means less fat around your middle. In addition, your body absorbs glucose more effectively, reducing your chances for adult diabetes. Scientists also know that strength training improves balance and flexibility, prevents bone loss, maintains the body's speed and power, and prevents injuries when playing Saturday morning softball.

Not too bad for a 30-minute, twice-a-week weight workout.

Bedazzled by bones

Most people have heard that women get osteoporosis as they age, but men do, too. Maybe they don't lose as much bone mass as women do, but if they're not careful, over time, their bones also become thin, porous, and brittle — and a fall can break a hip.

At first glance, bones seem to be, well, lifeless. Even the word *skeleton* comes from the Greek word meaning *dried up*. But your bones are just the opposite. There're dynamic, living tissue that is continuously renewing itself. Over 600 separate bones provide the internal framework for your body, giving you support, shape, and a place for your muscles to attach. Bones protect more vulnerable, softer internal organs such as your heart, lungs, and brain. The calcium you need for healthy nerve and muscle cells comes from your bones. Plus, the soft-center bone marrow forms red blood cells, certain disease-fighting white blood cells, and blood platelets. Given what they do for you, shouldn't you keep a healthy set of bones?

Until recently, it was believed that after 30 years of age, you could only slow down bone loss. However, the latest research at the Human Nutrition Research Center on Aging at Tufts University indicates that strength training, at any age, actually adds bone, instead of just reducing bone loss. Weight-bearing exercises cause your bones to become stronger and thicker in order to accommodate the pull from your muscles. (Now that's what you call good planning and engineering.)

Wild about weights

The winds of change are not only disrupting the way experts think about strength training, but also how to actually pump those irons. Originally, weight trainers emphasized lifting a moderate amount of weight for ten to 12 repetitions, for two or three sets. In other words, if you were doing biceps curls, you ended up producing 20 to 36 repetitions in total. When you add the biceps time to working out 12 other muscle groups, you're now spending an hour or more moving weights around a mirrored room. Add in the fact that you should be exercising three times a week in order to show improvement, your life outside of work becomes one continuous set of weight repetitions. No wonder health clubs have a high dropout rate.

Long, drawn out hours in the weight room are becoming history. About two decades ago, the winds began shifting from multiple-sets weight training to single-sets training — called High Intensity Training (HIT). It all started with Arthur Jones, the inventor of the Nautilus equipment. He developed his machines as tools for making exercise more intense, efficient, and productive, while at the same time safer than free weights and the older equipment. Based on his extensive research, Jones discovered that a workout where you pushed muscles to failure (can't move the weight no matter how hard you try) produced faster muscle strength than did the traditional two or three sets using lighter weights. Because HIT is so intense, you train just twice a week allowing your body time to rest and repair. Jones followed his Nautilus breakthrough with another success in 1987. He designed the MedX equipment for medical and rehabilitation centers to help patients recover faster from orthopedic surgery and sports injuries using the HIT method.

"When it comes to exercise, your time and energy are finite . . . so use what little you've got wisely," said Glen Peavey, President of High Efficiency Training in Wadsworth, Illinois. As a HIT trainer for almost a quarter of a century, Peavey has seen the powerful effects of "quality" training over the "quantity" approach. Applying the HIT philosophy to training professional athletes and competitive body builders, as well as a husband and wife in their 80s who wanted to continue playing tennis, Peavey knows that HIT works for all fitness levels and ages. He believes that "business professionals demand efficient use of their time in the gym. With HIT, they gain significant muscle strength with only 30- minute sessions, twice a week." If you want a little more information about HIT, read the sidebar "High Intensity Training (HIT) in a nutshell."

High Intensity Training (HIT) in a nutshell

We'll be up front with you: HIT is tough, so you'd better be stout of heart if you want to get the most out of it. Most people lifting weights usually avoid the last couple of grueling repetitions because they think they're avoiding the danger of injury, when in fact they're actually avoiding the most productive of all their muscle-building repetitions. With HIT, individuals must override their instinct to quit when they start feeling their body failing — for some people that's physically and mentally uncomfortable (to say the least).

Investigators at the Center for Exercise Science, University of Florida, have shown that "one-set

of failure" strength training produces results equal or superior to the traditional multiple-sets workout. In other words, when using HIT, your muscles receive the most effective workout.

You may be wondering what prevents injuries when a person lifts such a heavy weight to failure. The secret is slow, controlled movements with perfect form and continuous breathing. Then injuries never occur, but your strength increases significantly.

Because HIT is not your run-of-the-mill strength training, we recommend that you find an experienced trainer to give you a safe and solid foundation. You can find excellent information about HIT on the Internet at www.cyberpump.com. The site also offers extensive links to other related sites.

Mind-body renewal

If you're going to pound your body into a firmer, stronger you, then you'd better also give it plenty of rest. All that stress and strain causes microscopic muscle tears that need repair. All that pushing to "your personal best" requires limbering and stretching to prevent loss of flexibility. Therefore, take time to let your body heal and rebuild, making you even stronger.

Don't get warm-ups and stretching confused. They're different animals. Warming up is a lighter version of your exercise. It gets the heart, lungs, and muscles ready to perform at an optimal and safe level. Some sports require their own specific warm-ups, which may also include light stretching. But focused stretching is more for cool down. It prevents your muscles, tendons, and ligaments from tightening, begins the recovery process by allowing tired muscles to replenish nutrients, removes toxins, and prevents injuries during your next exercise session. You need both a warm-up and an end-of-exercise stretch.

If you're going to force your mind to endure exhaustive runs and push into failure with HIT, then it needs a little recovery time. Meditation (we discuss it earlier in the chapter) is an excellent way to detoxify your mind. And/or you can incorporate yoga, Pilates or tai chi (we discuss these workouts in the following three sections) into your exercise regime, as a way of balancing mind-body and helping release stress that accumulates with a tough workout. The last thing you want to do is over exercise, which intensifies the stress that you're already lugging around with you.

Yoga

Around 5,000 years ago in India, yoga was born. *Yoga* is a Sanskrit (ancient Indian language) word that means *yoke* or *join*. It's the practice of uniting the mind and body while moving, slowly and consciously, from one posture to another. What yoga was like five millenniums ago nobody knows for sure because, over the years, it adapted to the time and place in which it found itself. Today, about eight different branches of yoga exist. The most popular with Westerners is Hatha yoga (a Sanskrit word pronounced *haht-ha*). In fact, it's this form of yoga that is mostly widely practiced today. It's what you find taught in health clubs, offered at spas, demonstrated on videotapes, and presented in how-to yoga books. And it's the form that we focus on in this section.

Some people believe that Yoga is a Hindu religious practice. True, some followers of Hinduism practice it, but yoga came into being about 1,500 years before the religion did. And yes, many of the great yoga masters have come from India, but in the past decades, western yoga teachers have also developed styles to meet the needs of 21st-century practitioners. Yoga, like yogurt and won tons, has become universal.

Discovering the benefits

What hasn't changed during yoga's journey through history is its focus on balancing the mind and body — for providing health and healing. While yoga hasn't yet received the same scientific scrutiny by the western medical community that meditation has, many doctors still recommend it, and some insurance companies provide coverage for yoga. Some of the areas in which researchers have begun discovering yoga's healing powers include

- ✔ Stress
- ✔ Hypertension (high blood pressure)
- ✔ Injuries
- ✔ Epilepsy
- ✔ Arthritis
- ✔ AIDs
- ✔ Multiple Sclerosis

  ✔ Carpal tunnel syndrome

  ✔ Physical disabilities

  ✔ Aging — loss of muscle, flexibility and balance

  ✔ Bronchial asthma

  ✔ Diabetes

  ✔ Pain management

Looking at Hatha Yoga

In western countries, Hatha yoga (which we now refer to as simply yoga) has 11 to 13 different styles (depending upon whom you read). You can go from the very gentle Restorative yoga developed by Dr. Judith Lasater, a physical therapist, all the way to sweat-drenching, muscle-quivering Power yoga founded by Beryl and Thom Birch. And in between, you can dance your way through Kali Ray's flowing Tri-yoga. And for those of you who want a more traditional yoga experience there are centers and institutes all over the world providing Kundalini, Anaada, or Integral yoga (just to name a few).

Regardless of which style of yoga you choose, the foundation remains the same — stretching and strengthening movements enhanced by focusing on your breath and maintaining concentration. Some people have called yoga "meditation in movement" because it requires the same mental discipline that sitting meditation does. Therefore, for those of you who get too antsy in a sitting meditation, yoga is a great place to begin reducing stress, with the added benefits of increasing strength and flexibility.

The following sections look at yoga's three fundamental components.

Postures

Postures are the *asanas* (a Sanskrit word pronounced *ah-sah-nahs*) or yoga exercises that you do. Of the 2,000 possible postures (some of which only highly trained, pretzel-twisting contortionists can master), you'll probably learn about 20 basic ones. If you're just starting out in yoga, don't worry — each asana has a level for beginners, intermediates, and advanced.

Whatever your skill level, you begin where you're most comfortable. Yoga isn't a competition to see who can stretch the farthest or contort their body into the most bizarre postures. It's all about understanding and respecting your own abilities.

Asanas were designed to work together. Therefore, every yoga routine has a specific sequence of moves — each position building on the one that came before it. Within each individual asana, you move through three stages: getting into the pose, holding it, and coming out of it.

If you practice yoga with more than one teacher, view more than one video-tape, or study more than one book, get ready for inconsistencies. You'll find that some asanas with the same name may have slightly different moves or body positions. Likewise, you'll notice that similar positions may have different names. This is all part of yoga being a "living," and dynamic system — not something mummified from ancient times.

Breath control

Pranayama (a Sanskrit work pronounced *Prah-nah-yah-mah*) is the science of correct breathing. In Sanskrit, *Prana* means "life's energy" and *yama* means "discipline." The breath fuels your body and focuses your mind. Breathing helps increase muscle and ligament flexibility, while releasing mental and physical tension. As you move through each asana, you have specific places for inhalation and exhalation, consciously structuring when and how you breathe.

Human beings can go for several weeks without food and several days without liquid. But after four minutes without taking a breath, you permanently damage the brain and other vital organs. You're so dependent upon oxygen that in a 24-hour period, you take about 20,000 breaths. During your lifetime, you'll probably inhale and exhale more than a hundred million times.

There is a saying from the lands in the East that gave the West meditation and yoga: As the breath goes, so goes the body.

Concentration

In yoga, mindfulness is called *Dharana* (a Sanskrit word pronounced *dhah-rah-nah*) or mental focus. You spend less time fuming about the past or fretting over the future. You turn off the automatic pilot and tune in to the sensations that arise moment-by moment — while stretching, lifting, balancing, or simply holding a position.

Most people live disconnected from their bodies — that is, until they get high blood pressure, injure a joint, tear a muscle, experience heart pains, get cancer, or face death. For some individuals, yoga re-introduces them to the bodily structure that houses them 24 hours a day. Going through the asanas and focusing on their breath, people begin noticing what's actually happening in their bodies, including where they've been storing a lifetime of stress, hurt, and anger. They also learn how to consciously release that tension and avoid adding to it.

Ancient yoga masters describe five possible mind-states that relate to concentration. Most people's minds bounce around the first three states, which reduce their productivity, increase mistake making, and intensify stress. But some fortunate individuals master their minds, entering the last state — which athletes call *the zone*. Practicing yoga can help you achieve the maximum concentration in all areas of your life, not just on your mat.

The following are the states in which your mind can exist:

- **Agitated.** You feel distressed and anxious.
- **Distracted.** You're preoccupied with the past or future, making it difficult to focus on what's in front of you.
- **Dull.** You lack energy and alertness.
- **Focused.** You determinedly hold your thoughts on one activity.
- **Absorption.** You're totally engaged. You and the activity have become one. This is the ultimate in concentration — and the goal of yoga.

Finding yoga for every body

Whether you're a well-toned, limber, vegetarian, nonsmoking runner, or a flabby, stiff, meat-eating, smoking couch-potato, or some where in between, you can do yoga. There are postures that challenge your athletic toughness and those that offer a nonthreatening starting place. Plus, "every body" needs time to release stress and rejuvenate before going back out to the glass-and-steel jungle.

If you're intrigued by yoga, do we have a great place for you to begin — *Yoga For Dummies* (Hungry Minds, Inc.) by Dr. Georg Feuerstein and Dr. Larry Payne. (You knew we were going to recommend a *...For Dummies* book, didn't you?) The authors provide an outstanding down-to-earth, comprehensive reference for exploring all aspects of yoga. At the end of the book, you even get a wide-ranging list of resources for practicing at home, in a health club, or at a yoga center.

Pilates

Until the early 1990s, Pilates (pronounced *puh-lah-tease*) was the best-kept secret in the world of health and fitness. Practiced mainly by athletes and performing artists — people whose paycheck depended upon maintaining strong and healthy bodies — Pilates entered the world of health clubs, spas, and bookstores only after Hollywood celebrities had discovered it.

Pilates isn't another Sanskrit word, but the last name of Joseph H. Pilates, a German immigrant who created this method. You might say that Pilates is similar to yoga — but with a Westerner's approach to mind-body exercise. With Pilates, you:

- Strengthen muscles
- Improve flexibility

✔ Release stress

✔ Correct spine and body alignment

✔ Reduce back pain

✔ Heal athletic injuries

✔ Improve balance and posture

✔ Develop deep breathing

✔ Release neck and shoulder tension

✔ Strengthen your abdomen/core/powerhouse

Because Pilates is relatively new to the world of mind-body techniques, scientists haven't yet put it through their rigorous double-blind studies. Instead, support for this exercise practice comes in testimonials from people who stay in shape as they age, stay injury-free as they push their bodies (on the playing field or the movie set), and stay balanced during demanding and stressful performances (on the ski slopes or in the office).

The journey: From a prisoner-of-war camp to your local health club

Born outside of Dusseldorf, Germany, in 1880, Joseph Pilates grew up sickly, suffering from asthma, rickets, and rheumatic fever. Deciding to transform his body and health, he trained in yoga, karate, gymnastics, and boxing. Out of his various experiences, Pilates designed a method to strengthen both his mind and body that incorporated Eastern and Western principles. As his highly successful conditioning program spread through Germany during the early 1900s, Kaiser Wilhelm II asked Pilates to train the elite military troops. But being a pacifist, Pilates refused and left his homeland for England.

When World War I erupted, Pilates, with other Germans, found himself locked away in a prisoner-of-war camp. There, he began teaching his method to fellow prisoners. Their health and fitness improved so significantly that the prison guards also became Pilates' students. Eventually, Pilates' exercises became a mandatory fitness routine for everyone in the camp. After the war, Pilates continued improving upon and teaching his new method. With the help of one of his postwar students, boxing great, Max Schmelling, Pilates immigrated to New York City in 1926.

He opened his first studio on 8th Avenue, calling his method *The Art of Contrology* — a science and art for developing and coordinating the body-mind-spirit through movement under strict control of the will. (With a name and mission like that, he'd never have made it today.) Dance greats like Martha Graham and George Balanchine became avid followers and sent their own students to Pilates. Eventually, he caught the marketing spirit and changed the method's name to *The Pilates Method of Body Conditioning.* (Thank heaven.) By word of mouth, people like Madonna, Gregory Peck, Julia Roberts, Patrick Swayze, and Jessica Lange signed up. The San Francisco 49ers football team incorporated The Pilates Method into their training. Doctors, physical therapists, and chiropractors have also turned to Pilates for healing injuries.

The two best ways for learning about Pilates is to attend a class or watch a videotape, but neither of these opportunities come with your book. Therefore, the next best alternative is to understand how Pilates came into being. (See the sidebar "The journey: From a prisoner-of-war camp to your local health club.")

The ins and outs

Pilates and yoga are kissin' cousins. Both techniques focus on integrating the mind and body, using slow controlled movements, maintaining a deep concentration, and controlling your breath. The main difference is that in yoga you often hold positions, but in Pilates, your body often engages in repetitive movement focusing on a specific area of the body or muscle group. For those of you who get bored and restless staying in one yoga position for awhile, Pilates offers a more active alternative to releasing stress, improving balance, and conditioning your body. With almost 500 different movements from which to choose, Pilates requires a lifetime of learning.

Regardless of what type of equipment you use (we tell you more about that later in the section "The stuff you need and don't need") or what particular exercise you're doing, Pilates requires that you:

- ✓ **Keep your mind focused.** Here it is again — mindfulness — a total concentration on your body. You feel each muscle as it contracts and stretches. You're aware of how each joint rotates. You make each movement with precision. It's all about mental discipline.

- ✓ **Move with flow.** Every exercise takes you through a wide range of motions, requiring multiple repetitions (anywhere from five to ten reps). The goal is to avoid rushed or jerky movements. Rather, you develop a slow, natural rhythm as you progress through a specific routine.

- ✓ **Coordinate your breath with movement.** Pilates looks deceptively simple, but, when done correctly, it's exhaustive work. Your body needs plenty of clean oxygen for nourishment and lots of opportunity to flush out toxins.

- ✓ **Work from your *powerhouse*.** In Pilates the single most important section of your body is deep within your abdomen. It's your physical core, an area between the bottom of your ribs and the "line" across your hips. All movement originates from your powerhouse, even when you're using your arms and legs. A strong powerhouse aligns your posture, improves your balance, and protects you against back pain.

The stuff you need and don't need

People who experience Pilates for the first time shake their head in wonder at all the bizarre contraptions that line the room. You almost feel like you're in a torture chamber of the Inquisition. But never fear, you get a lot of gain from all the "equipment" without the pain.

When you think about it, the strange paraphernalia that Joseph Pilates created is a natural result of his time in a prisoner-of-war camp. He used what was readily available to him, such as walls, mattresses, bedsprings, ropes, chairs, barrels, and metal bands. Here's a lineup of the equipment:

- **The mat.** Just that — a simple exercise mat. But there's nothing simple about the tough, gymnastic-like workout you can do on it.

- **The wall.** You use a wall to limber the spine and stretch the hamstrings. It's a great way to release tension and you can do it anywhere.

- **The Cadillac (or the springs).** This is a table with trapeze-like bars, straps, and cuffs. Usually found in only The Pilates Method of Body Conditioning studios, it's for stretching, moving, and stabilizing the spine. (For home use, you can attach special springs and hooks to a door frame.)

- **The Barrel.** Think of a barrel cut in half lengthwise with the open-end face down. Using the curved top, you get a wonderful back and side workout. (Large firm pillows also work here.)

- **The Magic Circle.** It's a round metal band about 12 inches in diameter. Pushing it in with your hands or thighs increases muscular strength in the arms, chest, and leg. (You can substitute a 12- to 16-inch diameter ball.)

- **The Universal Reformer and the home version called the Pilates Performer.** You've got straps, bungee cords, springs, and a sliding platform all on one weird-looking piece of equipment. By lying, sitting, kneeling, and standing, you get an intense total-body workout.

- **The Chair.** Actually it looks like a box with a padded top and a step or pedal in the front that you push down. Because it requires so much strength, The Chair is reserved for the advanced students.

The wave of the future?

As the 77 million Baby Boomers (born between 1946 and 1964) increase in years, their physical injuries, their loss of flexibility, and the time their bodies need for self-repair will increase, too. A Sunday afternoon on the soccer field, a high-intensity step class, or a six-mile run (which was once a piece of cake) now begins leaving the body stressed, stiff, and sore. And that's not to mention all the free radicals rushing about destroying cells and speeding up the aging process. Therefore, you may have tolerated the no-gain-without-pain ways of staying fit when you were young, but with mounting birthdays, that kind of exercise eventually contributes to the loss of health.

This is where Pilates comes in. Rather than cause injury, it heals. Rather than stress the body, it helps you relax. And at the same time Pilates is doing those great things, it's also increasing your strength and flexibility. While it's still too early to predict if Pilate's strange equipment will ever become as mainstream as a treadmill or stepper, interest in it is certainly gaining momentum.

In October 2000, a Manhattan federal district court judge ruled that Pilates, like yoga and karate, is a recognizable type of exercise. In other words, it has become so universal and generic that Pilates has lost the uniqueness that would entitle it to legal protection as a trade name.

If you want more information about the Pilates mind-body fitness method, here are two books for you to check out. The first is *The Pilates Method of Body Conditioning* by Sean P. Gallagher and Romana Kryzanowska. Gallagher, a physical therapist, is the founder of the Pilates Studios and Kryzanowska was one of Joseph Pilates lead teachers. The other book, while not focused solely on Pilates, does a good job giving you an easy to understand overview. It's *Mind-Body Fitness For Dummies* by Therese Iknoian. (Yes, another *For Dummies* book, but Iknoian does a great job describing Pilates.)

Tai Chi

Tai chi (pronounced *tie chee*) is short for *tai chi chuan* (pronounced *tie chee chwan*). (We use the shorter name in this chapter.) You've probably seen on television or in the newspaper a park showing 3,000 Chinese men and women participating in their morning workout using slow, relaxed, controlled movements. That was tai chi.

But tai chi wasn't always the country's national exercise. In fact, the Communist government originally banned the practice of tai chi because party leaders felt that it was elitist and represented the old ways. After years of extensive research, however, the government concluded that tai chi indeed provided huge health and healing benefits. Now it's required in all schools, and factory workers take daily tai chi exercise breaks. Tai chi has finally returned to the place where it began many centuries ago.

Unfortunately, the majority of medical research on tai chi hasn't yet been translated from Chinese. A wealth of valuable information remains out of our reach. Only recently have Western scientists examined the health benefits of tai chi. Most of the studies were conducted with older people, usually living in retirement communities or care centers. The results unequivocally demonstrated that tai chi improved the balance of these adults, thereby reducing falls and subsequent broken hips. Harvard Medical School's *Women Health Watch Journal* (December 2000) reported that practicing tai chi regularly appeared to help maintain strong heart and lung functions as people got older — functions which usually deteriorate with age.

A way to a stronger and healthier you

If you're not one of those "older" adults who worry about broken hips, what does practicing tai chi give you? Long-time practitioners of tai chi describe the following benefits:

- Improved concentration
- Greater relaxation
- Stronger bones and muscles
- Better balance and coordination
- Stronger immune system
- Improved health
- Lower hypertension (blood pressure)
- Better posture
- More flexibility
- Stronger back and less back pain
- Improved mindfulness
- Less stress chemicals flooding your body
- More energy

Whether you're 16-years-old or 96, an athlete or physically challenged, you can gain the mind-body benefits of tai chi.

The supreme ultimate fighting system

In Chinese, *tai chi* means *The Supreme Ultimate* and is symbolized by the black and white yin-yang circle (described in the sidebar "Balance"). *Chuan* means *fist* or *fighting system*. Therefore, tai chi chuan is the supreme and ultimate martial arts system. In the next section, we compare tai chi with the other martial arts schools, but for now we want to give you a little more information about how tai chi works.

So, what exactly is tai chi? On the outside, it looks like a series of slow-motion dance-like movements. On the inside, it's intense mental concentration, meticulous awareness of what every part of your body is doing, and ironclad self-discipline. It's your mind and body working together to strengthen, energize, and heal you.

Don't let yourself get taken in by the dance-like movements that you see. In fact, they are actually specific martial arts positions used during combat. In tai chi, however, these movements have become choreographed into a routine called The Form. Each position flows slowly and seamlessly into the next. Each position has specific foot, leg, knee, torso, arms, elbows, hands, and head placement as you progress through the form. And when used by an experienced person in combat, those beautiful movements become one of the most powerful methods of self-defense.

In his book *Tai Chi: The Supreme Ultimate,* Dr. Lawrence Galante gave a personal example of how tai chi is used in one-on-one combat. As a man in his late 20s who held a black belt in karate, Galante was told by his tai chi instructor, Master Wong, to attack him. Master Wong "easily out-maneuvered me and deflected all my attacks," Galante wrote. Using tai chi moves, Master Wong evaded Galante's karate blocks, landed light punches on him, or sent him flying across the room. With all of young Galante's karate training, he could neither avoid nor attack his master — who was in his late 80s.

The problem you face studying tai chi is that there are multiple forms, and no two are taught exactly alike — even when they have the same name. If you attend a tai chi class, you'll hear terms like *The Long Form* and *The Short Form.* (But don't let the word *short* fool you. It'll still take you about 20 minutes to correctly complete, probably a year for you to learn it, and a lifetime to perfect.) Then you'll also hear terms like the *Chen style, the Yang style, the Wu style,* and the *Sun style.* (Those are the names of people who created their own forms of tai chi many centuries ago. The Yang style is the most prevalent in the United States.) However, you'll find that no two instructors doing the Yang style will perform it the same way.

What's important is not the form you use, but that you find an *experienced* tai chi instructor with whom you're comfortable. While there are lots of Tai chi videos and books floating about, the only way to learn the positions correctly and get the greatest healing benefits from it is to have a real-live person teaching you. If you want to know more about tai chi, Therese Iknoian's book *Tai Chi For Dummies* is a great place to begin. If you want to find a tai chi instructor, look in the Yellow Pages under the heading martial arts. Also, start talking with your friends; you may find someone who has been practicing for years.

The two faces of martial arts

When most people think of martial arts, they associate them with the flying kicks and knockout chops seen in movies. Rarely do they think of the slow, controlled flow of tai chi. But like everything else in nature, the martial arts also have a Yin and Yang. You find that there are the Yin or *Soft Schools* and the Yang or *Hard Schools.* Usually people prefer one or the other. It's no different than choosing skiing or snowboarding — individuals just have different personal preferences.

Balance

For the Chinese, the ancient tai chi circle shown in the figure symbolizes how opposing, but complementary, forces in nature combine to create harmony and balance. Yin, the dark portion, represents night, feminine, unconsciousness, air, flexibility, inner, and hot. Yang, the light half, stands for day, masculine, consciousness, earth, rigidness, outer, and cold. But you also notice that each half also contains a small circle of the other color, which means that in everything rests the seed of its opposite. Night holds the promise of day, and summer harbors the beginnings of winter.

All things in life contain both yin and yang. Only when they exist in balance — neither one dominating — do health and happiness exist. According to ancient Chinese medical texts, when yin and yang are out of balance, the body becomes susceptible to disease. In fact, if you examine the word *disease,* you see that it actually has two parts — dis + ease — which is the *absence of ease.* When stress destroys equilibrium and harmony, disease and sickness result.

Here's a quick comparison of the Hard and Soft Schools.

- **Hard Schools.** In this external style of martial arts, you attack your opponent. You can strike with your hands, elbows, knees, or feet, such as in karate, kung fu, and tae kwon do. Or you can grapple your opponent with throwing or locking techniques as in jujitsu, judo, and aikido. Even though each martial arts form has its own rules, regulations, and body-part focus, their goals are the same — to better one's self and increase self-control, not to dominate others. However, muscle strength, force, speed, and ferocity remain important in the hard schools.

- **Soft Schools.** In this style, neither speed nor muscular power determines success. Even though the forms, on the surface, look gentle, slow, and dance-like, great force is being generated internally. Of the three main Soft Schools of fighting, tai chi chuan, hsing-i, and pa-qua, tai chi is the softest and most popular. Force is never met with counterforce, but instead the defender attaches to and redirects each attack. Turning a Soft Schools form into self-defense requires years of training your muscle memory for each movement, your internal and external balance, your timing, as well as learning how to read what your opponent is planning.

Variations on a word

Don't be surprised to see chi written another way — as in qi or Qi. When translating from Chinese to English, you usually end up with a variety of ways to write a word. At one time China's capital, Beijing, was written as Peking.

Most individuals who practice tai chi do so for health and/or mindfulness training. Rarely do they learn the underlying martial arts foundation. But like everything else, the more knowledge you possess, the more meaningful the experience is for you. So when you search for an instructor, check to see whether he or she also understands the self-defense component. It's important to understand it, even if you never use it.

The mind and body challenge

The ancient Chinese based tai chi on nature. And nature doesn't stand still. Whether it's the stars, the air, the plants, your pet parakeets, or your own body, everything is always in motion. You can think of that motion in two different ways: externally, like leaves waving in the wind, or internally, an energy flowing through everything that exists.

The Chinese call it *chi* (pronounced *chee*), the Indians call it *prana* (see the section on yoga), and many Westerners call it *life force* or *life energy.* Whatever you want to name it, all living organisms have energy flowing through them — even if you can't see it on a CAT scan. When the energy or chi flows freely, plants, parakeets, and people stay healthy. When chi becomes blocked, organisms sicken and can even die.

As Dr. David Eisenberg, instructor in medicine at the Harvard Medical School said in Bill Moyers *Healing and The Mind,* it's the individual who is responsible for helping "to prevent illness or maintain health." This means keeping the chi flowing. And that's why, Eisenberg explained, millions of Chinese people practice tai chi in the park every day — to keep their chi circulating freely and to keep themselves healthy.

The goal of tai chi is to face all of life's ups and down with mental, physical, and emotional balance.

If you give tai chi a try, be prepared for times of confusion and awkwardness. You're challenging both your mind and body to new ways of thinking and moving. But you'll find the rewards life-enhancing.

Choices

To Westerners growing up in a centuries-old culture that separates the mind from the body, tai chi can appear alien and irrelevant to their lives. Similarly, to people who discuss their latest sports injury, knee surgery, or ski mobile thrill, yoga definitely feels puny. When you're concentrating on "abs of steel" or going for the burn, focusing on becoming more relaxed, rooted, and flowing doesn't at first compute.

However, while you sweat up a storm pounding that uncooperative body into shape or spend massive hours fighting through a merger, you're also flooding that same body (the only one you've got) with health-destroying stress chemicals. But your life doesn't have to become a treadmill of exhaustion and frustration. Thirty minutes a day of mind-body strength training does wonders for how you look and feel, as well as how you respond to tensions and traumas.

When you're body's healthy, your mind is calmer. When your mind is calm, your body's healthier. And when mind and body work well together, you've got the resources to meet whatever changes life or your boss throw at you.

The following is from the book *Healing And The Mind*. It's a conversation between Jon Kabat-Zinn, founder of the Stress Reduction Clinic at the University of Massachusetts Medial Center and Bill Moyers, author and television journalist.

> ***Kabat-Zinn:*** *"The only time that any of us have to grow or change or feel or learn anything is in the present moment. But we're continually missing our present moments, almost willfully, by not paying attention. Instead of being on automatic pilot, we can explore what's possible if we start to kindle the flame of being fully alive."*

> ***Moyers:*** *"I never thought I would be hearing this kind of talk in a major American hospital."*

> ***Kabat-Zinn:*** *"Well, times are changing. . . ."*

Part VI
The Part of Tens

The 5th Wave   By Rich Tennant

"It's hard to figure. The concept was a big hit in Nome."

In this part . . .

If you like things short and quick, then this part is for you. It contains three lists of ten that tell you exactly what you need to do if you want to become a change winner.

Chapter 23

Ten Things That Every Change Winner Does

In This Chapter

▶ Starting your personal check list for winning

▶ Protecting everyone's self worth

*C*hange winners do not come into this world winning. Somewhere along the path of growing up and charging into the world, they have watched, listened, sorted out, or stumbled over, but in any case captured enough wisdom and fortitude to become winners. Because the majority of major changes fail or quietly just fade away, more change losers than winners must be leading organizations (unless a small number of losers are firing off a whole lot of changes every day). Trivial logic aside, the real message is that any leader can develop the skills needed to win in this wonderful world of change.

The first five parts of this book provide the detail on leading change. This chapter is intended to give you a summary list of things you can do to improve your odds of winning at it. If you have read the book, use this chapter as a quarterly review exercise. If you haven't read the book, skim this chapter for your amusement and amazement and then go back and read the chapters that tickle your curiosity.

Gains Commitment from the Management Chain

Many a change has floundered and failed because the leader was not aware of or just ignored the need for buy-in in the manager ranks. Without the strong support of every management level, the leader's task of trying to motivate the employees is similar to that proverbial task of trying to push a wet noodle.

Employees naturally resist change. In order to live with themselves, they need valid reasons and/or excuses for resisting. While the change leader may be a dynamic, well-respected person, the employees will always watch and listen closely to their immediate supervisor. Any perceived lack of support for the change by a manager above them is great justification for resisting. It is easy for employees to conclude, "If the manager is not pushing this change, it's probably not a good idea, and it will eventually go away anyway."

The noncommitted manager also brings a second logical excuse for employee resistance. This immediate supervisor assigns their work, judges their performance, and has control over how they advance in the business. The employee's parents did not raise any dumb kids. Why would anyone want to openly invest time and energy in something their manager thinks is questionable at best? Without the support of your management team, your change effort has little chance of survival.

Sometimes leaders forget that managers are people, too. Managers also resist changes. Managers have reasons and excuses for resisting just like other folks. As you are planning your change, make sure that you get the commitment of your managers early in the game. That old cliché about only being as strong as the weakest link is also true about your management commitment chain. See Chapter 7 for more detail on the resistance of managers.

Celebrates Successes

Why do you say thank you when someone opens or holds a door for you? It's courteous. It makes someone feel good. It makes them want to do it again. It also makes you feel good. It's the way you want to be treated if you help someone. In your organization, saying thank you to and recognizing and applauding the folks who help accomplish your change is not only the courteous and right thing to do — it brings big time benefits.

Employees want to feel respected and appreciated. They want to go home after work feeling a sense of accomplishment — knowing they made a contribution. If they have really invested their blood, sweat, and tears into improving your customer service center, they would like to know that you realize and appreciate their effort. If you do recognize their effort and sincerely applaud the results, those employees feel good about themselves and will be ready to follow you up the next hill that needs climbing. If you don't acknowledge their effort and achievements, you will find a group of very reluctant warriors for that next challenge. Why should they pour their heart and soul into a black hole with no feedback or reward in sight?

A related, but different, benefit comes from letting employees know you are serious and committed to completing your change. Most employees are cautious about immediately jumping into something new — particularly if they have been stung by some previous program(s) of the month that failed or disappeared (a history of several programs of the month makes them very cautious). Publicly recognizing small successes as the change effort is under-way can send several messages to those who are still on the sidelines: You are closely following the progress of the project, you know what's happening, and you are rewarding those who are making the change happen. This trans-lates into "Whoops, she's serious about this. Looks like she will stay involved to the finish. Maybe we should jump in so that we don't get left behind."

Celebrating successes encourages, stimulates, and motivates those being recognized to stay the course and, if anything, work harder. It also nudges, pushes, and causes the skeptical, wait-and-see types to get off the bleachers and join the march. You can find the how and why of recognition in Chapter 19.

Creates a Single Direction

Would you want to hike with someone who seems to be continually changing directions? If you were following that person's lead, you would shortly start questioning whether the individual knew where he or she was going. You may not want to follow him or her too far.

Have you seen leaders that announce individual, unconnected changes that leave employees wondering if their leader knows where he or she is going with the organization? The changes seem to arrive with no cohesiveness or common purpose. For example, say that Sales is reorganized to create a single point of contact for the customer. Three months later, a decision is made to sell some products on the corporate Web site. That is followed by a decision to develop an 800 number customer service center, which is fol-lowed by a decision to outsource the customer billing work to another com-pany. These are probably good decisions, but where is this going? This may all be part of a grand plan, or the leader may be making disconnected, spur-of-the-moment decisions.

This scenario of disconnected changes raises employee doubts and ques-tions. Where are we going? Does our leader know where he is going? Is our leader capable of planning and leading? Do we want to follow this leader? Lack of confidence in the leader is not a good start toward building an ener-gized, go-take-on-the-world team.

If you have a clear picture of where you want to go, share it. If you do not have that mental picture of your desired state, create it and share it. As you announce changes, show how each change fits into your picture. And plan, package, and communicate your changes so that they clearly complement each other and are collectively moving the organization in a single direction. Chapters 13, 14, and 15 provide specific detail and examples of how to plan, package, and communicate your changes.

Undertakes Only Necessary Changes

Each change you decide to do has an impact on your employees. Implementing a change always causes extra work. By its very nature, a change also causes disruption or altering of the employee's present world. This leads to confusion and uncertainty. When a group of people are confused and even mildly unsure of what's happening, conflict, anger, and stress are more evident. Misinformation and rumors add fuel to the increasing levels of frustration. Employee attention and energy is diverted from their work, so quality and productivity may take a hit.

People can be totally overwhelmed by too much simultaneous change in their life. So don't overwhelm them — right? The leader at work may say, "I'm only asking them to change the way they walk, chew gum, and whistle — that's not a big deal." That leader is forgetting that each employee also has their own set of changes and stresses occurring in their personal life outside of work. The impact of personal and work changes are additive. Most of an employee's coping capacity can be consumed by events such as caring for a sick child, going through a divorce, or facing tough financial problems. A combination of smaller things like leaking plumbing, running out of gas in the car, or an F on Junior's report card will also reduce that coping capacity.

There is no way to know what's happening in employees' personal lives. There is no unit of measurement such as feet, pounds, or gallons to mathematically determine coping capacity or the impact of a specific change on the employees.

However, a change winner understands that too much change can overload employees to the point that their ability to function is reduced and performance will suffer. So the name of the game is to minimize the number of changes underway in your organization at any time. Restrain yourself and only do those changes that are absolutely required for the long-term growth and survival of the organization. Turn to Chapter 5 if you want to further pursue the dangers of too many changes.

Takes Time to Plan

Our society has a do-it-now philosophy. The rate of technical and business change says decisions must be made quickly. Those who respond to crisis are applauded and rewarded. Few gold stars are given for planning. The older leaders and employees can also remember a bureaucratic age when large committees created large books of plans that just sat on shelves and gathered dust. It is no wonder that people would like to avoid planning. It is more fun to just go do something.

An attitude of winging it is okay if it's a game and you don't need to win in order to buy food and shoes for your children. It's okay if you don't need to communicate where you are going and how to get there to a group of employees. For sure, it is okay to avoid large binders of stuff to set on the shelf.

Unfortunately, the truth is that time spent in planning is recouped many times when the action or project is implemented. Effective planning actually saves time. Building a well-developed plan for your change also provides a number of other positive attributes. The plan provides a means to communicate and reach common understanding among the employees. Employees can work together effectively if they know the plan.

Problems identified during planning can be resolved or at least included in the plan before you start the change. The same problem appearing as a surprise while making the change can be costly in time and money. A major problem appearing midstream during implementation may even scuttle the change effort.

A documented plan also provides intermediate milestones, which allow you to track the progress of making the change. You are in a position to know and intervene quickly if the change starts to go off course. Change winners take the time to quickly, but thoroughly develop a plan for their change. Of course, they then follow the plan. A broader discussion of the need and value of planning is in Chapter 11.

Communicates Well and Continually

In this day and age, good communication is a prerequisite for leading any group of people to do anything (assuming that you want them to do it well). Communication is even more important if you're asking employees to change. You're asking them to do something they naturally do not want to do. You're asking them to change the way they work, learn new things, ignore any feelings of inadequacy, leave the comfort of today's routine — maybe in tough cases to even jeopardize their own job. You need to be a good communicator to lead change. And you need to know what to communicate.

People are more inclined to follow you if they know why they need to change, where you want them to go, and how you plan to get there. It's probably helpful to know those three things yourself, if you expect to lead them. So make sure that you and your planning team answer those three questions as part of your planning process. Those three subjects should be the core of the communication package for your kick-off meetings.

Change winners also know that they must continue the flow of communication during the time the change is underway. They need to continue to reinforce and strengthen understanding of the why, where, and how. They need to convince the uncommitted. They need to give everyone updates on the status of implementing the plan. And most importantly, they need to demonstrate that the leader is committed and staying personally involved in this change effort — in other words, the change is here to stay and will be successful. Chapters 15 and 18 discuss how winners use communication in much more detail

Listens to People's Issues and Concerns

A leader has a number of reasons for carefully listening to employee issues and concerns. If employees know their input is heard and considered, they feel valued and respected. That leads to feeling a sense of commitment, responsibility, and loyalty to you and the organization. That's important even if you're not introducing changes.

Employees hear you more clearly if they know they have been heard.

Cultivating and listening to upward input can flag problems that you had not noticed before. You may hear of potential technical glitches that would be damaging to making your change — "the software they just purchased is not compatible with our time reporting software." If you know about the problems, you have a shot at taking care of them during the planning phase.

On the human side, you will hear concerns such as "I am already overloaded. How do I find time to work on this?" You may also hear comments like "It takes three weeks to get my money back on expense vouchers," or "There is no cooperation between groups." Some of these people issues may be potholes or major roadblocks to your change. Change winners include action items for the most critical of these issues in their implementation planning. If you want more information on hearing peoples concerns, try Chapter 6.

Stays Personally Involved

People really do not want change. No one wants their nice comfortable world upset and disrupted. No one wants that feeling of uncertainty. At the same time, everyone wants to feel that they are a good person. Good people support their leaders and teammates. Resisting the change and being a good person are incompatible — unless there is a good excuse for resisting. So employees will naturally look for excuses to stay on the sidelines as a non-participant or, heaven forbid, actively oppose the change.

One of the best excuses for resisting is "The leader is not really serious about this thing. It will go away. It is a waste of my time to work on it!" Employees will always watch your actions and behavior to determine how committed you really are to this community relations program or whatever you've just announced.

So, how do you show them that you're committed? Role modeling sends a strong message — so what can you role model for the employees? Can you role model the new behavior? Can you take the same training courses or seminars? Can you participate on a process management team? Can you go visit customers? Employees will respond enthusiastically if they see you're in the same boat with them and are willing to do whatever you are asking of them.

Aside from role modeling, ask yourself what you can do to show that you are staying involved. Your list may include reviewing progress of the change in every staff meetings, visiting groups involved in the change to get first-hand input, making the change a subject of formal and informal communication, and publicly recognizing people and teams. The key is to show people you are still involved and know what's happening. For a broader discussion of your role in leading change, see Chapter 17

Protects People's Self-Worth

Damaging employees' sense of self-worth creates massive resistance to change. There seems to be software in the brain programmed for the sole purpose of recognizing when something hits our self-worth, aggressively opposing the cause of the hit, and trying hard to restore our damaged image of ourselves. Immediate opposition to any self-worth arrow is a natural reaction.

Employee's self-worth is typically not a major subject in management seminars. It's not normally high on the list of concerns. So leaders can (and often do) damage employees self-worth and never know it. Perhaps the greatest example of unknowingly hitting employees' self-worth was in the 1980s when formal quality programs were being adopted all over the country. In one form or another, leaders told their employees that "now we are going to start a quality program." Employees immediately assumed that their leaders were saying they had been doing poor quality work. And leaders wondered why there was so much resistance to quality.

Fortunately, you can help protect self-worth. You can talk with people in a way that helps them feel respected, valued, and proud of their contributions — even when you're discussing a problem or a need to make changes. You can be careful to explain that the need for the change is not caused by something they did wrong. Remember that employees' self-worth and resistance are very tightly linked. Protecting their self-worth avoids a lot of resistance to your change.

Protecting self-worth to avoid resistance works the same way with spouses, children, friends, and neighbors. It builds cooperation and helps people to feel good about themselves. How can you beat that? Further discussion of this self-worth factor is in Chapter 5.

Works with Resistance — Not Against It

The notion of resistance to change being a natural reaction for human beings has been a big secret to most people. Without understanding this "natural" reality, opposition or challenge to the latest change announcement immediately looks like disloyalty, sabotage, inflexibility, and perhaps stupidity. This opposition often looks like a personal attack on the leader. So the leader's self-worth takes a hit, and the leader lashes back at the employees. The employees get hurt and disengage, and the resistance goes underground. How's that for a scenario for failure? Happens all the time, doesn't it?

Change winners know that resistance is a natural phenomenon. They also know that they can plan and implement the change in a way that minimizes employee resistance. They do not like resistance — no leader wants the confusion, arguments, and tensions that occur. They view working with resistance as a necessary part of leading successful change.

Change winners also know that there is a positive side to working with resistance. Leaders do not know everything there is to know about their change. Some may think they do, but they're probably not among the winners. A fuller discussion of the nature of resistance and how to work with it can be found in Chapters 3, 4, and 5.

Chapter 24

Ten Barriers to Successful Change

Change winners use every tool and technique they know in order to help their employees cope with and implement change. They know that a number of potential barriers or roadblocks on the human side of their change can really get in the way. These barriers cause people pain, frustration, and uncertainty, or they may simply provide reasonable excuses for not changing. Change winners develop their plans with a specific objective of removing, or at least minimizing, human side barriers.

Your first challenge is to identify the potential barriers. This chapter is intended to give you a running start at that challenge. If you can identify your potential list, common sense will at least partially guide your planning to avoid these obstacles to success. If necessary, refer back to the relevant chapters, as indicated in each of the following sections. In any case, please use the list with success.

Employees Feel Treated like Robots

You already know what this barrier is all about. But you may not realize how it also relates to changes that don't work. The extreme example of employees feeling treated like robots was the assembly lines in the first half of the last century. Employees punched a timecard coming in, used their back and arm muscles to do some repetitive task, and punched the same timecard when they left. The descriptive phrase was "leave your brain at the door." Yes, assembly lines and repetitive tasks still exist. However, it is now clear that those same workers, with brains engaged, bring valuable knowledge and creativity to their work. The power of the whole quality improvement effort of the last several decades is testimony to that knowledge and creativity.

Suffice it to say that today's employee wants to be viewed and treated as a whole person with feelings, goals, values, ambitions, creativity, and valuable information about their workplace. They want to be trusted, respected, and valued. Creating a work environment that meets these basic needs engages their heart and mind to assist with your change. Feeling that they are treated as an expendable resource will cause them to be unsupportive at best or opposing at the worst — and represents a barrier to your success. You need action item(s) in your plan to improve this work environment issue. Chapters 2, 5, and 6 all provide valuable insight on this subject.

Change Has a Flavor-of-the-Month Track Record

Experience is a great teacher. Fortunately or unfortunately, that statement is true for your employees. In the world of change, they clearly remember and learn from their experience with past changes or announced changes. That is the track record for this organization. Notice we said track record of the organization — not your track record. Employee response to your change will be influenced by their personal experience with past changes — not yours.

Put yourself in the employee's chair. Is their experience one of changes continually popping up and then eventually dying a quiet death? You know some leaders grab any "trumpeted silver bullet" that flashes across magazine covers and give it a try. Worse yet, does your employees' experience include supporting their leader by investing their own time and energy in these abandoned efforts? If so, the past track record is a major barrier to the change you want to implement. You will not find people anxious to tackle and commit themselves to any change — regardless of how good it is.

If you encounter this barrier, design your plans to communicate and demonstrate that this change is different than those they experienced in the past. Chapter 5 gives additional information on this problem, and Chapter 17 gives you personal tools for convincing the employees this change is for real.

Resistance Goes Undercover

Employees will resist your change. The question is how will they resist. Will they openly tell you about their problems and concerns with your change? Or will they complain to their family members at home and remain quiet as a fence post in the office? Here comes that proverbial question — do you shoot messengers? Perhaps that's too strong, so ask yourself whether your employees know it is safe to express doubts or raise unpleasant issues with you.

All human beings have a natural desire for self-protection. Don't expect employees to speak up if they feel threatened by your reaction. Input (positive and negative) from employees gives you the advantage of considering their knowledge, concerns, and recommendations, perhaps modifying plans, and avoiding problems during the implementation of your change. If the employees choose to hide their resistance and input, you may get blindsided with unexpected problems during the implementation.

You can't afford to gamble with this barrier of underground resistance. Your plans should include action items that bring resistance and communications into the open. If you want some ideas for getting the employee resistance on top of the table where you can deal with it, try Chapter 8.

Employees Are Saying, "I Don't Know How This Affects Me"

It is difficult for employees to jump on your change bandwagon unless they have some idea of how the change affects them personally. Written announcements and verbal presentations at change kick-off meetings can often provide a high-level view of the need for the change, where the organization needs to go, and hopefully a description of how to get there. Many leaders will then assume their communications task is finished, leaving a serious barrier to the success of the change.

After employees hear your initial big picture, they will immediately want to know what this change means to them individually. Is their job secure? Does their work change? If so, what are they expected to do? Is the pay the same? And the list goes on.

You can significantly reduce this barrier by building your communications plan so employees have the opportunity to discuss their concerns in more detail on a face-to-face basis with someone — if not you, then a knowledgeable manager. These discussions remove major uncertainty for the employees so that they can then concentrate on helping you with the change. Chapters 4 and 15 can help you understand this common excuse and help you design your communications to deal with it.

The Culture Is Different than the Change

Employees look for legitimate excuses for resisting your change. One of the fertile fields for such searching is comparing the change to the attitudes and behaviors (read *culture*) of their leadership. If they find a disconnect between the existing culture and the behaviors required for the change, they have found all the justification they need. They have their excuse for resisting — they can assume that the change will fail, and they are usually right. That excuse is really a barrier to success.

A typical case of culture disconnect starts with the priorities that leaders silently communicate by their attitudes and behaviors. Assume that the culture has had a quantity output and financial focus. The goals and measurements match that focus. Overtime is automatically cut any time the expense budget is in jeopardy. Meeting revenue, expense, and production output goals brings recognition and bonuses. Customers are evident in speeches and advertising, but there are no goals or measurements related to the customer.

Now let the leaders announce a new gee-whiz drive to increase customer retention. Employees immediately believe the leader is not serious. The existing culture is not customer-focused. They expect the change to fail and will be very reluctant to invest themselves in a predetermined failure. So, they create a self-fulfilling prophecy — unless you simultaneously change the culture to match the requirements of the change. Changing the culture will remove this barrier to success. If you want more detail, Chapter 4 expands on this barrier of culture disconnects, and Chapter 14 shows you how culture is included in your implementation planning.

HR Policies Are Different Than the Change

This discussion can be brief, since it is the same song — different verse — as the culture disconnect described in the preceding section. Employees will also find legitimate excuses for resisting where the personnel policies and procedures do not include or support the change.

Examples of disconnect or nonsupport are

- A strong program for improving teamwork, without "teamwork" appearing in the appraisal or recognition plans
- A quality program without quality goals, measurements, recognition of accomplishments, or consequence management
- A program on employee development without adequate funding, time off for classes, tracking of accomplishments, and recognition of those accomplishments

You get the picture.

Disconnects between your change and HR policies or procedures create the same type of barriers to success as the culture differences. Your plan can include steps to review and modify policies and procedures where needed to avoid this barrier. Chapters 4 and 14 are good references here.

Your Employees Are Stressed Out

Have you ever been in total overload — physically worn out and mentally exhausted? If so, the last thing you needed was for someone to beat the drums, wave banners, and announce the start of a new grand and glorious change. You would resist any added task, regardless of how great it may be.

Employee stress overload is a barrier to successful change. What do you know about the stress conditions in the organization? What are overtime levels running? What are you hearing through those open communication channels? What does your absence data say? And when all else fails, what do you hear when you ask the employees how they are doing?

It is obviously better to avoid the problem of a stressed out workforce in the first place, but that is not always possible. You do not control all of the events that stress an organization. However, you can discipline yourself to only introduce those changes that are absolutely necessary. If stress is a problem for you or your employees, take a look at Chapter 5.

Turf Battles Occur

Successfully implementing significant changes requires cooperation and teamwork amongst the involved groups. Unfortunately, turf battles often occur. The conflict, tension, finger-pointing, frustration, and wasted time are counterproductive to basic work performance and a major barrier to successful change.

A root cause of turf disagreements is poorly defined processes and lack of clarity regarding roles and responsibilities. These disagreements undermine any semblance of teamwork. Therefore, make sure that your implementation plan includes actions to define roles and strengthen teamwork.

If you have turf issues, but don't want to deal with this barrier, forget the change — it won't work anyway. If you see turf issues in your organization, Chapter 14 shows you how to include the "process" solution in your implementation plans.

Employees Believe Change Is Not Needed

Employees' view of the world, and particularly of your organization is different than yours. Backgrounds are different. Experiences are different. The information you have is at least partially different than the information employees normally see as part of their jobs. So don't be surprised if they occasionally reach different conclusions than you do. The employees are not ignorant. In this case, they're just examining and judging the need for change with different perceptions and facts.

How hard would you work on a change that you felt was not needed? You don't want to do it anyway — it is extra work and causes unnecessary confusion. Believing it is not needed gives you an excellent excuse for not jumping in to help. The bottom line is that "believe change not needed" is a barrier to successful change. If you want more information, Chapter 4 discusses this resistance issue, Chapter 12 describes identifying the need, and Chapter 18 talks about keeping all communications channel open.

Make sure that your change implementation plans include multiple communications channels and opportunities to help employees understand the need for changing.

Leader Lacks Credibility

Don't expect enthusiastic support if employees have doubts about the capability of the leader. Trust in the leader is a basic requirement if people are going to go that extra mile needed for successful change. Obviously, you want to lead changes in a way that does not wreck your credibility as a change leader — so don't lead failures.

If credibility has been damaged, recovering lost credibility is a slow process. You can jumpstart the recovery by following a disciplined planning approach and then ensuring the implementation plan is accomplished as designed. Employees only follow winners. If you have or simply want to avoid a change credibility problem, try following the process described in Chapters 12 through 15.

Index

focus group
  agenda for, 97
  example of, 98
  facilitator for, 97
  forming, 96
  knowing when to use, 95–96
  optimum number, 96–97
  overview of, 94–95
  for physicians, 95
  survey and, 101, 103
  use of, 21, 65, 87
focus for meditation, 300
following through, 100, 115
food, emotional response to, 296
Ford, Harrison, 284
Fortey, Richard, 275
four-word mantra, 239
free agent, worker as, 31, 33
free radicals, 306
Friedman, Howard, 271
friendship, disruption of, 18
Future Shock (Toffler), 27–28

• G •

Galante, Lawrence, 320
Galbraith, John Kenneth, 93
Gandhi, Mahatma, 221
General Electric Company, 229, 232
generational needs in workplace, 32–33
gestures when speaking, 245–246
Gidé, Andre, 22
Glaser, Jay, 298
globalization, 28–29
goals, unchanging, 36
Golden Rule, 90–92, 291–292
Gordon, James S., 302
gratitude, 281
Great Pyramid, The, 14
groupthink, 163
growth, need for, 36
gut reaction as reason for change, 151

• H •

Hanging Gardens of Babylonia, The, 14
Harman, Denham, 306
Hatha yoga, 311, 312–314

health. *See also* mind-body effect; stress
  balance and, 321
  compassion and, 289
  emotions and, 271, 282
  meditation and, 298–299
  psychoneuroimmunology, 270–271, 298–300
  support groups for, 295
High Intensity Training, 309–310
Hill, Napoleon, 156, 231
Holmes and Rahe scale, 23–25
honesty, 137
Honeywell, 14
Hooker, Richard, 57
hostility and health, 271. *See also* anger
hot buttons, 131–132
Huddleston, Peggy, 271
human face
  of change, 16–17, 192
  implementation plan and, 197–203
  of leader, 232–233

• I •

immigration, 29–30
immune system and stress, 271
impatience of manager, 116–119. *See also* patience
impermanence as permanent, 13–16
implementation plan. *See also* action item; successful implementation plan, characteristics of
  benefits of, 192–193
  communication plan and, 248
  description of, 194
  domino effect, 194–195
  elements of, 48
  human side action item menu, 200–201
  importance of, 47, 64–65
  kickoff meeting, 211–212
  prioritizing issues for, 80, 152–153, 334
  resistance, preparing for, 127–128
  reviewing and revising, 202
  as roadmap, 162, 193
  targeting excuses, 199–200
  targeting resistance, 197–199
  technical side, 196
  updating, 65, 162

Michelangelo, 280
mind-body effect. *See also* health; stress
  choices, 322–323
  demonstrating, 272
  exercise, 305–311
  meditation, 296–304
  overview of, 294–295
  Pilates, 314–318
  research on, 270–271, 294–296
  tai chi, 318–322
  yoga, 311–314
mindfulness
  definition of, 275
  difficulty of practicing, 276
  implications of, 277
  meditation and, 297
  present moment, living in, 277
  stuck-in-traffic practice, 278
  teeth brushing practice, 278
mindmapping, 171–173
mission statement, 126
mistakes. *See also* terrible idea reason for
    resistance
  being kind to self after making, 283
  increase in, 18–19
  learning from, 42
  making in public, 112–113
  resistance and, 128
model
  biological filter, 44–45
  cultural filter, 45–46
  filters and, 43–44
  individual filter, 46
  types of filters, 44, 45
modification, messiness of, 12–13
modifying workplace behavior, 184
Molière, Jean-Baptiste, 274
money, wasting, 154
monitoring resistance, 126–127
Montgomery Ward, 13
morale, reinforcing, 170
Mothers Against Drunk Driving (MADD),
    221
motion, law of, 11–12
motivation
  coaching and, 222–224
  importance of skill of, 42, 50–51
  leadership and, 222

recognition and, 254, 257
role modeling, 50, 71–72, 111, 112–113
of self, 131
Motorola, 241
movie industry, free agent in, 33
Moyers, Bill, 323
multivoting, 177
myths of resistance
  good managers eliminate resistance,
    55–56, 60
  people only resist changes they don't
    want, 57–58, 60
  people who resist are disloyal and bad,
    58–59, 60
  resistance has no value, 59, 60
  resistance is avoidable, 55, 60
  resistance is bad, 56–57, 60
  turning into reality, 60

• N •

needs, unchanging, 36
negative reaction to employee, controlling,
    135–136
Nelson, Miriam, 308
Newton, Sir Isaac, 11
nonjudgmental attitude in meditation, 301

• O •

Occupational Safety and Health
    Administration, 13
one-way communication
  employee to manager, 243
  manager to employee, 242
opportunity, missing, 154
opposition, role of, 59
optimism and longevity, 282
organizational development, 124
Ornish, Dean, 295

• P •

past-failure reason for resistance
  description of, 85–86, 198, 336
  resistance as messenger, 86–87
  trust, earning, 87

time, wasting, 154
timeframe
  for change, 119
  for survey return, 102
Toffler, Alvin, *Future Shock,* 27, 28
tools. *See* skills
TQM (Total Quality Management), 17, 117,
  154, 240–241
tracking change, 159
training
  avoiding, 114
  implementation of change after, 118
trial run. *See* pilot test
trust
  Change Management Team, 160
  earning, 87
  failure and, 155
  need for, 36
  promising what can be delivered, 136–137
turf battles, 339
two-way communication, 243

• U •

uninformed optimism, 57
unrealistic expectations, 117–118, 119
updating
  implementation plan, 65, 162
  policy and procedure, action item for,
  201–202
  recognition plan, 260
upward communication
  feedback, obtaining, 107–108, 243
  implementation phase, 128
  improving, 124
  input, encouraging, 214, 243, 336
  team building and, 230
upward-feedback survey, 77, 85, 116
use before this date syndrome, 117

• V •

values
  diverse thinking, 163–164
  Golden Rule, 90–92, 295
  recognition plan and, 259–260
  unchanging, 36

viewing
  change, 10
  merger, 17
  problem from employees' eyes, 22–23,
  133–134
  reality, 43–44
  resistance, 83–84
  situation, 274
  world, 46–47
virtual team, 35
vision, 181–182, 230. *See also* desired state
vocal technique, 245–246
vulnerability. *See* self-worth

• W •

walking the talk. *See* role modeling
Wallace, R. Keith, 298
Walters, Larry, 58
watchful cynicism phase, 148
Watson, John, 132
Weil, Andrew, 302
Welch, Jack, 63, 232
what's-going-right list
  benefits of, 169–170
  brainstorming versus mindmapping,
  171–173
  examples of, 173–175
  input for, 170–171
  kickoff meeting, 208–209
  organizing information for, 173
Williams, Redford, 271
Winfrey, Oprah, 277
wise versus ordinary person, 37
Woods, Tiger, 277
work
  changes at, 10
  self-worth and, 19, 20
workforce for 21st century example, 189
working with resistance
  change winner, 334
  emotional intelligence, 130–131
  finding common issues, 134–135
  focusing on problem, 135–136
  options for, 54
  promising what can be delivered, 136–137
  respecting people, 138–139

Notes

Notes

Notes

YOUR ONLINE RESOURCE

WWW.DUMMIES.COM

Discover Dummies Online!

The Dummies Web Site is your fun and friendly online resource for the latest information about *For Dummies* books and your favorite topics. The Web site is the place to communicate with us, exchange ideas with other *For Dummies* readers, chat with authors, and have fun!

Ten Fun and Useful Things You Can Do at www.dummies.com

1. Win free *For Dummies* books and more!
2. Register your book and be entered in a prize drawing.
3. Meet your favorite authors through the Hungry Minds Author Chat Series.
4. Exchange helpful information with other *For Dummies* readers.
5. Discover other great *For Dummies* books you must have!
6. Purchase Dummieswear exclusively from our Web site.
7. Buy *For Dummies* books online.
8. Talk to us. Make comments, ask questions, get answers!
9. Download free software.
10. Find additional useful resources from authors.

Link directly to these ten fun and useful things at
www.dummies.com/10useful

WWW.DUMMIES.COM

SURF THE NET

For other titles from Hungry Minds,
go to **www.hungryminds.com**

Not on the Web yet? It's easy to get started with *Dummies 101: The Internet For Windows 98* or *The Internet For Dummies* at local retailers everywhere.

Find other *For Dummies* books on these topics:
Business • Career • Databases • Food & Beverage • Games • Gardening
Graphics • Hardware • Health & Fitness • Internet and the World Wide Web
Networking • Office Suites • Operating Systems • Personal Finance • Pets
Programming • Recreation • Sports • Spreadsheets • Teacher Resources
Test Prep • Word Processing

Hungry Minds™

FOR DUMMIES
BOOK REGISTRATION

Register This Book and Win!

We want to hear from you!

Visit **dummies.com** to register this book and tell us how you liked it!

✔ Get entered in our monthly prize giveaway.

✔ Give us feedback about this book — tell us what you like best, what you like least, or maybe what you'd like to ask the author and us to change!

✔ Let us know any other *For Dummies* topics that interest you.

Your feedback helps us determine what books to publish, tells us what coverage to add as we revise our books, and lets us know whether we're meeting your needs as a *For Dummies* reader. You're our most valuable resource, and what you have to say is important to us!

Not on the Web yet? It's easy to get started with *Dummies 101: The Internet For Windows 98* or *The Internet For Dummies* at local retailers everywhere.

Or let us know what you think by sending us a letter at the following address:

For Dummies Book Registration
Dummies Press
10475 Crosspoint Blvd.
Indianapolis, IN 46256

BESTSELLING BOOK SERIES